The London Muse

Victorian Poetic Responses to the City

South Atlantic
Modern Language Association
Award Study

The London

Victorian Poetic Responses to the City

The University of Georgia Press · Athens

Muse

William B. Thesing

Copyright © 1982 by the University of Georgia Press
Athens, Georgia 30602

Designed by Richard Hendel
Set in 11 on 12 Garamond
The paper in this book meets the guidelines for
permanence and durability of the Committee on
Production Guidelines for Book Longevity of the
Council on Library Resources.
Printed in the United States of America

Library of Congress Cataloging in Publication Data
Thesing, William B.
    The London muse.
    (South Atlantic Modern Language Association
award study)
    Bibliography: p.
    Includes index.
    1. English poetry—19th century—History and
criticism.   2. London (England) in literature.
3. Cities and towns in literature.   4. Industry in
literature.   I. Title.   II. Series.
PR595.L64T4   821'.8'0932421   81-23148
ISBN 0-8203-0619-3   AACR2

For my parents, who gave me poetry,
and for my wife, who gave me the city.

Contents

Chapter Four. The Poetry of the Nineties

Epilogue

Those who can only detect beauty in pastoral and primitive pursuits, those who can only find sentiment in struggling streams and dreamy sunsets, will be unable to discover either in the incessant roar of the machinery . . . or in the murky clouds that float above them. Yet, those who dip below the surface will be able to trace the broad outlines of a mighty poem of moving human interest in those bellowing blast-furnaces and grimy workshops. They are carving out of raw materials the means of social elevation, amelioration and enjoyment. They are breaking down old asperities, indefinitely adding to the usefulness of existence, linking town to town, uniting in the bonds of amity long-estranged and oft-embattled lands, and binding all classes in the rough but genial poetry of real life.

From a speech, "The Rise and Strength of Great Towns," given by Joseph Cowen, M.P., October 1881.

Acknowledgments

It is a pleasure to acknowledge my personal and professional debts. At Indiana University I gained many scholarly insights and strategies from my teachers, Professors Patrick Brantlinger, J. Albert Robbins, and Paul N. Zietlow, all of whom read early drafts of my manuscript and made valuable comments. My greatest debt, however, is to Professor Donald J. Gray, who has read and shaped the study over a period of several years. His perceptive insights and his helpful suggestions as well as his humane support have been a continuing source of inspiration to me. I also thank my colleague Patrick G. Scott for suggesting several useful revisions. Because William H. Nolte, my past chairman, and George L. Geckle, my present chairman, have provided me with research time and funds, I have been able to pursue my scholarly work to better advantage. My research and interests have also been enriched in the past by such special friends and professionals as Donald Reitzes, Tony Shipps, Denis Thomas, Frank Coyne, Stuart Sperry, Martha Vicinus, Glenn Burne, Carol Carlisle, Robert Oakman, Ina Hark, Nancy Lane, Meili Steele, and Arnold Hirshon as well as by others—both colleagues and students—too numerous, unfortunately, to elaborate here. I shall always be grateful, too, for the expert care given to my manuscript by the 1980 SAMLA Studies Award Committee and by the staff of the University of Georgia Press.

Sections of my book appeared originally in somewhat different forms as the following articles: "'Tom's Garland' and Hopkins' Inscapes of Humanity" in *Victorian Poetry* 15, no. 1 (1977): 37–48; "Tennyson and the City: Historical Tremours and Hysterical Tremblings" in the *Tennyson Research Bulletin* 3, no. 1 (November 1977): 14–22; "London and the Poetry of the 1890s" in *Journal of the Eighteen Nineties Society*, no. 11 (December 1980): 10–15; "Matthew Arnold and the Possibilities of the Nineteenth-Century City" in *College Language Association Journal* 24, no. 3 (March 1981): 287–303; and "Robert Buchanan and Late Victorian Scottish Poetry of the City" in *Scottish Literary Journal* 8, no. 2 (December 1981): 44–60. I am grateful to the editors and publishers of these journals for permission to adapt and republish the materials here.

Finally, I owe a great personal debt of gratitude to my parents, William V. and Harriet C. Thesing, who always valued education and the arts. At many points in my career they have shared in triumphs and defeats; they have provided me with both emotional and financial support. My greatest personal debt, of course, is to my wife, Jane Isley Thesing, who endured the years of the composition of this study and offered many critical insights. In the years ahead, I look forward to repaying her with affection and dedication.

W.B.T.

Introduction

In the nineteenth century British society became predominantly industrial and urban at an unprecedented pace. As Raymond Williams points out, "By the middle of the nineteenth century the urban population of England exceeded the rural population: the first time in human history that this had ever been so, anywhere. As a mark of the change to a new kind of civilisation the date has unforgettable significance. By the end of the nineteenth century, the urban population was three-quarters of the whole." [1]

The urban experience in Victorian times was, of course, not everywhere the same; life in London differed markedly from life in Manchester, Liverpool, or Birmingham. Yet in many ways the London experience was the most representative and the most important. London's population equalled or outran the population trends of the country as a whole. In 1800 the city's population was one million; in 1850 it grew to almost three million; and in 1900 it reached nearly six million. Although London did not have the overwhelming industrial atmosphere of Manchester or Birmingham, it did have many of the health and welfare problems associated with rapid industrial growth. For most of the nineteenth century, London was the largest city on earth—an international economic, political, and cultural center. Throughout that century London was the literary and publishing capital of Great Britain. The diverse urban experience of London, then, invited a variety of responses.

More late-century novelists than poets described the city in their work. In their studies of Victorian London since the appearance of Charles Dickens's novels both readers and critics have focused on the fictional response. One important reason for the dominance of the novel as a literary form—especially in the second half of the nineteenth century—may be the fact that fiction captured and recorded the topical, immediate, everyday life of both the city and the country. Fiction is the mode of the actual, the literary form of the middle class uniquely suited to capture the social, moral, and psychological tensions of the city. [2]

Conversely, one of the conventional ideas about nineteenth-century poetry holds that Victorian poets were predominantly poets of the countryside who had little, or little that was interesting, to say about city life. Between William Blake's "London" and T. S. Eliot's *The Waste Land*, so the received opinion goes, the major poets turned their backs on urban life. Like all such opinion, this conception has its grain of truth, but recent scholarship has shown the oversimplification of this picture. Books like R. A. Forsyth's *The Lost Pattern: Essays on the Emergent City Sensibility in Victorian England* and Raymond Williams's *The Country and the City*, as well as G. Robert Stange's essay "The Frightened Poets" in *The Victorian City*, show the widespread poetic interest in the city theme. Stange especially indicates the complexity of the topic when he claims that the Victorian city aroused "fear, fascination, horror, and ennui" in many Victorian poets who made attempts at "domesticating our apprehension of the terrifying or the unknown."[3]

Stange's pioneering essay first sparked my interest in how Victorian poets responded to the diverse and challenging phenomena of the urban experience, particularly in London. In a more general way, however, my study has been influenced and informed at many turns by the writings of Raymond Williams. Williams's reaction to the "sense of possibility" in the metropolis continued to dominate my thoughts. After quoting some lines from the sonnet in which Wordsworth looks out from Westminster Bridge and admires the "ships, towers, domes, theatres and temples . . . all bright and glittering in the smokeless air," Williams records his own modern response to the city: "It is true that this was the city before the rush and noise of the working day, but the pulse of the recognition is still unmistakable, and I know that I have felt it again and again: the great buildings of civilisation; the meeting-places; the libraries and theatres, the towers and domes; and often more moving than these, the houses, the streets, the press and excitement of so many people, with so many purposes. . . . I have known this feeling . . . [and said,] 'This is what men have built, so often magnificently, and is not everything then possible?'"[4]

This "sense of possibility" as an element of a poet's response to the city was most pronounced around 1850. Within three years, three writers challenged poets—in the words of Arthur Hugh Clough—to "own the positive and the present" and to speak "the Second Reverence, for things around." F. G. Stephens, Charles Kingsley, and Clough all asked poets to perform essentially the same tasks: to abandon rural verse overlaid with mythological machinery and to focus directly upon the exciting new energies and materials to be found in the contemporary city. To their way of thinking, the new poetry should help bring a sense of order to urban details and a new understanding of city experience to urban dwellers. It should also be a criticism and a commentary on their lives that they could recur to, just as they read the Bible for resolutions, inspiration, and understanding. In reading these mid-century statements, some questions come to mind: Did poets respond to the challenge of the three critics to deal directly in verse with the contemporary urban experience? How did society receive such poetry? Were some kinds of poetry about the city more popular than others? What forces or concepts prevented or deflected the expression in poetry of the possibilities and the problems of Victorian London? What was the range of responses? Should a poet offer literal transcriptions of the facts of the contemporary city in the form of journalistic observations or condemnations for social reform purposes? Should he offer high, visionary transformations of the city into an imaginative ideal? In short, what happens to poets and poetry under the impact of the urban experience?

I have never worked on a project where I was more surprised by the expanding directions in which it led. What began as a study of the development in theme and form of five or ten poets (from Blake to Eliot) who attempted to make social and political sense of the city, grew to include nearly twenty-five poets. In examining the varying uses that poets made of the city as setting and symbol, problem and promise, the study continuously raised questions about what poets in different decades of the nineteenth century conceived to be the functions and proper topics of poetry. The answers proved interesting but somewhat disturbing, for most nineteenth-century poets did not consistently realize the promise of the diverse subject of the city and of the ambitious program which Clough, Kingsley, and Stephens proposed to them. A large number of poems present, on the one hand, the entertainment, excitement, cultural enrichment, and social community of the city, and, on the other, its ugliness, danger, economic deprivation, and social alienation. But the point that comes across so strongly is that the various poets' subscription to an impossibly high ideal of an elevated poetic diction as well as noble subject matter and purpose prevented them from achieving the feats accomplished by a novelist like Dickens. Certainly the lure of the countryside and of the mythological past was also a distracting factor. In the final analysis, however, the dearth of truly first-rate poetic works between Blake's *Jerusalem* and Eliot's *The Waste Land* is explained by the traditions, partly inherited, and the conceptions, partly self-imposed, that most Victorian poets held concerning what a poet should be and what he should write about. Poetic traditions as nineteenth-century readers and poets understood them were not comprehensive enough to embrace consistently and fully the great challenge presented by the experience of the city. It took a Blake or an Eliot to break out of the prescribed forms and traditional notions, to write about the raw materials of the city in the context of the positive dream of London as the New Jerusalem or as a surrealistic world of nightmare alienation.

But Victorian poetry was often able to record the "structures of feeling" that respond to various social and historical facts. As urban dwellers, who more than likely came to the city for the first time in their early twenties, many Victorian poets were moved enough by the vitality of London to try at least once or twice, and sometimes sustainedly, to capture and record it from a poet's perspective. In the last half of the nineteenth century, poetry was a vital form as many poems sensitively and variously reflected the dynamics of urban change. In the poetry written between 1850 and 1900, there is a combined richness that deserves attention, even though no single dominant poet emerged. For five decades a variety of poets—from Clough to Henley, from Hopkins to Morris, from Buchanan to Davidson—responded to the historical facts of Victorian London and enriched their poetry by doing so. A study of this canon of poetry reveals much about the poets and their imaginative sense of the city. It was an exciting fifty-year period when the challenge to make poetry from the energy and devastation of the city was often met by fresh uses of the premises and conventions of Victorian poetry. In so many ways not yet even fully realized, Victorian London is a vital territory in the annals of Victorian poetry.

My intention in this study is not to provide a comprehensive descriptive catalogue, but to analyze in some detail several of the major strains of response by poets to the Victorian city. Not all of the relevant nineteenth-century poets are included and not all of the varieties of responses are treated. This work omits any discussion of working-class poets' treatment of the city because Martha Vicinus's excellent study *The Industrial Muse* amply covers this topic. Also, I have only suggested the topic's comparative literature dimensions—relationships between Victorian poets and such foreign writers as Baudelaire, Whitman, and others. Thus, several unexplored city streets remain for future days and future scholars.

Chapter One
Romantic Versions of the City

The Celestial City in the Poetry of Blake, Wordsworth, and Tennyson

Although William Blake, William Wordsworth, and Alfred Lord Tennyson envisioned what it would be like for humanity to live in an ideal city—a harmonious community of peace and fulfillment—they also experienced the reality of the nineteenth-century city. Of the three poets, Blake welcomed and most completely accepted metropolitan London. Blake lived in London all but three years of his life, while Wordsworth and Tennyson visited the city only to conduct business or to participate in special events. This does not imply that Wordsworth and Tennyson were ignorant of or indifferent to the growth of urban industrial communities in the nineteenth century. They both thought deeply about the disturbing and widespread changes in nineteenth-century life. Yet neither poet chose to become directly and permanently involved in the nineteenth-century urban environment. Beyond that, they chose not to make the city a major theme or setting in their poetry. But Blake, Wordsworth, and Tennyson did write about the celestial-city ideal, although each poet experienced the city of London differently.

In Blake's poetry the celestial city is most completely and essentially intertwined with the materials and inhabitants of the earthly city of London. Each earthly urban inhabitant contributes to the creation of the true vision that will build heaven on earth. The New Jerusalem on earth will be ushered in by the generous and compassionate attitudes of individuals who lead diverse but integrated, fulfilled lives. Blake is the first and only romantic poet to establish such a comprehensive and optimistic version of the celestial city. His vision always starts from and continues with the actual details and human attitudes of the earthly city. The New Jerusalem will be the capital of a perfect but real society. Although Blake admits a tension between the ideal and the real cities, he believes that his poetry can and will help to reconcile the disparity between the two states of being.

Blake most fully explores the two ideas—actual and ideal, unredeemed and glorified—of the city. In Wordsworth's poetry, however, versions of the celestial city appear less predictably or systematically. Glimpses of transcendent urban harmony appear in the "Westminster Bridge" sonnet as the actual city before the poet's eyes is transformed into an imagined symbol of natural and silent bliss. Several visions of an earthly celestial city are described in *The Excursion* and are nearly always associated with a particularly striking natural occurrence such as a storm upon a mountain-top. Only in *The Prelude* does Wordsworth present the details of his imme-diate and often confusing contact with the reality of London.

In the poetry of Alfred, Lord Tennyson, the celestial city is reached through the passage of historical imagination. Camelot, a city in the dis-tant past, always appears shrouded in mist and mystery. Although Cam-elot and Arthur seem closest to the celestial state when the poem begins, *Idylls of the King* is the story of a decaying social order. Instead of elevating the city to social and spiritual harmony (as in Blake's vision), the actions of Camelot's citizens hasten its social and moral dissolution. In other poems, like "Timbuctoo," when Tennyson contemplates how things really are, the city of imagination vanishes instantly. In *Maud* and in some shorter political poems when Tennyson considers specific details of the actual Lon-don of his time, he writes with a hysterical fear of the hard, indifferent force of the city as do some other poets of the Victorian period.

Blake's Urban Vision: The Poetry of Communal Renewal

With the exception of the years 1800–1803 spent in a cottage in Felp-ham, Sussex, Blake lived all of his life in London. Prophecy and visionary creation early became Blake's tasks as a poet. Hazard Adams makes a use-ful distinction between two types of prophecy: "If we examine the idea of what a prophet does, we see that prophecy takes two forms—criticism of existing conditions and visionary creation of a better world. The two forms are not apart, for in the fallen world the objects of indignation are the debased or inverted forms of that better world in the prophet's vision-ary grasp."[1] Although the two forms may not be "far apart" in Adams's terms, a considerable difference exists between Blake's treatment of the city in the early short sonnet "London" (1794) and the later long pro-phetic poem *Jerusalem* (1820). The development of Blake's entire career, his urban sensibility, and his prophetic mission intercede between the "microcosmic lyric" and the "macrocosmic epic."[2]

In the early volume *Songs of Experience* (1794), Blake's criticism of the social evils of London is direct and fiercely scrupulous; it has only muted symbolic resonances. Martin K. Nurmi, for example, has demonstrated how accurately Blake recorded the details of the wretched living and working conditions of chimney sweepers well before they appeared in "Extracts from Minutes of Evidence" taken by a committee of the House of Commons in June 1817.[3] Blake needed no investigative committee; the words of the small child speaker throughout the volume constitute a devastating attack on "Priest" and "King." The treatment of poverty by society in "Holy Thursday" (1794) is hypocritical and aloof. The speaker sees little hope for the "land of poverty"—"bleak and bare" and plagued with "eternal winter."[4] Although the poet's use of the surrealistic detail of the "cold and usurous hand" that hypocritically throws a few crumbs to the "Babes reduced to misery" (ll. 3–4) effectively presents the problem, he offers few solutions to urban suffering.

In "The Chimney Sweeper" (1790–92) and "Holy Thursday," Blake shows the rich and poor, the exploiters and the victims hardly meeting in the urban setting. The institutions of church and state are remotely present in "The Chimney Sweeper," and the special Ascension Day service which brings the poor orphans and the "cold and usurous hand" together only takes place annually. The lyric "London" is the most important statement on urban society in the volume because its symbolic figures suggest the intricate and continuous webs connecting classes in the capitalistic city. The speaker in the poem is neither a child nor a remote observer, but William Blake, a mature and responsible individual.

> I wander through each chartered street
> Near where the chartered Thames does flow,
> And mark in every face I meet
> Marks of weakness, marks of woe.   [ll. 1–4]

Implicit in this stanza and in the phrase "mind-forged manacles" in the next is the perception that societal repression is at least partly self-imposed: that there is a relation between one's weakness and one's woe. The remaining two stanzas of the poem develop dramatically and specifically what Raymond Williams calls "the submerged connections of this capital system."[5]

> How the chimney-sweeper's cry
> Every blackening church appalls,
> And the hapless soldier's sigh
> Runs in blood down palace walls;

> But most through midnight streets I hear
> How the youthful harlot's curse
> Blasts the new-born infant's tear
> And blights with plagues the marriage hearse. [ll. 9–16]

The city encompasses and reflects the welfare of all. As Williams stresses, Blake's vision in this poem is

> very far from the traditional way of seeing innocence in the country, vice in the city. The innocence and the vice are in and of the city, in its factual and spiritual relations. The palace which impressively symbolises power has to be seen as running with blood: the real but suppressed relationship is made visible, as also in the conventions of church and marriage against the reality of those who suffered and were despised and outcast. . . . . It is a making of new connections, in the whole order of the city and of the human system it concentrates and embodies. This forcing into consciousness of the suppressed connections is then a new way of seeing the human and social order as a whole.[6]

By the time Blake wrote *Jerusalem* (1820), he had expanded the symbolic dimensions of his poetic prophecies and was ready to describe the increased complexities of urban life. A celestial city that stood for a perfect society strongly attracted Blake, as it did Wordsworth and Tennyson. For all three poets, the road to the great, good place was through creative imagination and poetic vision. The uniqueness of Blake's achievement is that details and conditions of the real city of London continue to stimulate his imagination. He wants to make the actual city ideal, but in yearning after the ideal, he does not lose sight of the fact that only people can create a new, just, and harmonious social order. The Jerusalem that Blake envisions is a community of individuals who share the creative vision of a holy city rather than an unholy one of rational oppression and moral law. To build the holy city requires an expansion of creative, sensitive response to the real city. Jerusalem would not descend ready-made out of the sky, but would have to be built with the help of all in "England's green and pleasant land." The building plans are complex. Pages of commentary are intricately devoted to the streets and inhabitants of Blake's Jerusalem. The symbolic figures, events, and concepts most relevant to this study are in the contrast between the city of Golgonooza, built through Los's imaginative inspiration, and the unholy City of Babylon, filled with social and mental oppressions.

In trying to unravel Blake's view of the city in *Jerusalem*, one is immediately struck by the dense variety of possibilities associated with what are actually several separate cityscapes. One basic organizational device of the poem is a comparison and contrast between the City of Golgonooza and Babylon. Thus, two separate passages of long, detailed description of the building of both cities are given. The leaders and their multitude of followers invest tremendous energy and labor into this building. Both of these descriptive pieces appear early in the poem (plates 12 and 24). Throughout the remainder of the poem, Blake expands the significance of the cities as symbols by what could be called the process of associative addition. This process is very effective because it shows the cities to be constantly growing and changing. It also makes for effective symbolism because the basic symbol gathers resonance as qualities are later added one by one throughout the long prophetic poem. These expanding construction sites are worth exploring. Babylon should be visited first, followed by Golgonooza, which leads directly to Jerusalem in the temporal eternal dimension.

The long, detailed passage describing the building of Babylon is in plate 24.

> O human imagination! O divine body I have crucified,
> I have turned my back upon thee into the wastes of moral law.
> There Babylon is builded in the waste, founded in human
>   desolation.
> O Babylon, thy watchman stands over thee in the night;
> Thy severe judge all the day long proves thee, O Babylon,
> With provings of destruction, with giving thee thy heart's desire.
> But Albion is cast forth to the potter, his children to the builders
> To build Babylon, because they have forsaken Jerusalem.
> The walls of Babylon are souls of men, her gates the groans
> Of nations, her towers are the miseries of once happy families.
> Her streets are paved with destruction, her houses built with death,
> Her palaces with hell & the grave, her synagogues with torments
> Of ever-hardening despair, squared & polished with cruel skill
>   [pl. 24. ll. 23–35]

The precision with which Blake informs his urban vision of the unholy city throughout the poem is impressive. The spiritual degradation that plagues the fallen city is not simply a generalized feeling of uneasiness or ennui but a series of specific instances of desolation which link the various dimensions of spiritual malaise to certain tangible objects of the city. Thus, the "souls of men" become mortar for the "walls of Babylon," just as the soldier's blood becomes a grotesque decoration on the palace wall in the lyric "London." The gates consist of groans, while the increasing "miseries of once happy families" build ever-soaring skyscrapers or "towers." This surrealistic vision of an urban spiritual wasteland is depicted over one hundred years before T. S. Eliot's famous poem.

Such a panoramic view of Babylon appears only once. Throughout the rest of the poem, the speaker focuses on specific episodes and locales as Babylon takes on ever grimmer dimensions. In plate 42, for example, Albion appeals to the "twenty-four rebellious ingratitudes" who "curse their human kindness and affection" as he "calls aloud for vengeance deep!" (pl. 42. ll. 48, 54, 60). By appealing to the inhabitants' baser emotions of fear, cruelty, and vengeance, Albion offers to lead the disgruntled to the new citadel.

> "Come up, build Babylon! Rahab is ours & all her multitudes
> With her in pomp & glory of victory. Depart,
> Ye twenty-four, into the deeps; let us depart to glory!"
>
> [pl. 42. ll. 63–65]

But the important fact that Babylon is no citadel on a hill but really either underground or under heavy smoke is established in plate 60 where the images of captivity in the forms of dungeons and mills are described.

> But Jerusalem faintly saw him [the Divine Lamb], closed in the
> dungeons of Babylon.
> Her form was held by Beulah's daughters, but all within unseen
> She sat at the mills, her hair unbound, her feet naked,
> Cut with the flints—her tears run down, her reason grows like
> The wheel of Hand, incessant turning day & night without rest.
>
> [pl. 60. ll. 39–43]

Several lines later, Jerusalem affirms her belief in human imagination and the divine body even though she is a captive in Babylon: "But I know thee, O Lord, when thou arisest upon / My weary eyes, even in this dungeon & this iron mill" (pl. 60. ll. 58–59). Several commentators have stressed the misleading notion that Blake equates London/England with "the dark Satanic mills." Actually, the mills are only one small dimension of the London/Babylon landscape.

Indeed, many other rich symbolic dimensions of Babylon, the fallen city, are developed even as the prophecy moves toward its apocalyptic conclusion. In plate 74, for instance, Blake presents the city as a labyrinthine maze and as a storehouse for the errors of human history.

> I behold Babylon in the opening streets of London. I behold
> Jerusalem in ruins wandering about from house to house.

This I behold; the shudderings of death attend my steps,
I walk up and down in six thousand years; their events are present
   before me.   [pl. 74. ll. 16–19]

This figure of the narrator "wandering about," seemingly devoid of all
purpose except to observe the snares of errors, recurs often in nineteenth-
century poetry as an important motif. The aspect of the city as the reposi-
tory of the errors of human history (mainly under the forms of the wastes
of "abstraction opposed to the visions of imagination" and "cruel laws" [ll.
26–27]) is elaborated more fully several lines later.

Babylon, the rational morality deluding to death the little ones
In strong temptations of stolen beauty. I tell how Reuben slept
On London Stone, & the daughters of Albion ran around admiring
His awful beauty; with Moral Virtue the fair deceiver, offspring
Of good & evil, they divided him in love upon the Thames & sent
Him over Europe in streams of gore out of Cathedron's looms.
                                           [pl. 74. ll. 32–37]

In this passage and in the following, Blake identifies the false outlooks
that oppress mental states. Falsehoods are outward, artificial delusions
that prevent the realization of the individualized state of true inward vi-
sion. Besides these delusions, falsehoods include uncreative work and reli-
gious creeds—"Moral Visions"—that obscure God's true purposes. The
symbolic and associative resonances continue as lures of fleshly passion and
other destructive falsehoods—subtle deceits and sometimes violent in-
trigues in both personal and business relationships—are associated with
Babylon in plate 82.

So saying, she took a falsehood & hid it in her left hand,
To entice her sisters away to Babylon on Euphrates.
And thus she closed her left hand and uttered her falsehood.
                                           [pl. 82. ll. 17–19]

And, again, a few lines later:

See how the fires of our loins point eastward to Babylon.
Look! Hyle is become an infant love. Look, behold, see him lie
Upon my bosom! Look! Here is the lovely wayward form
That gave me sweet delight by his torments beneath my veil.
                                           [pl. 82. ll. 36–39]

Besides lust and the violence of materialistic power, Blake identifies a final
set of human errors that enslave mental life in Babylon: "pride," "oppres-
sion," and "delusion" (pl. 85. l. 31).

In the closing plates of the poem, just before the Apocalypse, the situation becomes bleaker. At the nadir of nastiness, Babylon is indeed "The Abomination of Desolation" (pl. 75. l. 19). In these last days, Blake reverts to images that he used earlier in his "London" lyric and also borrows heavily upon figures that appear in the Book of Revelation.[7] Thus, in plate 84, the aged blind man being led through the streets by a child reappears: "I see London blind & age-bent begging through the streets / Of Babylon, led by a child: his tears run down his beard" (pl. 84. ll. 11–12). But the misery extends beyond London so that it taints the entire world.

> The voice of wandering Reuben echoes from street to street
> In all the cities of the nations; Paris, Madrid, Amsterdam.
> The corner of Broad Street weeps, Poland Street languishes,
> To Great Queen Street & Lincoln's Inn, all is distress & woe.
>
> [pl. 84. ll. 13–16]

At the eleventh hour before the Apocalypse, Babylon is no longer described in terms of perverted human traits, but in terms of larger emblems. Babylon—now called "Babylon the Great"—is referred to several times as "religion hid in war, a dragon red & hidden harlot" (pl. 75. l. 20 and pl. 93. l. 25).

So far as similarities between Blake's presentations of Babylon and Golgonooza are concerned, strenuous energy and dedication are invested in the constant construction of both cities; Blake wishes to stress that for the present, at least, it is a struggle between "two opposite but equal orders."[8] On the Golgonoozan side of London, Los and his laborers bear the pressures of "terrible eternal labour" (pl. 12. l. 24) and exhibit "vast strength" (pl. 11. l. 1). The specter of Los is also seen

> labouring at the roarings of his forge,
> With iron & brass building Golgonooza in great contendings
> Till his sons & daughters came forth from the furnaces
> At the sublime labours. . . .   [pl. 10. ll. 62–65]

Furthermore, just as in the description of the building of Babylon, an extended passage details the metaphorical building materials used to construct Golgonooza.

> What are those golden builders doing?
>
> .   .   .   .
>
>   Is that Calvary & Golgotha
> Becoming a building of pity & compassion? Lo!
> The stones are pity and the bricks well-wrought affections,
> Enamelled with love & kindness, & the tiles engraven gold,

Labour of merciful hands. The beams & rafters are forgiveness;
The mortar & cement of the work, tears of honesty; the nail
And the screws & iron braces are well-wrought blandishments,
And well-contrived words, firm fixing, never forgotten,
Always comforting the remembrance; the floors, humility,
The ceilings, devotion; the hearths, thanksgiving.

[pl. 12. l. 25, ll. 28–37]

These materials are shaped into a distinctive "fourfold" pattern that distinguishes Golgonooza's architecture as a mental state. In Blake's system, a "fourfold" pattern indicates completeness, proportion, and near-perfection.

Fourfold the sons of Los in their divisions. And fourfold
The great city of Golgonooza: fourfold toward the north
And toward the south fourfold, & fourfold toward the east & west,
Each within other toward the four points—that toward
Eden, and that toward the world of generation,
And that toward Beulah, and that toward Ulro.
(Ulro is the space of the terrible starry wheels of Albion's sons.)
But that toward Eden is walled up till time of renovation;
Yet it is perfect in its building, ornaments & perfection.

[pl. 12. ll. 45–53]

The significant difference between Babylon and Golgonooza first appears in this passage. Whereas the inhabitants of Babylon suffer the confining limits of single or perverted vision, the citizens of Golgonooza have the gift of expansive vision ("every inhabitant fourfold" [pl. 13. l. 20]). Each expansion of imaginative vision, each creative act is a step toward Eden, the gates of which are "all closed up till the last Day" (pl. 13. l. 11). The expansion of Golgonoozan vision leads to the regeneration of Albion/England and beyond that, the redemption of the world. Given this temporal-eternal dimension, one is hard-pressed to find specific passages concerning single locales, episodes, and errors as is evident with Babylon. Yet just as Blake uses the device of building up the symbol of Babylon by adding aspects of the city one by one, so too he uses the process of associative addition to establish the symbolic importance of Golgonooza.

Golgonooza is shown to be an ever-expanding community of creative imagination. The reentry to eternity through Golgonooza is not guaranteed. The "terrors of Entuthon"—the land of dark, gloomy forests—surround and nearly engulf Golgonooza (pl. 5. l. 24). In the early plates of the poem Blake establishes the tremendous odds Golgonooza has to overcome and its need for a vigorous reclamation program. Further details of the environs are given: "Around Golgonooza lies the land of death eternal, a land / Of pain & misery & despair & ever-brooding melancholy" (pl. 13. ll. 30–31) and there are "deep vales beneath Golgonooza" (pl. 14. l. 34). For many lines a high construction fence blocks the reader's view of the building of Golgonooza because new details and aspects of the symbolic city do not surface again until plate 53. Here Blake stresses that the building of Golgonooza, like the evolution of any great city, will be a matter of "continually building and continually decaying" (pl. 53. l. 19). Both art and urban renewal involve regeneration and reassessment; both are sustained by continual, active creation and reworking of fading material. As London/Golgonooza becomes more secure in its position, it becomes a hub of activity. In the struggle to rescue Jerusalem from her Babylonian captivity, London/Golgonooza, as the nucleus of a network, enlists the aid of the Twenty-Eight Cathedral Cities of England. The expansion continues until

> All these centre in London & in Golgonooza, from whence
> They are created continually, east & west & north & south,
> And from them are created all the nations of the earth,
> Europe & Asia & Africa & America, in fury fourfold!
>
> [pl. 72. ll. 28–31]

London, although it becomes a world city, never loses its distinctive character for Blake, and he captures its awesome but actual charm in one of the nineteenth century's most beautiful lyric tributes to the city's industry and human vitality.

> So Los spoke to the daughters of Beulah, while his emanation
> Like a faint rainbow waved before him in the awful gloom
> Of London, city on the Thames, from Surrey hills to Highgate.
> Swift turn the silver spindles, & the golden weights play soft
> And lulling harmonies beneath the looms from Caithness in the
>   north
> To Lizard Point & Dover in the south. His emanation
> Joyed in the many weaving threads in bright Cathedron's dome,
> Weaving the web of life for Jerusalem; the web of life
> Down flowing into Entuthon's vales glistens with soft affections,
> While Los arose upon his watch, and down from Golgonooza
> Putting on his golden sandals to walk from mountain to mountain,
> He takes his way, girding himself with gold, & in his hand
> Holding his iron mace; the spectre remains attentive.

Alternate they watch in night, alternate labour in day,
Before the furances labouring, while Los all night watches
The stars rising & setting, & the meteors & terrors of night.
With him went down the dogs of Leutha, at his feet
They lap the water of the trembling Thames, then follow swift.

[pl. 84. ll. 66–83]

As the poem moves toward the Apocalypse—the revolution that will assure peace, harmony, and unity—the City of Golgonooza, Los's City of Art, is seen "in the shadowy generation" (pl. 98. l. 55). The art works themselves may fade into a penumbra, but the creative gestures that produced them are eternal and properly are transferred from Golgonooza to Jerusalem.

Another feature of Blake's vision merits particular attention: his doctrine of "Minute Particulars," or the conviction that "Everything exists, & not one sigh nor smile nor tear, / One hair nor particle of dust, not one can pass away" (pl. 13. l. 66; pl. 14. l. 1). In *Jerusalem* Blake constantly stresses that the actions and thoughts of individuals cause the social and imaginative order to be formed gloriously or deformed grotesquely. Raymond Williams has written extensively concerning how the term *masses* is used to focus the aggregate of our unknown and irrational fears. The *masses* never includes us or our friends, but always some vague, mysterious other group of people or forces.[9] Blake would have none of this. Unlike many later nineteenth-century poets, he had no fear of people working together for constructive change. The term *masses* occurs only once in *Jerusalem* and that reference is to a heap of stones (pl. 83. l. 10). Blake does, however, use the terms *multitudes* or *innumerable multitudes* often, but he is always careful to keep his social descriptions in focus by stressing the minute particularity or individuality that is the underlying foundation of a group's deeds or misdeeds.

Besides the social implications of Blake's urban vision, several commentators provide other interesting perspectives on the poem. In *Fearful Symmetry* Northrop Frye makes significant connections between *Jerusalem* and the archetypal myth of "The City of God." In *Blake: Prophet against Empire* David Erdman takes a more historical perspective, linking events in the poem to trends and actualities of early nineteenth-century England and France. Kenneth R. Johnston's essay "Blake's Cities: Romantic Forms of Urban Renewal" is perhaps the most balanced of the studies because it points out that although Blake viewed the city as "a place of infinite possibility," "a giant mythic entity," there is also a realistic understanding in his prophetic vision that the building of the New Order would require strenuous exercise of the creative power of imagination and would suffer many setbacks along the way. In Johnston's words, Blake "brings urban myth and urban reality together in his illuminations as well as his texts." Furthermore, "we build a Jerusalem or a Babylon depending on how we choose to exercise our imaginations."[10] A valuable appendix to Johnston's article compares Blake's urban vision to those of other nineteenth-century poets. Johnston points out, for example, that although Wordsworth's distaste for London is well known, "we tend to forget the mythopoeic stature of the images in which he expressed it—or attempted to reconcile himself to it."[11] This tension between celebration and alienation, between the ideal and the actual, that the city produces in Wordsworth and Blake is most significant. Raymond Williams seems to second Johnston in agreeing that "Blake's London and Wordsworth's London are equally alienated, but the standpoint is different."[12] The reasons behind the tension and the standpoints of the two poets are worth exploring.

Wordsworth's Urban Vision: Distant Glimpses and "Hurdy-gurdy" Involvement

Although a fundamental impulse behind Blake's urban poetic vision involved a transliteration of the actual into the ideal, this generalization is only partially valid with regard to Wordsworth's poetry about the city. Whereas Blake spent only three years of his life away from London, Wordsworth spent just under three years of his long life in the "vast metropolis." Wordsworth's response to London, then, was fundamentally that of a rural man who found himself both eager and bewildered in the densely concentrated center of humanity. Indeed, Wordsworth focuses on *distance* in nearly all of his poems and passages concerning the city. For Wordsworth, distance from the city is a means of order. It is not only mere physical distance—the stance on a bridge, or in an outlying field— but also the distance of memory and tradition along with the device of viewing the city experience through another character's eyes or through a pastoral veil. An understanding of the workings of this complex response requires a more detailed elaboration of some of Wordsworth's poems.

In "The Reverie of Poor Susan" (1797) Susan, a recent migrant to London from the countryside, is still able to receive sensations and to daydream of the "green pastures," "the mountain ascending," and the "single small cottage" she has left behind.[13] Yet in the barren midst of the city and at a time when she most needs to rely on the sustaining powers of imagination, she is unable to associate or to recall intensely enough in order to transport her daydreams to a vital vision.

> She looks, and her heart is in heaven: but they fade,
> The mist and the river, the hill and the shade:
> The stream will not flow, and the hill will not rise,
> And the colours have all passed away from her eyes!   [ll. 13–16]

Susan's plight is meant to evoke pity, but Wordsworth treats a similar situation with humor in "The Farmer of Tilsbury Vale" (1800). Old Adam "dwells in the centre of London's wide Town" (l. 5). Most of his life, however, was spent as a farmer and innkeeper until he decided one day to declare bankruptcy. The rascal solicited charitable contributions from his neighbors and "Then (what is too true) without hinting a word, / Turned his back on the country—and off like a bird" (ll. 39–40). Old Adam's first few days in the city are pathetic.

> To London—a sad emigration I ween—
> With his grey hairs he went from the brook and the green;
> And there, with small wealth but his legs and his hands,
> As lonely he stood as a crow on the sands.   [ll. 45–48]

Soon, however, the crafty farmer feels the vitality and diverse stimulation of the city.

> He seems ten birthdays younger, is green and is stout;
> Twice as fast as before does his blood run about;
> You would say that each hair of his beard was alive,
> And his fingers as busy as bees in a hive.   [ll. 53–56]

Although the tone of light humor is sustained throughout, a subtle form of salvation is introduced at the poem's turning-point.

> In the throng of the town like a stranger is he,
> Like one whose own country's far over the sea;
> And Nature, while through the great city he hies,
> Full ten times a day takes his heart by surprise,   [ll. 61–64]

The semicolon separates and holds in tension two prevailing structures of feeling. On the one hand, the recent arrival feels strange and alienated amidst the excitement of the new place with its thronging masses of people; on the other hand, the sights, sounds, and smells of familiar country life uplift him. Like Blake, Wordsworth can specifically inform his idealized vision of contentment with actual details. Unlike Blake, Wordsworth's actualities and particularities create a pastoral cityscape.

'Mid coaches and chariots, a waggon of straw,
Like a magnet, the heart of old Adam can draw;
With a thousand soft pictures his memory will teem,
And his hearing is touched with the sounds of a dream.

Up the Haymarket hill he oft whistles his way,
Thrusts his hands in a waggon, and smells at the hay;
He thinks of the fields he so often hath mown,
And is happy as if the rich freight were his own.

But chiefly to Smithfield he loves to repair,—
If you pass by at morning, you'll meet with him there.
The breath of the cows you may see him inhale,
And his heart all the while is in Tilsbury Vale.   [ll. 77–88]

Wordsworth also wrote poems about specific historical characters trying
to come to grips with the urban experience. The poem "Michael" (1800),
for instance, is based on factual stories of the Lake Country region. As
Isabel and Michael try to envision a way out of their impoverished situa-
tion, they recall the story of the boy Richard Bateman, who, with the
good wishes of the neighborhood, "went up to London [and] found a mas-
ter there" (l. 264). Chosen as a "trusty boy," Richard soon became "won-
drous rich" as he took charge of overseas merchandise (ll. 265–67). Never
forgetting his humble origins, he gave monies and services to the poor.
Based on this local exemplar, the old couple decide that it is in their son
Luke's best interest to send him to the city so that he may also become a
prosperous and generous man. Luke does well for a time, but all too
quickly his career becomes a grim parody of Richard Bateman's.

                    Meantime Luke began
To slacken in his duty; and, at length,
He in the dissolute city gave himself
To evil courses: ignominy and shame
Fell on him, so that he was driven at last
To seek a hiding-place beyond the seas.   [ll. 442–47]

The city breaks not only the spirit of a fine country boy but also the hearts
of his parents. All productive work halts at home: "Many and many a day
he thither [Michael to the sheepfold] went, / And never lifted up a single
stone" (ll. 465–66).

Wordsworth's poem "Written After the Death of Charles Lamb" (1835)
treats the circumstances of an urbanite who was an actual historical fig-
ure—a friend of Wordsworth's who chose to live his life in the city and an

individual who did not hesitate to express his antipathy toward the country way of life. To Wordsworth, Lamb's urban existence was dreary indeed; London was the place where he

> humbly earned his bread,
> To the strict labours of the merchant's desk
> By duty chained. Not seldom did those tasks
> Tease, and the thought of time so spent depress,
> His spirit, but the recompense was high.   [ll. 4–8]

In the statement "the recompense was high" Wordsworth refers to the personal qualities of Charles Lamb that enabled him to transcend the sordidness and irritations of his London life. Lamb spread his humane joy through the streets of the city: ". . . while he ranged the crowded streets / With a keen eye, and overflowing heart" (ll. 13–14). The city inspired Lamb to produce creative literature filled with "affections," "humour," and "wit."

> So genius triumphed over seeming wrong,
> And poured out truth in works by thoughtful love
> Inspired—works potent over smiles and tears.   [ll. 15–17]

To generalize, then, from some of Wordsworth's shorter poems, when the poet looks at the city in the experience of others, he sees it as a good place when it becomes laden with pastoral trappings, as a stimulant to virtue for those few who can struggle against its hardness, or as a destructive spoiler of those of weaker character.

As far as strictly personal responses to "the vast metropolis" are concerned, Wordsworth's canon has two sonnets, one book of *The Prelude*, and some other scattered references. The two sonnets, "Composed upon Westminster Bridge, September 3, 1802" and "London, 1802" reinforce the Blakean divisions of London as ideal versus London as the emblem of all corrupt things. Although neither poem captures in a detailed way Wordsworth's experience of the metropolis, the two poems prefigure strains of response that would appear many times in the course of the century. The "Westminster Bridge" poem is one of the first examples in nineteenth-century poetry of the tendency not really to look at or to become involved with the city before the viewer's eyes. Instead, the countryside from which the poet has just come stays predominantly on his mind as he sees the city from a distance. The urban forms and structures metaphorically expand outward "unto the fields, and to the sky."

> This City now doth, like a garment, wear
> The beauty of the morning; silent, bare,

> Ships, towers, domes, theatres, and temples lie
> Open unto the fields, and to the sky;
> All bright and glittering in the smokeless air.   [ll. 4–8]

"London, 1802" focuses on the deteriorating condition of England's virtues and traditions. Not one line of the poem specifically deals with London. Rather, the distancing device of an appeal to past tradition or to something outside the city is operative as the spirit of John Milton is invoked as a saving power.

> Milton! thou shouldst be living at this hour:
> England hath need of thee: she is a fen
>
> .   .   .   .   .   .
>
> Oh! raise us up, return to us again;
> And give us manners, virtue, freedom, power.
> Thy soul was like a Star, and dwelt apart.   [ll. 1–2, 7–9]

By this appeal to something other than the city's internal energy or to the potential of its inhabitants, Wordsworth suggests that the city must be understood and saved by the imposition of an order different from that of a metropolis. This suggestion recurs in Wordsworth's poetry and in works by poets as late as T. S. Eliot.

Wordsworth's fullest, most complex, and most direct responses to the city are found in *The Prelude*. Although there are some significant differences between the 1805 and the 1850 versions of the text, the 1805 version is the fresher, more immediate of the two responses. By 1850 Wordsworth had settled into a hardened conservatism and tended to be unrealistic and vituperative in his attitude toward the city.[14] The 1805 version is based on memories of a stay in London from January to September 1795. Although the most extended discussion of the "vast metropolis" occurs in book 7, "Residence in London," both the city and the characteristic Wordsworthian tendency of distancing it in order to concentrate on creative work occur in the opening lines of book 1.

> O welcome messenger! O welcome friend!
> A captive greets thee, coming from a house
> Of bondage, from yon city's walls set free,
> A prison where he hath been long immured.
> Now I am free, enfranchised and at large,
> May fix my habitation where I will.[15]

Even though Wordsworth leaves the city behind in the opening lines of *The Prelude*, he returns to study and savor it in book 7. The more one reads "Residence in London," the more one is struck by the intricacy and complexity of Wordsworth's response to the great metropolis. Wordsworth's moods in the city fluctuate so strikingly between eagerness and bewilderment, celebration and alienation, admiration and detestation, anticipation and disappointment. Basically, book 7 divides into four categories of responses: (1) an early enchantment with the very idea of London, (2) an uneasiness at the theater and other entertainment shows about town, (3) a distressed confusion amidst the plethora of sensations and the masses ("rabblement") at Bartholomew Fair, and (4) a reaffirmation of individual identity and a rather swift departure from the city.

Wordsworth recalls that as a boy at Cockersmouth Grammar School, a classmate with leg trouble had to go to London for an operation. Wordsworth states that the more he thought about London while the boy was away, the more his vision of the city took on the exciting qualities of "wonder and obscure delight." He associates London with all that he has heard and read about Rome, Alcairo, Babylon, and Persepolis; he remembers those alluring reports given by "pilgrim friars / Of golden cities" (bk. 7. ll. 81–91). Wordsworth, then, sets up the city as a grand ideal vision in his mind. Soon, however, reality undercuts the idealized city as the crippled boy returns and Wordsworth recalls his own reaction.

> I was not wholly free
> From disappointment to behold the same
> Appearance, the same body, not to find
> Some change, some beams of glory brought away
> From that new region. Much I questioned him;
> And every word he uttered, on my ears
> Fell flatter than a cagèd parrot's note,
> That answers unexpectedly awry,
> And mocks the prompter's listening. Marvellous things
> My fancy had shaped forth, of sights and shows,
> Processions, equipages, Lords and Dukes,
> The King, and the King's Palace, and, not last,
> Or least, Heaven bless him! the renowned Lord Mayor.
> {bk. 7. ll. 100–112}

Rich in its responses, this passage has an underlying assumption that the city is a region so glorious and new that it should inevitably work some drastic, even redemptive change in a person. The fact that the boy traveler was a cripple adds to the expectation of the city's miraculous curative or restorative power; a person would go to London as a pilgrim would journey to a religious shrine. As Wordsworth listens to the boy tell of his visit, his words sound "flatter than a cagèd parrot's note." Thus, Wordsworth touches on the captive artificiality, the "puppet show" aspect of figures in the city—spectacles such as the poets of the 1890s would celebrate as interesting and valuable material for poetry about the city. Wordsworth also envisions the city as a showplace for royal establishment-type figures (bk. 7. ll. 110–12). He makes no mention yet of the thronging, mass crowds.

Wordsworth's disappointment over the young cripple's report about London not matching the reports "by pilgrim friars / Of golden cities" was not enough to restrain him from visiting the metropolis himself. Wordsworth's first impressions of the city are probably unsurpassed in their candor and insight in nineteenth-century poetry. He records that he is immediately overwhelmed to see "how men lived / Even next-door neighbours, as we say, yet still / Strangers, and knowing not each other's names" (bk. 7. ll. 118–20). And yet, the sheer physical scale of the city fascinates him—"Streets without end, and churches numberless" (bk. 7. l. 133)—as does what Raymond Williams calls "the press and excitement of so many people, with so many purposes."[16]

> The endless stream of men, and moving things,
> From hour to hour the illimitable walk
> Still among streets with clouds and sky above,
> The wealth, the bustle and the eagerness,
> The glittering chariots with their pampered steeds,
> Stalls, barrows, porters; midway in the street
> The scavenger, who begs with hat in hand,
> The labouring hackney coaches, the rash speed.
>   [bk. 7. ll. 158–65]

In this passage Wordsworth initially distinguishes types in the crowd; he neither fears the thronging crowds nor sees them as an undifferentiated blur. He sees individuals going about their various trades in the work-a-day world of the city. Later in the poem Wordsworth also admires and appreciates the cosmopolitan aspects of the city which blended individuals from all nations of the world into the crowds.

Besides viewing the variety of London's people and their serious activities, in book 7 Wordsworth also describes the various entertainments about town.

> At leisure let us view, from day to day,
> As they present themselves, the spectacles
> Within doors, troops of wild beasts, birds and beasts
> Of every nature, from all climes convened;
> And, next to these, those mimic sights that ape

> The absolute presence of reality,
> Expressing, as in mirror, sea and land,
> And what earth is, and what she has to show.   [bk. 7. ll. 244–51]

The artificial, mimic-of-reality aspect of the city's entertainments along with the real shows of exotic beasts and birds strike Wordsworth's attention. His perspective in recording the various events likewise strikes the reader's attention. The great poet in the city is indeed a passive consumer of popular culture; he has no control over the "spectacles" that "present themselves." The passage also reminds the reader that Wordsworth is not a citizen of London but a tourist passing through, a lone man walking about the town "at leisure." Wordsworth's perspective, then, is different from Blake's, and this partially explains why Wordsworth focuses so extensively on puppet shows and the like and never sees the "dark Satanic mills" that sometimes appear in Blake's poems.

Although Wordsworth's and Blake's perspectives on the London scene differed in several respects, it would be a mistake to imply that Wordsworth was only a passive tourist who took in the sights of the city. Like Blake, Wordsworth sees things in London which distress him deeply. Thus, important shifts from mere observation to concerned condemnation occur in book 7 of *The Prelude*. For example, Wordsworth, like Blake, was appalled by the number of harlots about town. Wordsworth is uneasy about theater entertainment because it attracts all sorts of disreputable people.

> Upon a board
> Whence an attendant of the theatre
> Served out refreshments, had this child been placed,
> And there he sate, environed with a ring
> Of chance spectators, chiefly dissolute men
> And shameless women; treated and caressed,
> Ate, drank, and with the fruit and glasses played,
> While oaths, indecent speech, and ribaldry
> Were rife about him as are songs of birds.   [bk. 7. ll. 382–90]

Wordsworth also senses and berates the sudden shifts in mood and fashion which have become a characteristic of urban life.

> Folly, vice
> Extravagance in gesture, mien, and dress,
> And all the strife of singularity,
> Lies to the ear, and lies to every sense—
> Of these, and of the living shapes they wear,
> There is no end. . . .   [bk. 7. ll. 571–76]

As it turns out, this "sterile of singularity," this bewildering spectacle of everybody trying to mark himself off from the masses, increasingly obsesses Wordsworth in the vast metropolis. The foregoing discussion of Blake's _Jerusalem_ introduced Raymond Williams's theories concerning the writer's perceptions of the masses. Blake always saw the city as a conglomerate of individual thoughts, actions, and feelings. For a time, Wordsworth maintains such an outlook. It soon becomes apparent, however, that Wordsworth fears the merging of his own identity with the "many-headed mass." Such a loss of bearings and identity disturbs him deeply. The problem was not unique to Wordsworth, but it is an indication of the poet's modernity. The late-nineteenth-century sociologist Georg Simmel studied the screening mechanisms that individuals use to protect themselves and to preserve their autonomy in the crunch of metropolitan life. He argued that a predominant defense is an increased emphasis on intellectual activity, as opposed to strong emotional relationships, which are more characteristic of rural or small town communities. "Metropolitan life, thus, underlies a heightened awareness and a predominance of intelligence in metropolitan man. . . . Intellectuality is thus seen to preserve subjective life against the overwhelming power of metropolitan life." [17]

Simmel's emphasis on the predominant reliance on intellect as a response to metropolitan life sheds a more flattering light on Wordsworth's constant return to Milton's spirit and verse and makes Wordsworth's references to "even highest minds" (bk. 7. l. 705) as opposed to "untaught minds" (bk. 7. l. 297) appear a little less elitist and snobbish. With Simmel's explanation in mind, such perplexing passages as the following invitation by Wordsworth become more understandable.

> Meanwhile the roar continues, till at length,
> Escaped as from an enemy, we turn
> Abruptly into some sequestered nook,
> Still as a sheltered place when winds blow loud!
>
> [bk. 7. ll. 184–87]

At first this passage appears to be indulgence in pure escapism by a man frustrated with the press of the city. Is "some sequestered nook" a dark alley or a park square? Who is the "we" Wordsworth invites to accompany him in his retreat from the "enemy" on the streets? Here Wordsworth's mind turns to a passage in Milton's _Comus_ in which a shepherd talks of finding shelter in "a dark sequester'd nook" (l. 500). Thus, the lines under discussion are not merely rural fantasizing, but a subtle commingling of Wordsworth's reliance on the distancing devices of nature and tradition.

By implication the "we" in the passage refers to the body of educated readers who could also share in the transporting and restorative intellectual relief that the Miltonic passage could provide.

At other times in the city, however, Milton and intellect were not enough succor as Wordsworth became overwhelmed with the emotional sensations he felt in the midst of a large crowd. Such gatherings also sparked irrational fears in Wordsworth's political conscience. The most famous record of this response is, of course, that of his visit to St. Bartholomew's Fair with Charles Lamb in 1802. Even before Wordsworth presents his own disturbance at the fair in detail, he strictly links such entertainment with dangerous tendencies in the city.

> What say you, then,
> To time, when half the city shall break out
> Full of one passion, vengeance, rage, or fear?
> To executions, to a street on fire,
> Mobs, riots, or rejoicings? From those sights
> Take one, —an annual festival, the Fair
> Holden where martyrs suffered in past time,
> And named of St Bartholomew; there, see
> A work that's finished to our hands, that lays,
> If any spectacle on earth can do,
> The whole creative powers of man asleep!   [bk. 7. ll. 644–54]

As in the veiled use of Milton in the "sequester'd nook" passage cited earlier, Wordsworth immediately calls on poetry to rescue him in his confusion.

> For once, the Muse's help will we implore,
> And she shall lodge us, wafted on her wings,
> Above the press and danger of the crowd.   [bk. 7. ll. 655–57]

But the call for the Muse's help is to no avail. In the confusion of the crowd, Wordsworth loses his individual human identity. As Williams stresses, the loss of self-identity leads inevitably to the loss of social identity, to the destruction of society itself.[18] Wordsworth becomes an alienated entity wandering amidst a "swarm" of urban inhabitants.

> To the whole swarm of its inhabitants;
> An undistinguishable world to men,
> The slaves unrespited of low pursuits,
> Living amid the same perpetual flow
> Of trivial objects, melted and reduced

> To one identity, by differences
> That have no law, no meaning, and no end—
> Oppression, under which even highest minds
> Must labour, whence the strongest are not free.
>
> [bk. 7. ll. 698–706]

As Williams points out, "Under the pressure of alienation, delusion is generated."[19] Not only does Wordsworth come to see Bartholomew Fair as a "Parliament of Monsters" that is "monstrous in colour, motion, shape, sight, sound" (bk. 7. l. 661) and full of "All-out-o'-the-way, far-fetched, perverted things / All freaks of nature" (bk. 7. ll. 687–88), but in his confusion extends the perception delusively so that it comes to stand for the entire city of London: "Oh, blank confusion! and a type not false / Of what the mighty City is itself" (bk. 7. ll. 795–96). (In the conservatism of his old age, Wordsworth changed "type" to "true epitome" in the 1850 revision.)

The "Oh, blank confusion!" passage, however, is not the "true epitome" of Wordsworth's response to the city. Wordsworth never ceases to amaze readers and critics in his ability to recover his sense of perspective and to grow immensely from a confusing experience. Throughout *The Prelude* there are various scenes such as the boat-stealing incident, the ice-skating experience, and the gibbet landscape, which at the time of their occurrence leave the poet in a state of confusion; their full revelatory significance and restorative power are understood only in retrospect. The Bartholomew Fair incident is also one of these "spots of time." By the close of book 7, Wordsworth looks back at the experience from the distancing perspective of his mind, aided by "The Spirit of Nature." As Williams says, "Wordsworth responds to his own remarkable vision of an alienated social condition with a reaffirmation of the power of his own mind, educated by Nature, to retain order, relation, and composure."[20] At the end of book 7, Wordsworth convinces himself that there is a way out, that he can move "Through meagre lines and colours, and the press / Of self-destroying, transitory things" to "Composure, and ennobling Harmony" (bk. 7. ll. 738–40).

Wordsworth never again devoted so many lines to the city as in book 7 of *The Prelude*. Even though longer poems followed, a detailed treatment of the city did not. In *The Excursion* (1814) Wordsworth's Solitary Sage does allude to a city; in fact, he alludes to many cities. The Sage's thoughts on cities demonstrate revealing disparities in viewpoint. The Wanderer's ability to hold two contradictory tendencies—the real and the ideal city—in one mind is an astonishing accomplishment. At one level, the Wanderer knows that the city glaringly displays the "deformities of brutish vice" as well as the "transitoriness of things." Thus, the Wanderer refers to the "turbulence of murmuring cities vast" (bk. 3. l. 104), to the "obstreperous city" (bk. 4. l. 369), to the city's "fickle pleasures, and superfluous cares, / And trivial ostentation" (bk. 4. ll. 821–22), to the city inhabitants' "wretched hearts, or falsely gay" (bk. 4. l. 358), and finally, to the industrial city's dark, outrageous rape of the countryside (bk. 8. ll. 117–56). At another level, many of these derogatory or realistic presentations of the city are balanced with passages that idealize the city. For example, soon after the Wanderer deplores the rape of the English countryside he announces

> yet do I exult,
> Casting reserve away, exult to see
> An intellectual mastery exercised
> O'er the blind elements; a purpose given,
> A perseverance fed; almost a soul
> Imparted—to brute matter. I rejoice,
> Measuring the force of those gigantic powers
> That, by the thinking mind, have been compelled
> To serve the will of feeble-bodied Man.
> For with the sense of admiration blends
> The animating hope that time may come
> When, strengthened, yet not dazzled, by the might
> Of this dominion over nature gained,
> Men of all lands shall exercise the same
> In due proportion to their country's need. [bk. 3. ll. 199–213]

Elsewhere, in the course of his long discourses, the Wanderer refers to "the great City, an emporium then / Of golden expectations" (bk. 2. ll. 216–17), to "thousands of cities, in the desert place / Built up of life, and food, and means of life!" (bk. 4. ll. 437–38), and to "the city vast / Of his devoted worshippers, far-stretched, / With grove and field and garden interspersed" (bk. 4. ll. 689–91). If these allusions seem disjointed, the fault is not in the selection; Wordsworth's Wanderer refers to cities across the sea and to golden cities that existed in ancient times. At two points in the long narrative, however, the Wanderer's visions of golden, celestial cities are strikingly well-integrated because they have ties to reality; they demonstrate that man makes cities as one way of showing physical and imaginative mastery over "the blind elements." The first of these visions is found at the end of book 2 (ll. 827–81). Far too long to quote here, the vision is carefully informed with precise details in the true Blakean fashion. Furthermore, although the apparition that is felt—"I saw not, but I felt that it was there"—is that of "a mighty city," it has its birth in a "watery storm" and its very streets are commingled with the dull mists over the country's hillsides. The Sage's final vision of a golden city of hope is expressed near the end of the poem. This particular vision has an air of utopian scheming, but it is impressive because the Sage believes that the great society will be based on a fruitful balance between the city and the country. (Here again, Blake's lines, "Our souls exult and London's towers, / Receive the Lamb of God to dwell / In England's green and pleasant bowers," echo in the reader's ear.) Thus, Wordsworth's Sage half-queries and half-prophesies:

> Shall that blest day arrive
> When they, whose choice or lot it is to dwell
> In crowded cities, without fear shall live
> Studious of mutual benefit; and he,
> Whom Morn awakens, among dews and flowers
> Of every clime, to till the lonely field,
> Be happy in himself?—The law of faith
> Working through love, such conquest shall it gain.
>
> [bk. 9. ll. 666–73]

Tennyson's Urban Vision: Historical Tremors and Hysterical Tremblings

The development in poetic attitudes toward the city after Blake and Wordsworth is a relatively unexplored topic. G. Robert Stange's pioneering essay "The Frightened Poets" is the most important introductory survey of the subject. Stange begins his discussion of Victorian poetic responses to the city by examining some of the poetry of Alfred Lord Tennyson. After erecting a guidepost generalization that proclaims "Wordsworth's poetic successors tended either to inveigh against the city or to pretend that it didn't exist," Stange devotes a long paragraph to proving that "The city that one feels is most real to him is Camelot, . . . the celestial city."[21] To understand fully the variety and complexity of Tennyson's uses of the city one must examine carefully the relevant poems that span the decades of Tennyson's poetic career (from the late 1820s to the early 1890s). Ultimately, it is not a contest as to which concept of the city is more significant; the full significance can be seen only by examining all of the variegated attitudes toward the city. Tennyson's poetry about the city has four distinct stages, and these stages often relate to or reflect contemporary historical situations. In the first stage, ideal or visionary conceptions mold the cities portrayed in "Babylon" (1827) and "Timbuctoo" (1829); the second stage shows a new realism as the middle-aged Tennyson looks at the actualities of contemporary London in "Locksley Hall" (1842), *In Memoriam* (1850), and *Maud* (1855); the third stage is one of perplexing tensions as the real challenges the ideal in *Idylls of the King* (completed 1872); the final stage displays a realism that is indeed frightening as the aged and more conservative poet tries to make sense of what London has become in "Locksley Hall, Sixty Years After" (1886), "Beautiful City" (1889), and "The Dawn" (1892).

Although in 1829 Tennyson may have been unsure that poetry should be his lifetime career, his absolute sovereignty over the imaginary cities that he erected in his early visionary poems was indisputable. Tennyson, however, was not naively attracted only to celestial cities in his visionary moments. In fact, his first poem in this vein presents the infernal city of Babylon. The stance of the "I" narrator in "Babylon" is brashly defiant and intensely confident. This is to be expected since the narrator's voice throughout is that of the Lord. The sinful city is obliterated totally and the tone conveys the consuming vehemence.

> Like a wine-press in wrath will I trample thee down,
> And rend from thy temples the pride of thy crown.
> Though thy streets be a hundred, thy gates be all brass,
> Yet thy proud ones of war shall be withered like grass;
> Thy gates shall be broken, thy strength be laid low,
> And thy streets shall resound to the shouts of the foe![22]

In the end the Lord and "the foe" under the leadership of Cyrus destroy Babylon and, simultaneously, the intense glow of the poem's vision consumes itself.

> I will sweep ye away in destruction and death,
> As the whirlwind that scatters the chaff with its breath;
> And the fanes of your gods shall be sprinkled with gore,
> And the course of your stream shall be heard of no more!
>
> [ll. 37–40]

The prize-winning poem "Timbuctoo" also shows a competent narrator in full control of his vision of the city, at least until the last few lines of the poem. The disturbing intrusion of reality at the end of "Timbuctoo" gives the poem a glimmer of contemporary relevance, something "Babylon" totally lacks. Critics have long been aware of the tension in "Timbuctoo" between the ideal and the real. Jerome Hamilton Buckley speaks of "the warning of the Spirit of Fable, the mythic imagination, that Discovery, which is the temper of scientific rationalism, threatens to darken and destroy the fair city of the ideal."[23] In a similar vein, Christopher Ricks maintains that a fundamental question in the poem is "whether myths and legends are consolatory but ultimately false." He answers that "in Tennyson the outcome is often, though not always, desolation and loss."[24] Critics have overlooked the fact that the narrator's perception of city structures serves as an integral part of the poem's structure. This organization is easily missed because "the waving of her [Discovery's] wand" near the end of the poem seems to dissolve the vision in great haste. Throughout the poem, however, the narrator focuses more carefully on the city's forms and architectural structures in order to prepare for the dissolution. At first the narrator sees the city in all its ethereal high majesty: "Deep in that lion-haunted inland lies / A mystick city, goal of high emprise."[25] This commingling emphasis on the geographical-visionary height of Timbuctoo continues in the early part of the poem, even as the narrator begins to question the city's attainability.

> Then I raised
> My voice and cried, 'Wide Afric, doth thy Sun
> Lighten, thy hills enfold a City as fair
> As those which starred the night o' the elder World?
> Or is the rumour of thy Timbuctoo
> A dream as frail as those of ancient Time?' [ll. 56–61]

Much like the observer's perspective in a modern airplane descending on a metropolis from above the clouds, the Tennysonian narrator's first glimpse of the city is of a wide, glittering expanse just below the clouds.

> I saw
> The smallest grain that dappled the dark Earth,
> The indistinctest atom in deep air,
> The Moon's white cities, and the opal width
> Of her small glowing lakes, her silver heights
> Unvisited with dew of vagrant cloud. [ll. 96–101]

The narrator's next perspective is that of a traveler by land. However, the highest structures in the imperial capital draw his eyes upward.

> Then first within the South methought I saw
> A wilderness of spires, and chrystal pile
> Of rampart upon rampart, dome on dome,
> Illimitable range of battlement

On battlement, and the Imperial height
Of Canopy o'ercanopied.   [ll. 158–63]

As the narrator becomes more and more caught up in the actuality of the
city around him, reality begins to negate the ethereal vision. The press of
the crowds—"multitudes of multitudes" (l. 179)—and the unending
puzzle of streets—"all the intricate and labyrinthine veins" (l. 217)—
overwhelm him. The realization that the idealized fabric of the vision
must be replaced by the earthy materials of sand and mud is painfully
disgusting to the Tennysonian narrator.

Oh City! oh latest Throne! where I was raised
To be a mystery of loveliness
Unto all eyes, the time is well-nigh come
When I must render up this glorious home
To keen *Discovery*: soon yon brilliant towers
Shall darken with the waving of her wand;
Darken, and shrink and shiver into huts,
Black specks amid a waste of dreary sand,
Low-built, mud-walled, Barbarian settlements.
How changed from this fair City!   [ll. 236–45]

Even though the vision of Timbuctoo's "mystery of loveliness" dis-
solved all too suddenly and disappointingly into the reality of "Low-built,
mud-walled, Barbarian settlements," the actualities of the contemporary
city—specifically London—captured and held Tennyson's attention in the
second stage of his poems about the city. The great city of London is itself
"a mystery of loveliness" as the narrator in "Locksley Hall" recalls the day
that he first beheld the metropolis from the countryside.

Yearning for the large excitement that the coming years would
     yield,
Eager-hearted as a boy when first he leaves his father's field,
And at night along the dusky highway near and nearer drawn,
Sees in heaven the light of London flaring like a dreary dawn;
And his spirit leaps within him to be gone before him then,
Underneath the light he looks at, in among the throngs of men;
Men, my brothers, men the workers, ever reaping something new;
That which they have done but earnest of the things that they shall
     do.   [ll. 111–18]

This new concentration on the actualities of the contemporary city con-
tinues in *In Memoriam* and *Maud*, which have more city street scenes than

any other works by Tennyson. The significance of this fact is somewhat obscured, given that in *In Memoriam* the observer is overcome with desolation and in *Maud* with madness. Although the two narrators are certainly untypical of nineteenth-century urbanites, by 1850 Tennyson was beginning to focus on the actual street surfaces (and social conditions) of London, rather than on airy towers.[26] The two most significant references to London in *In Memoriam* are, as Stange points out, in sections 7 and 119: "In Section VII the poet-speaker visits the dark house of his dead friend in 'the long unlovely street.' In this passage the city is a symbol of desolation, but when, after a lapse of time, the poet has partly overcome his despair, he returns to Wimpole Street (Section CXIX) and finds that its metropolitan horror has been mysteriously dissolved by nature." After quoting from two stanzas in which the speaker finds the city asleep even as he smells "the meadow in the street," and "hear[s] a chirp of birds," Stange concludes that "like Wordsworth, Tennyson can find beauty and value only in a city permeated by nature, one that offers itself to his imagination as something other than a busy metropolis."[27] Whether Nature or the spirit of Hallam redeems the city and lifts the poet out of his desolate state could be debated, but the important point is that something that is *not* the city, something other than indigenous urban potential is called upon to rescue the city. This redeeming tendency became a recurring and important theme in nineteenth-century poetry about the city.

City streets and crowds are also used in both *In Memoriam* and *Maud* to convey the speakers' nightmarish states of mind. In *In Memoriam*, he envisions an urban wasteland.

> I dreamed there would be Spring no more,
> That Nature's ancient power was lost:
> The streets were black with smoke and frost,
> They chattered trifles at the door.   [sec. 69. ll. 1–4]

And at another psychic moment, surreal figures move through his mind.

> Cloud-towers by ghostly masons wrought,
> A gulf that ever shuts and gapes,
> A hand that points, and pallèd shapes
> In shadowy thoroughfares of thought;
>
> And crowds that stream from yawning doors.   [sec. 70. ll. 5–9]

This nightmarish exaggeration of the city becomes even more intense in *Maud* as the speaker's perspective heightens to a madman's vision. In poetic language that T. S. Eliot reechoed sixty years later, the disturbed young man hears a "sullen thunder" and a "tumult [that] shakes the city," sees "the yellow vapors choke / The great city sounding wide," and feels a hatred for indifferent inhabitants—"And I loathe the squares and streets, / And the faces that one meets" (pt. 2, sec. 4. ll. 189–90, 203–4, 232–33).

Although the suicide's grave at the crossroads of the street (or high road) is a common theme from Tennyson's Lincolnshire youth, in *Maud* the new populousness of the street carries connotations of urban alienation, and the loneliness of the crowd. The madman imagines himself to be buried in a suicide's grave beneath the street.

> Dead, long dead,
> Long dead!
> And my heart is a handful of dust,
> And the wheels go over my head,
> And my bones are shaken with pain,
> For into a shallow grave they are thrust,
> Only a yard beneath the street,
> And the hoofs of the horses beat, beat,
> The hoofs of the horses beat,
> Beat into my scalp and my brain,
> With never an end to the stream of passing feet,
> Driving, hurrying, marrying, burying,
> Clamour and rumble, and ringing and clatter.
>
> [pt. 2, sec. 5. ll. 239–51]

Clearly, in such passages in *In Memoriam* and *Maud*, Tennyson moved toward exciting poetic reflections of urban psychic existence. True, the speakers of the two works just begin to touch on the actual realities of the city; however, those realities *do* touch the very depths of their psyches. Seen in this light, the glittering, medieval towers panoramically displayed in *Idylls of the King* on initial consideration appear to be a reactionary daydream. Some critics argue that in Camelot, Tennyson presents "an allegory in the distance," an ideal symbol of a past civilization worth revering and emulating. These critics stress the possibility of Prince Albert becoming King Arthur's ideal knight. But on the other side, John Rosenberg says that the *Idylls* are "the subtlest anatomy of the failure of ideality in our literature." [28]

What, then, is the true nature of Camelot? Literally and figuratively Camelot is shrouded in a "dim rich," "spiritual" mist. The most thorough blueprints of Camelot appear in "Gareth and Lynette." Here, the city is located on a high summit (l. 192); it moves "so weirdly in the mist" (l. 245); and it has palaces that are "shadowy," but "stately" (l. 303). In short, it is a city "built / To music, therefore never built at all, / And therefore built forever" (ll. 277—79). Camelot appears to be a glittering center of majestic towers in the distance. The cold winds of reality, however, do blow through the cracks of the "shadowy palaces." And here is the heart of the tension and complexity of the *Idylls*: in Camelot the ideal is challenged on all sides by the real, and in the end the realities of human nature succeed in undermining the ideal. Donald J. Gray hinted at this interplay between an ideal (Arthur) and the realities of human nature (the deficiencies of the Round Table's members) in an article in which he pointed out that Arthur's major effort is "to make the ideal actual, the dream flesh," and that in the end Arthur "does not defeat himself; others [those engaged in social action] betray him to his defeat." [29] In a more recent study, Patrick Brantlinger traces Tennyson's growing doubts about the potential of human nature to unite in the meaningful social action that would be needed to usher in a fair and just community on earth. The *Idylls* seem to stand as an allegorical testament to the fact that "the desire for social improvement is subverted by doubt about its possibility." Brantlinger elaborates on this principle in his discussion of the conception and execution of the *Idylls*.

> But the *Idylls* themselves describe the rise and fall of a nation, and the emphasis is on fall: only the first two books are hopeful, full of springtime idealism; waxing through the other ten books, deceit and disillusionment eat away at the foundations of Camelot. And what unsturdy foundations they are! Camelot is a reflection of the heavenly city, but it is founded upon an abyss. In what seems to have been Tennyson's earliest plan for the *Idylls*, he describes "the sacred Mount of Camelot" as "the most beautiful in the world. . . . But all underneath it was hollow, and the mountain trembled, when the seas rushed bellowing through the porphyry caves; and there ran a prophecy that the mountain and the city on some wild morning would topple into the abyss and be no more." [30]

During the last decade of his life, Tennyson became more realistic in his perceptions of social conditions in the burgeoning urban centers. In July 1884 he voted for extension of the franchise. In his memoir, Hallam Tennyson reports that his father called it "the first step on the road to the new social condition that is surely coming on the world." [31] Other statements appear in the memoir from around this same time which show that Tennyson was being driven by what Buckley calls "apocalyptic fears" to a more realistic appraisal of the contemporary social conditions. [32] Thus, Tennyson is said to have remarked: "When I see society vicious and the poor starving in great cities, I feel that it is a mighty wave of evil passing over the world, but that there will be yet some new and strange development, which I shall not live to see." He followed this very quickly with a statement that betrays a deep questioning of his former idealism: "I tried in my 'Idylls' to teach men these things [old reverence and chivalrous feeling], and the need of the Ideal. But I feel sometimes as if my life had been a very useless life."[33]

If Tennyson seems bitter in the remarks just quoted, if Tennyson meant to say in the *Idylls* that human reality never matches humane ideals to sustain a celestial city on earth, then it is also true that Tennyson hysterically amplifies this message in several of his late poems in which he reacts against contemporary social and political unrest. In "Locksley Hall, Sixty Years After" Tennyson begins to present the ugliest aspects of the real city, but hysterical fear nearly overwhelms his perception. In the 1880s Tennyson had a general interest in housing conditions and he read *The Bitter Cry of Outcast London* by Andrew Mearns and similar works. The poet asks penetrating questions of his society and renders his version of the *inside* of a tenement dwelling.

> There among the glooming alleys Progress halts on palsied feet,
> Crime and hunger cast our maidens by the thousand on the street.
>
> There the Master scrimps his haggard sempstress of her daily bread,
> There a single sordid attic holds the living and the dead.
>
> There the smouldering fire of fever creeps across the rotted floor,
> And the crowded couch of incest in the warrens of the poor.
>
> [ll. 219–24]

Though the poet's vision of the realities of urban life is relatively clear and accurate in this passage and in others, such as the one which condemns "roofs of slated hideousness!" (l. 246), he delivers the penetrating observations in such a frenzied tone of hysteria that it becomes impossible to assign any blame for the contemporary conditions. As Buckley points out, Tennyson "strove through heavy revision of several early drafts to control the invective." Furthermore, "late in the composition of the poem he added several lines which permitted the narrator a brief self-conscious retreat from his violence":[34]

> Heated am I? you—you wonder—well, it scarce becomes mine
>   age—
> Patience! let the dying actor mouth his last upon the stage.

Cries of unprogressive dotage ere the dotard fall asleep?
Noises of a current narrowing, not the music of a deep?

[ll. 151–54]

This confused, bitter, hysterical tone appeared in several other poems by poets responding to social conditions in the 1880s, notably in the poetry of Coventry Patmore and Roden Noel, and in one poem by Gerard Manley Hopkins. With them, as in Tennyson, it stems from the dilemma of deciding who is responsible for the existing conditions in the cities—is it Providence, Progress, or Science? Most Victorian poets seem reluctant to conclude that only people make and change the social order. A confused social perspective also accounts for the terror evident in two late poems by Tennyson, "Beautiful City" and "The Dawn." The Paris Commune uprising of 1871 deeply troubled Tennyson, along with several of the other poets mentioned. Although some of the other poets wrote long poems that constantly refer to the events across the channel, in "Beautiful City" Tennyson devoted only four lines to the turmoil.

Beautiful city, the centre and crater of European confusion,
O you with your passionate shriek for the rights of an equal
    humanity,
How often your Re-volution has proven but E-volution
Rolled again back on itself in the tides of a civic insanity!

[ll. 1–4]

One must agree with Stange that the poem "comes close to incoherence" because the principal emotion underlying the quatrain is fear.[35] "The Dawn," a poem written in the last year of Tennyson's life, proclaims that things are cannibalistic now as "The press of a thousand cities is prized for its smells of the beast, / Or easily violates virgin Truth for a coin or a cheque" (ll. 14–15). After "a hundred, a thousand winters," however, the human race may have developed enough so that the humane society may be realized. As Buckley points out, the poem is "gnarled and gnomic in style."[36] "The Dawn," then, seems to be a modification of some of Tennyson's previous positions because he sees himself and human society at an actual point in history moving *toward* an ideal that may be realized many years in the future.

In an important article published in the *North American Review* in 1853, Arthur Hugh Clough called for a new realism in poetry which would treat the city as it actually and presently existed. Tennyson, who succeeded Wordsworth as poet laureate in 1850, demonstrated incipient leadership in making the realities of the city a "fit and proper" subject of Victorian poetry. Other poets coming to prominence after 1850—such as Matthew

Arnold, Robert Buchanan, and Alexander Smith—had to work out their own guidelines as to how much and what types of city life could be introduced successfully into poetry. For a time after midcentury the concept of the celestial city that was so alluring in the poetry of Blake, Wordsworth, and Tennyson was forgotten or thought of as excessively romantic. In another sense, increasingly nostalgic feelings for the country and the village community refashioned and replaced the celestial city idea. In the two decades after Clough's review, this feeling of what Raymond Williams calls "rural retrospect" was at least as strong a deterrent to making the contemporary city a legitimate topic of poetry as Wordsworth's celestial city ideal or Tennyson's hysterical fear of social facts. The tensions between the real and the ideal city would continue in new strains as poets attempted to determine what would or could redeem the nineteenth-century city and its teeming masses—forces within the city (people building a new and just social order) or forces from without (God, nature, tradition). In his poetry Tennyson worked with many of the tensions inherent in real versus ideal conceptions of the city. The four stages of Tennyson's treatment of the city over his long poetic career seem to alternate between the visionary and the real but each is unique and interesting in its own right. From the visionary escapism of "Timbuctoo" to the fresh look at the realities of contemporary London in the poems of the 1850s, from the exciting tension between visionary ideals and the realities of human nature in Camelot to the hysterical and reactionary response in the late poems, the canon of Tennyson's poetry about the city is rich and diverse.

Chapter Two
Realism Versus Escapism, 1850–1870

The Call to Treat the City Realistically

As Walter Houghton demonstrates, the basic and almost universal conception of the mid-Victorian period is that it was an age of transition, a unique moment in history when "men thought of their own time as an era of change *from* the past *to* the future."[1] Houghton defines some of the characteristics of such a period: "By definition an age of transition in which change is revolutionary has a dual aspect: destruction and reconstruction. As the old order of doctrines and institutions is being attacked or modified or discarded, at one point and then another, a new order is being proposed or inaugurated." The question is then asked, "At the center of the Victorian period, what new construction had emerged?"[2] Because the primary interest of Houghton's study is "doctrines and institutions," it is necessary to look elsewhere for a fuller understanding of the age. Even as new systems of religious and philosophical belief were being erected, the physical appearance as well as the social problems of London were also changing markedly. Along with this expansion there were new ideas about how poetry should play a part in capturing the city's burgeoning reality. Thus, at least three important writers called for a new realism in poetry—in both technique and subject matter. This chapter, then, examines the functions of poetry as it either embraced or avoided the new urban problems and promises that became manifestly evident in the 1850s and 1860s.

The years between 1850 and 1870 were years of prosperity and accomplishment. In London there was a quickened pace to the energy of change. The list of urban improvements around London is impressive. With the destruction of the old House of Commons by fire in 1834, construction plans for a new Gothic complex were begun so that by 1860 the Houses of Parliament and Big Ben towered over the Thames. In 1843 a crane placed the statue of Admiral Nelson on its column in the Trafalgar Square layout designed by Charles Barry. Perhaps the most exciting event of the age was the opening in 1851 of the Crystal Palace, the first great international exhibition of modern industry's products. For centuries St. Paul's Cathedral had been the most imposing London structure; but it was certainly rivaled in 1851 by Paxton's Palace, whose internal length was four times that of St. Paul's. In the year that the Crystal Palace stood in Hyde Park, it attracted over six million visitors.

An increasingly complex network of railroads assured the importance of the city as a center for a variety of concerns and activities. The world's first underground railway, from Paddington to Farringdon Street, was completed in 1863. Underground sewage construction was also evident everywhere. Near the railway terminals, some of the grandest hotels ever conceived were built—among them Gilbert Scott's St. Pancras Hotel (1865–1872) and the Great Western Hotel (1852). With their prominent mansard roofs and towers, the hotels must have made visitors imagine they sojourned in a medieval castle. Cultural edifices also helped to make London a center of civilization: the British Museum Reading Room opened in 1857; Mudie's Select Circulating Library was remodeled in 1860; and the Albert Hall opened in 1871. Clearly then in terms of sheer transformation of the local scenery, in the quarter century before 1866, London underwent the most extensive building boom since reconstruction after the Great Fire of 1666.

But if the metropolis at mid-century fulfilled many promises in its exciting growth and in its impressive new construction sites, it also was the source of numerous social problems and discomforts. Residents and visitors alike complained of the noise, confusion, and pollution of the burgeoning metropolis—"an atmosphere which seemed in the nostrils of one regular visitor to the district to be a concoction of haddocks and oranges, of mortar and soot, of hearthstones and winkles, of rotten rags and herrings."[3] Perhaps the most unsettling areas of the city were the ones that had sustained garden farming on a small scale for years. The momentum of change and construction "rubbed out almost overnight the familiar landmarks of the townsman's evening stroll into the fields, and puzzled and shocked the suburbians themselves, who could measure the retreat of the open country in terms of furlongs per year."[4] H. J. Dyos quotes an obscure poetic lament that precisely records the common situation.

> The fields are broken up, and in their place,
> Form'd into narrow strag'ling streets, are seen
> Cold, scanty dwellings of a starvling race,
> And all around is silent, dim, and mean,
> And gone for e'er the flowr's, the fields, and meadows green.[5]

Sometimes resistance to urban expansion was so adamant that there was a "tendency towards overcrowding, the intermixture of cowsheds and piggeries with dwelling-houses" and "pigs, cows, and sometimes sheep [would] be made to perform the least of their natural functions even in the hideous conditions of a metropolitan slum."[6] Mid-century Victorians were especially alert to the factory fumes, soot, and social ills because many of them had spent their formative years in the fresh, healthy air of the English countryside. Between 1850 and 1870, the population of Greater London increased from 2.5 to 3.7 million; and according to the 1861 census only 45 percent of the males then living in London had been born there.

What casual visitors to London perceived to be the city's superficial allurements were in reality viewed with horror and fear by more seasoned inhabitants. With increasing vehemence, both pamphlets and periodicals condemned the increase of prostitution. In the 1850s one police report estimated that there were 2,828 brothels and 8,600 prostitutes in London. In a fifty-page article in the *Westminster Review* (1850), W. R. Greg categorized prostitution as "the worst and lowest form of sexual irregularity, the most revolting to the unpolluted feelings, the most indicative of a *low* nature, the most degrading and sapping to the loftier life" and relegated prostitutes to the position of "outcasts, pariahs, lepers."[7] From a more comprehensive point of view, the menacing confusion and fatal destitution (as well as prostitution) found in London's streets captured the eye of the French historian Hippolyte Taine in the 1860s.

> I recall the alleys which run into Oxford Street, stifling lanes, encrusted with human exhalations; troops of pale children nestling on the muddy stairs; the seats on London Bridge, where families, huddled together with drooping heads, shiver through the night; particularly the Haymarket and the Strand in the evening. Every hundred steps one jostles twenty harlots; some of them ask for a glass of gin; others say, "Sir, it is to pay my lodging." This is not debauchery which flaunts itself, but destitution—and such destitution! The deplorable procession in the shade of the monumental streets is sickening; it seems to me a march of the dead. That is a plague-spot—the real plague-spot of English society.[8]

The important point to keep in mind is that prostitution is basically an urban phenomenon and it was only one aspect of the many social problems that became increasingly complex and severe as nineteenth-century Britain underwent enormous urban growth. For many, prostitution was a welcome escape from a dreary work routine or meager income, and a city the size of London offered a comforting anonymity for practicing the profession. The victims of both destitution and prostitution appear in the poetry written at mid-century by Clough, Smith, and Buchanan.

While it is true that London was growing at an unprecedented rate between 1850 and 1870, the city's growth was both exciting in the scope of its new construction sites and depressing in the magnitude of its social problems. Poets of this period were faced with a series of vital, perplexing challenges. What function should poetry perform in the city? Should poets try to capture or perhaps even to celebrate the exciting and quickened pace of city life? Could poetry serve as a balm to help heal some of the suffering caused by poverty, squalor, and prostitution? Would poetry sacrifice a broad-based appeal if it attempted to deal with troublesome feelings of loneliness, alienation, or even desolation?

In the early 1850s three clear calls for a new realism in poetry emerged—a realism that would encompass the contradictory aspects of the growing city. The first such call came from Charles Kingsley in chapters 8 and 9 of his novel *Alton Locke, Tailor and Poet* (1850). Here a discussion, which amounts to a conversion, occurs between the artisan narrator, Alton Locke, who writes poetry about Pacific islands, and his Scottish mentor, Saunders Mackaye, who urges him to look not at the realms of Arcadian nostalgia but at the streets of London. Mackaye's arguments for an urban-based poetic consistently focus on the harlot figure and the evangelical mission of poetry to redeem victims of urban corruption.

> What do ye ken anent the Pacific? Which is maist to your business?—thae bare-backed hizzies that play the harlot o' the other side o' the warld, or these—these thousands o' bare-backed hizzies that play the harlot o' your ain side—made out o' your ain flesh and blude? You a poet! True poetry, like true charity, my laddie, begins at hame.
>
> But all this is so—so unpoetical. . . .
>
> Poetic element? Yon lassie, rejoicing in her disfigurement and not here beauty—like the nuns of Peterborough in auld time—is there na poetry there? That puir lassie, dying on the bare boards, and seeing her Saviour in her dreams, is there na poetry there, callant? That ault body owre the fire, wi' her "an officer's dochter," is there na poetry there? That ither, prostituting hersel' to buy food for her freen—is there na poetry there?—tragedy . . . Ay, Shelley's gran'; always gran'; but Fact is grander—God and Satan grander. All around ye, in every gin shop and costermonger's cellar, are God and Satan at death grips; every garret is a hail Paradise Lost or Paradise Regained; and will ye think it beneath ye to be the "People's Poet"?[9]

Initially Alton Locke responds to Mackaye's suggestions by insisting that the proposed urban material is not fit to be treated in poetry—"But all this is so—so unpoetical." Yet, after long and deep reflection, in the Wertherian style, Alton comes to a profound revelation that takes on the dimensions of conviction and conversion.

> I had made up my mind that if I had any poetic power, I must do my duty therewith in that station of life to which it had pleased God to call me, and to look at everything simply and faithfully as a London artisan. To this, I suppose, is to be attributed the little geniality and originality for which the public have kindly praised my verses—a geniality which sprung, not from the atmosphere when I drew, but from the honesty and single-mindedness with which, I hope, I laboured. Not from the atmosphere, indeed—that was ungenial enough; crime and poverty, all-devouring competition . . . the ceaseless stream of pale, hard faces, intent on gain, or brooding over woe; amid endless prison walls of brick, beneath a lurid, crushing sky of smoke and mist. . . . And it [London life] did its work upon me; it gave a gloomy colouring, a glare as of some Dantean *Inferno*, to all my utterances. . . . It crushed and saddened me; it deepened in me that peculiar melancholy of intellectual youth, which Mr. Carlyle has christened . . . "Werterism"; I battened on my own melancholy. I believed, I loved to believe, that every face I passed bore the traces of discontent as deep as was my own—and was I far wrong? Was I so far wrong either in the gloomy tone of my own poetry? Should not a London poet's work just now be to cry, like the Jew of old, about the walls of Jerusalem, "Woe, woe to this city"?[10]

This emphasis on psychic tension, this overweening melancholy, this divisive struggle between the sensitive artist and the crowd around him are of central importance in the poetry of Clough, Smith, and Arnold.

A second critical call for a new urban realism came from F. G. Stephens in an article called "Modern Giants," which appeared in the 1850 volume of the *Germ*. Stephens calls for "the development of our individual perceptions . . . to indicate the civilization of a period."[11] By "perceptions" Stephens means essentially the powers of visual observation or literary description. By "period" he means contemporary England—industrial and urban. Stephens maintains that for too long "the essentials of poetry" and poetic observations have been linked to "green grass, verdant meads, tall pines, vineyards" and "the past world, [where] you go on repeating in new combinations the same elements for the same effect . . . the glorious tale of Griselda."[12] Stephens calls for poetry to record immediate, alert observations of industrial urban facts. The newness of these facts gives them the aura of "mystery, the main thing required for the surprise of the imagination." It is Stephens's sincere critical conviction that "there is the poetry of the things about us; our railways, factories, mines, roaring cities, steam vessels, and the endless novelties and wonders produced every day." Stephens embraces progress on all sides and has no patience with reactionary rural Arcadians: "The Earth shakes under you, from the footfall of the Genii man has made, and you groan about the noise. Vast roads draw together the Earth, and you say how they spoil the prospect, which you never cared a farthing about before." [13] Stephens's critical message is clear and forthright: he challenges poets to make poems about the cities and machines being made by the progressive men of the age. This new "pure perception" would be based on a close observation of the new but still mysterious facts, and it presumably would be expressed in primarily descriptive poetry as opposed to lyric or narrative forms.

Still another critic—who was himself a poet—offered to set up critical standards based on a new realism for poets of the period. In an 1853 review of one volume of Alexander Smith's poems, two volumes of Matthew Arnold's, and one volume of William Sidney Walker's, Arthur Hugh Clough set down what pleased and disturbed him in the various volumes. At the same time, he revealed much about his own poetic tastes and contemporary concerns, as well as his own intellectual personality. Like Stephens, Clough is explicit in his distrust of poetry that concentrates exclusively on nature and ancient mythology. Poetry whose only muse is nature comes too easily and ignores the pressing challenges of the age. It is "an easy matter to sit under a green tree by a purling brook, and indite pleasing stanzas on the beauties of Nature and fresh air." Likewise, it is not "so very great an exploit to wander out into the pleasant field of Greek or Latin mythology, and reproduce, with more or less of modern adaptation" because it is derivative and unthinking. [14] The metaphor of wandering into fields is apt, because in Clough's eyes it is a wandering far afield, a denial of pressing contemporary problems and of the new urbanized, industrialized environment. But beyond his explicit injunctions against poetry that draws on the matter and conventions of nature and classical poetry, Clough's statements are much more tentative and implicit than those of the other two critics examined. When Clough indicates most openly the direction in which he would like to see poetry move, he states his ideas as a question and employs vague terminology.

> Yet there is no question, it is plain and patent enough, that people much prefer *Vanity Fair* and *Bleak House*. Why so? Is it simply because we have grown prudent and prosaic? . . . Or is it, that to

be widely popular, to gain the ear of multitudes, to choke the hearts of men, poetry should deal more than at present it usually does, with general wants, ordinary feelings, the obvious rather than the rare facts of human nature? Could it not attempt to convert into beauty and thankfulness, or at least into some form and shape . . . the actual, palpable things with which our every-day life is concerned; introduce into business and weary task-work a character and a soul of purpose and reality; . . . Could it not console us with a sense of significance, if not of dignity, in that often dirty, or at least dingy, work which it is the lot of so many of us to have to do, and which some one or other, after all, must do? Might it not . . . content itself merely with talking of what may be better elsewhere, but seek also to deal with what *is* here?[15]

Although Clough appreciates the "substantive and lifelike, immediate and first-hand . . . images drawn from the busy seats of industry" in Smith's *A Life Drama*, the aspects of the poetry that he most admires hinge upon the terms *struggle* and *purity*. Inevitably the terms are closely related. The most admirable passages of *A Life Drama* in Clough's eyes are the "states of feeling," which present an "ingenuous, yet passionate, youthful spirit, struggling after something like right and purity amidst the unnumbered difficulties, contradictions, and corruptions of the heated and crowded, busy, vicious, and inhuman town."[16] The hero in Smith's poem accepts the stark fact that man made the town. In Clough's eyes, he comes to the town, experiences disappointment and disloyalty, consorts with a prostitute, and at times seems overcome—"still we seem to see the young combatant, half combatant, half martyr, resolute to fight it out, and not to quit this for some easier field of battle,—one way or other to make something of it."[17] Indeed, Clough's words "we seem to see" are interesting, because a close reading of *A Life Drama* shows that the young hero in fact wavers constantly between the city and the country and very rarely exhibits the resolve that Clough "seems to see" in him amidst the diverse pressures of man's newly created urban industrial community. In his review essay Clough sees what he would like to see and what is important to him in Smith's work, even though it is clearly not supportable by close textual analysis.

Clough's comments on Arnold's poetry tend toward the same subjective revelation. While the Glasgow mechanic's poetic hero wore the "armor of pure intent," Clough sees behind Arnold's poetry a temperament that is "highly educated" and possessive of "a keener sense of difficulty in life." He asks if these leanings are not "too delicate for common service?"; are they not loomings of morbid paralysis and melancholy passivity?[18] In short, what Clough fears, but ironically condemns, is the immersion into the whirlpool of Wertherism that Mackaye warned against in *Alton Locke*. Clough almost uniformly devotes his attention to this concern in Arnold's poetry because it has a peculiar attraction/repulsion to his sensibility: "We listen, indeed, not quite unpleased, to a sort of faint musical mumble, conveying at times a kind of subdued half-sense, or intimating, perhaps, a three-quarters-implied question, Is any thing real?—is love any thing?— what is anything?"[19] The final points about Clough's treatment of Arnold's two volumes of poetry stand out. First of all, at one point in the review, Clough realizes that in reading and analyzing Arnold's poems he has unconsciously been engulfed in a Wertherian whirlpool: "But now, we are fain to ask, where are we, and whither are we unconsciously come? Were we not going forth to battle in the armor of a righteous purpose, with our first friend, with Alexander Smith? How is it we find ourselves here, reflecting, pondering, hesitating, musing, complaining, with 'A.'?"[20] Second, although Clough called for poetry to come nearer to life and realities, and especially for it to take a stand in the city, he never gets around to discussing the poems in Arnold's 1852 *Empedocles* volume which are set in London or deal with the place of the city in civilization—"A Summer Night," "The Buried Life," "Lines Written in Kensington Gardens," and "The Future."

Finally, Clough discusses the one volume *Poetical Remains of William Sidney Walker*. He has little to say about Walker's poetry but launches a vitriolic attack on Walker as a person who attempted to take on the role of poet.

> If our readers wish to view real timidity, real shrinking from actual things, real fear of living, let them open the little volume of Sidney Walker's *Poetical Remains*. The school-fellow and college friend of Praed, marked from his earliest youth by his poetic temper and faculty, he passed fifty-one years, mostly in isolation and poverty, shivering upon the brink, trembling and hesitating upon the threshold of life. Fearful to affirm any thing, lest it haply might be false; to do any thing, because so probably it might be sin; to speak, lest he should lie; almost, we might say, to feel, lest it should be a deception,—so he sat, crouching and cowering, in the dismal London back-street lodging, over the embers of a wasting and dying fire, the true image of his own vitality. "I am vext," is his weak complaining cry.[21]

At least one modern critic has picked up the "scornful" tone of Clough's attack on Walker and has surmised that the reasons are at least partly biographical. Wendell V. Harris maintains that "one can hardly avoid finding that the vehemence of this attack springs from Clough's aversion to qualities only lately exorcised from himself. It may have been unkind of Clough to condemn Walker for having lived his fifty-one years among fears that Clough knew only too well, but the real target of his disapproval is not Walker but the 'fear of living.' . . . He [Clough] was, however, so newly freed from a form of the malaise he sees in Walker that he could not behold it without reacting violently."[22]

While Kingsley, Stephens, and Clough quite clearly called for poets to treat the circumstances of the city realistically and to forego fanciful indulgence in either the legendary past or pastoral scenes, the three writers differed in their awareness of the emotional implications and consequences that might befall poets who responded to their call to live in and write about the city. For a poet to renounce the traditional subjects of the mythic past and pastoralism in favor of new urban material was a revolutionary demand in itself. To ask the poet to write about his emotional responses to the urban scene—material always thought to be intractable and unpoetic in the past—was to issue a radically new challenge, the implications of which were not yet fully understood. Of the three writers, only Kingsley seems to be conscious that a new kind of melancholy and hesitation may itself arise from the poet's thinking about the city and trying to write about it. An awareness that city life might produce a psychological wrench that could lead to subjective desolation is more faintly evident in Clough (when he speaks of the "struggle" for "purity," for example). A fuller awareness of the dilemma can be found in the poetry he wrote about the city before his 1853 review.

The Indeterminacy of Clough's Poetry about the City

Before his 1853 review, Clough wrote over a dozen shorter poems and one long poem, *Dipsychus*, about life in the city. Not all of the poems are about London, but they all raise questions about the proper mental stance and the appropriate action to be pursued in the contemporary metropolis. Clough's poems rely on description and talk about the need for an integrated life of purity, duty, work, and action. Yet little action is ever presented or narrated. As Walter E. Houghton points out: "From start to finish *Dipsychus* is simply a series of dialogues between only two characters in which nothing happens except a swim at the Lido and a ride in a gondola."[23] Thus, in poem after poem and in scene after scene, the city rumbles around the poet, but what is presented is a mental drama whose stage is Clough's own mind.

Clough's shorter poems about the city fall into four categories: (1) those which see the city as a religious battlefield between spiritual and secular forces, (2) those which see the city along the lines of an "I-them" dimension, (3) those which preach an ascetic gospel of work, duty, and labor, and (4) those which present a parade of descriptive urban images. Needless to say, the first two categories comprise the most interesting and successful poems; however, the last two categories are worth examining briefly because of their reminder that Clough is writing in an age of transition and trying to expand the boundaries of poetry. Put another way: the poems of the first two categories pose some of the problems and tensions of city life, but these difficulties are not satisfactorily resolved in the poems of the second two categories.

Two poems that fit the first category have very similar titles—"To the Great Metropolis" (1841) and "In the Great Metropolis" (1852). The point of departure for the speaker in "To the Great Metropolis" is his experience of the city.

> Traffic, to speak from knowledge but begun,
> I saw, and travelling much, and fashion—Yea,
> And if that Competition and Display
> Make a great Capital, then thou art one.[24]

Soon, however, the speaker thinks that certain noble traits, the requisite brick and mortar for the golden city, are not clearly evident about town.

> But sovereign symbol of the Great and Good,
> True Royalty, and genuine Statesmanhood,
> Nobleness, Learning, Piety was none.
> If such realities indeed there are
> Working within unsignified, 'tis well.   [ll. 6–10]

The last two lines are an important qualification. The speaker is not condemning the city, but withholding final judgment because he still thinks it possible that the highest refinements of civilization may be implicitly present. At present, however, they are not evident in the great metropolis. The poem comes to no resolution, but instead closes with what Stange calls "a lament, along conventional lines, for the fact that the stranger's fancy of London"[25]

> Is rather truly of a huge Bazaar,
> A railway terminus, a gay Hotel,
> Anything but a mighty Nation's heart.   [ll. 12–14]

Eleven years later, in "In the Great Metropolis," Clough seems to have arrived at the bitter conviction that Mammonism and competition in the form of the devil have taken over the city and that rapaciousness goes un-satisfied. Each of the seven stanzas of the poem closes in the tradition of a Chartist chant with the refrain "The devil take the hindmost, o!" The cap-italized abstractions found in "To the Great Metropolis" have disappeared to be replaced by more specific indictments of institutions about town.

> Each for himself is still the rule,
> We learn it when we go to school—
> The devil take the hindmost, o!
>
> .   .   .   .   .   .
>
> For in the church, and at the bar,
> On 'Change, at court, where er they are,
> The devil takes the hindmost, o!   [ll. 1–3, 7–9]

A second pair of closely allied poems is the "Easter Day" set. In these poems Clough foreshadows the urban wasteland of T. S. Eliot by depict-ing the city's power to concentrate hopelessness and loss of faith. The first, "Easter Day. Naples, 1849," wavers between personal and tribal despair; the second poem presents the mental and spiritual drama of an isolated speaker. The first poem begins with a lone figure wandering through the scorching urban landscape.

> Through the great sinful streets of Naples as I past,
> With fiercer heat than flamed above my head
> My heart was hot within me; till at last
> My brain was lightened, when my tongue had said
>
> Christ is not risen!   [ll. 1–5]

Walking in the city, the speaker comes to the realization that just as there is no center to contemporary life, so too the city is no center of hope, belief, or truth.

> As circulates in some great city crowd
> A rumour changeful, vague, importune, and loud,
> From no determined centre, or of fact,
> Or authorship exact,
> Which no man can deny
> Nor verify;
> So spread the wondrous fame;
> He all the same
> Lay senseless, mouldering, low.
> He was not risen, no,
> Christ was not risen!   [ll. 48–58]

The speaker's situation is not an isolated case, but a shared, universal dilemma. By the end of the poem, instead of salvation he finds a conspiracy of silence.

> Eat, drink, and die, for we are souls bereaved,
> Of all the creatures under this broad sky
> We are most hopeless, that had hoped most high,
> And most beliefless, that had most believed.
>
> .   .   .   .
>
> There is no glistering of an angel's wings,
> There is no voice of heavenly clear behest:
> Let us go hence, and think upon these things
> In silence, which is best.   [ll. 86–89, 150–53]

In "Easter Day II" the communication impasse is dramatically presented as the speaker walks through the streets beside a "blear-eyed pimp." Although the pimp vociferously points out such sights as "the lady in the green silk there" and "the little thing not quite fifteen," the speaker becomes increasingly locked within his own shell—"So in the sinful streets, abstracted and alone, / I with my secret self held communing of mine own" (ll. 11–12).

At other times Clough transcends solipsistic despair or Wertherism and gives over to a quasi-religious Victorian sentimentality. One such poem is "Blessed are those who have not seen," which is framed in the form of a prayer. The conclusion is that only a few good souls will dispense charity in the city.

> So let me think whate'er befall,
> That in the city duly
> Some men there are who love at all,
> Some women who love truly;
> And that upon two million odd
> Transgressors in sad plenty,
> Mercy will of a gracious God
> Be shown—because of twenty.   [ll. 9–16]

The second category of Clough's shorter poems about the city presents the "I-them" dimension or what Raymond Williams refers to as the perceived gulf between the individual and the masses. Three poems touch on the question of how to maintain individual integrity and purity in the city without being engulfed by the masses. This is a fundamental question for the hero of *Dipsychus*. In the shorter poems, however, Clough offers insights into the dilemma. For instance, in "These vulgar ways that round

me be" the speaker worries about losing the "purity of perception" that
F. G. Stephens valued in his *Germ* article.

> These vulgar ways that round me be,
> These faces shabby, sordid, mean,
> Shall they be daily, hourly seen
> And not affect the eyes that see? [ll. 1—4]

The speaker feels uneasy at the constant impulse to scorn and censor that
his fellows stir in his heart and he prays that the virtues of "patience, faith
and simple sooth" may help him to "poise all things in the scales of
truth." Another short poem is an ascetic prayer to "purity" and to the
"Good Lord" to deliver the speaker

> From that wealth that is not health
> But insecurity,
> From Self-will that is not sanity,
> From all the thousandfold inanity
> Of loving kindliness that turns to vanity,
> From worldly wisdom that is imbecility,
> From worldly help that gives us disability,
> From worldly joys that weaken, waste and wither us— [ll. 2—9]

The best poem in this second category of Clough's shorter poems, and one
of the best in the entire Clough canon, is "The contradictions of the ex-
panding soul." The poem presents a personal dilemma that has universal
implications for anyone who lives in a rapidly changing society.

> The contradictions of the expanding soul,
> These questionings of the manhood of our race,
> These views, these feelings like opposing tides
> Swaying and rolling, and beating against each other,
> Who does not feel them? [ll. 1—5]

At points in the poem, Clough loses his focus by indulging vague roman-
tic metaphors such as "I am a log of driftwood tost about / And moving
ever with the stronger stream" (ll. 10—11). At his best, Clough poses the
question that every sensitive artist who considers himself a democrat must
try to come to grips with—how to feel comfortable rubbing shoulders
with the man-in-the-street.

> In the meantime
> It is a little difficult, unconstrained
> By grand convictions about blood and caste

And quick exterior homage, to escape
Contamination in the jostling street
And foul contagion from diseased base souls.
To claim an isolation on the plea
And [*illegible*], as it seems, may be unfounded
Of native superiority,
To acknowledge brotherhood, yet not surrender
Integrity; to own the common soul,
Yet save the individual; love one's neighbour,
Yet keep unbroke the precious party wall;
Alas we seem as women in the world
Amongst rude men unlovered.   [ll. 31–45]

The contradictions regarding the proper balance between the individual
and society that are raised in these lines are persistent and ever expanding.
The closing metaphor links his sensibilities to that of a woman about to be
raped by a gang of men. With the overwhelming urban forces lined up
against him, Clough sees himself turning into a sort of prostitute if he
becomes an urban dweller. In a similar frame of mind, he wrote an article
entitled "Recent Social Theories" and expressed his conservative fears that
"the multitudes" were ravaging the sacred bastions of culture: "With us,
on the contrary, the miserable truckling to the bad taste of the multitude
has gradually stolen up into the very regions of the highest art—into ar-
chitecture, sculpture, painting, music, literature. Nay, has it not infected
even morality and religion?"[26]

In his 1853 review article, Clough asked if the poetry of the age could
"introduce into business and weary task-work a character and a soul of
purpose and reality." One of the functions of the new poetry would be to
lend a sense of significance to the "dirty, dingy work [with] which it is the
lot of so many of us to have to do."[27] Yet, when Clough's own consoling
attempts along these lines (his third category of city poems) are weighed
in the balance, the reader may very well find them lacking. The worker
figure in "To his work the man must go" comes across as the happy war-
rior being led off to the factory battlefield.

To his work the man must go
            Cheerily, oh cheerily
Like a soldier and fight the foe
Smiting strong, struggling stay,
Battling, conquering all the day
            Cheerily, oh cheerily.   [ll. 1–6]

The worker's wife remains at home, playing the role of the stereotypical Victorian caged lark. She is Tennyson's Mariana in the moated grange come to the city.

> In the house the woman bides
> > Wearily, oh wearily
> Waiting for the eventide.
> In her heart a nameless pain
> Fitful fancies in her brain
> > Wearily, oh wearily.   [ll. 7–12]

The fourth category of Clough's shorter poems about the city seems to be the least successful. In "Four black steamers plying on the Thames" Clough merely lines up four boats in order to form a descriptive parade of imagery.

> Four black steamers plying on the Thames;
> These are their names
> Printed on the paddle boxes anyone may know
> Painted up in white
> Morning and Evening and Noonday and Night.   [ll. 1–5]

In "Ye flags of Piccadilly" the poet's images are tinged with his feelings of homesickness. Seen through the filter of distance and memory, the crowds take on the dimensions of a huge still life: "Are the people walking quietly / And steady on the feet" [ll. 5–6). In the midst of a storm at sea, the distant London is juxtaposed in the poet's mind as an idyllic playground complete with kites floating in the balmy spring breeze over Green Park.

> Are the little children playing
> Round the plane-tree in the grass?
>
> This squally wild north-wester
> With which our vessel fights,
> Does it merely serve with you to
> Carry up some paper kites?   [ll. 15–20]

Throughout the decade of the 1840s, Clough wrote over a dozen shorter poems in which he discussed the necessity of writing poetry about the contemporary experience of the city. These poems were relatively simple in their structures and indeterminate in their solutions. While in Venice in 1850, Clough erected a far more complex poetic structure, which embodied even subtler contradictions and tensions. The product of that effort was the long poem *Dipsychus*. In an elaborate structure of feeling, the poem records the argumentative struggles between the divided per-

sona, Dipsychus, and the ambiguous Spirit. More than one critic of the
poem has called it a classic piece that states, but does not resolve, tensions
and contradictions.[28] The central importance of *Dipsychus* to this chapter is
that in the poem Clough continues to discuss the difficulties of the urban
experience and the difficulties of writing about it. He realizes that there is
a task for the poet to perform in the city (the call is concretely formulated
later in the 1853 review), but because his poetry focuses on his own men-
tal states, he offers few solutions to urban problems.

Clough's *Dipsychus* is far longer than his other poems about the city and
much more complex. The importance of seeing *Dipsychus* as the immediate
response—at a variety of psychic levels—of a mid-nineteenth-century man
to a kaleidoscope of urban situations and stimulations cannot be over-
emphasized. The format of the poem—fabular, complete with doppelgän-
ger figures, Mephistophelean voices, alluring temptresses—distances the
contemporary metropolis and removes the action and significance to an
almost medieval timesphere. At least one critic has been misled by the dis-
tancing perspective in the poem. Thus, Clyde de L. Ryals concludes that
the poem is not "a study of failure; on the contrary, it is, in my opinion, a
dramatization of human development. Speaking with the diffidence of
hindsight, Clough half ridicules the spiritual anguish he had suffered in
his youth . . . his reflections on former stages in his development are iron-
ically humorous."[29] Such a reading implies that the temptations and
dilemmas presented in the dialogues of the poem are mere adolescent pre-
occupations. However, the preoccupations, issues, and situations in the
poem are *lifetime* concerns, concerns that persist even to this day in the
adult urban environment. At least three are relevant here: (1) the con-
scious rejection of facile or romantic escape routes from the city's bustling
reality, (2) the temptation to experience the most impersonal financial re-
lationship of the city, prostitution, and (3) the problem of how extensively
urban work activity dissolves individual personality and integrity.

As pointed out earlier, there is little action in *Dipsychus*. The poem's
development relies on a series of mental impressions and discussions be-
tween Dipsychus and the Spirit, who is later labeled Mephistopheles. One
of the few events narrated is a gondola ride through the canals of Venice.
In the midst of the ride, however, the experience sours, just as real experi-
ence has a way of intruding on romantic dream visions. And that is pre-
cisely the point. The aquatic excursion in scene 5—"In a Gondola"—is
initially presented as a Shelleyan flight of romantic escapism. The voice of
Dipsychus is the voice of idealism.

> How light it moves, how softly! Ah,
> Could life, as does our gondola,

> Unvexed with quarrels, aims, and cares,
> And moral duties and affairs,
> Unswaying, noiseless, swift, and strong,
> For ever thus—thus glide along!
> How light we move, how softly! Ah,
> Were all things like the gondola!   [sc. 5. ll. 11–18]

Throughout the scene, the Spirit serves as the undercutting voice of realism and contemporary skepticism. He points out that nature meant for the oarsman to stay fixed in his position, to be "our most humble menial debtor." The notion that his pleasure is built on the foundation of another's oppression disturbs Dipsychus deeply. And yet, the reservoir of Dipsychus's idealism is deep enough that he can, for a time, answer and resist the Spirit's taunts. As they are about to approach the landing, however, the Spirit launches an all-out attack of skeptical undercutting.

> Nay;
> 'Fore heaven, enough of that to-day:
> I'm deadly weary of your tune,
> And half-*ennuyé* with the moon;
> The shadows lie, the glories fall,
> And are but moonshine after all.
> It goes against my conscience really
> To let myself feel so ideally.
> Make me repose no power of man shall
> In things so deucéd unsubstantial.   [sc. 5. ll. 258–67]

As the gondola hits the pier once again, Dipsychus momentarily succumbs to the Spirit's taunts and is forced to condemn partially his naive notions of romantic escapism.

> On to the landing, onward. Nay,
> Sweet dream, a little longer stay!
> On to the landing; here. And, ah,
> Life is not as the gondola!   [sc. 5. ll. 302–5]

Dipsychus represents a new outlook in Victorian poetry in that the hero's leanings toward romantic escapism rarely involve a recurrent backward look to the idyllic natural countryside. In fact, Dipsychus only once comes close to such an outlook in the poem. Bewildered by the pressures in the metropolis, the open countryside, the cloud-capt Alps, and the broad sea momentarily seem to offer him relief. The familiar romantic haunts, however, are considered only briefly because Dipsychus literally forces himself to be happy by making his stand *in* the city. Indeed, he may have been one of the first poets to take the step toward modern neurosis.

> No, no,
> I am contented, and will not complain.
> To the old paths, my soul! Oh, be it so!
> I bear the workday burden of dull life
> About these footsore flags of a weary world.   [sc. 11. ll. 85–89]

A second major aspect of urban life to which the Spirit repeatedly draws Dipsychus's attention is prostitution. At first the Spirit's arguments for Dipsychus's consorting with a prostitute rely on mildly fallacious logic. If it is done in the haystack, why should it not be done in an urban boudoir?

> It was a lover and his lass,
> With a hey and a ho, and a hey nonino!
> Betwixt the acres of the rye,
> With a hey and a ho, and a hey nonino!
> These pretty country folks would lie—
> In the spring time, the pretty spring time.   [sc. 3. ll. 126–31]

Or more succinctly, "But heavens! [prostitution is] as innocent a thing / As picking strawberries in spring" (sc. 3. ll. 33–34). This tactic of wrapping urban sex in natural metaphors only increases Dipsychus's resolve to forebear. The Spirit soon changes his strategy by alternatively appealing to physical immediacy and to skeptical morality. Thus, as Dipsychus and the Spirit examine some of the "flagrant women of the street," Clough becomes one of the first poets to describe the prostitute's physical appearance.

> 'Tis here, I see, the custom too
> For damsels eager to be lovered
> To go about with arms uncovered;
> And doubtless there's a special charm
> In looking at a well-shaped arm.
> .   .   .   .   ,   [sc. 2. ll. 49–53]
> Look, she would fain allure; but she is cold,
> The ripe lips paled, the frolick pulses stilled,
> The quick eye dead, the once fair flushing cheek
> Flaccid under its paint; the once heaving bosom—
> [sc. 3. ll. 105–8]

The Spirit quickly realizes, however, that mere physical allurement does not reach Dipsychus's psychic center. In trying to liberalize the hero's puritanical conceptions of his proper sexual identity, the Spirit soon bombards Dipsychus with Byronic capsules of freethinking urban morality. Thus, the Spirit argues that since the prostitutes have already lost their virginity, and thereby their chances for respectable marriage according to the Victorian social code, it is a moral and charitable act to support them by becoming their client.

> Nor can God's own self,
> Renew to Ina frail or Ana
> Her once rent hymenis membrana.
> So that it needs consideration
> By what more moral occupation
> To support this vast population?   [sc 3. ll. 143, 146–50]

Another argument the Spirit advances is that the girls are at ease in their work and that the city offers an assured anonymity.

> Where, as we said, *vous faites vôtre affaire.*
> They'll suit you, these Venetian pets!
> So natural, not the least coquettes—
> Really at times one quite forgets—
> Well, would you like perhaps to arrive at
> A pretty creature's home in private?   [sc. 3. ll. 239–44]

The Spirit then humorously overturns—as Byron took such delight in doing in *Don Juan*—all Platonic notions and advocates reliance upon common sense.

> This lovely creature's glowing charms
> Are gross illusion, I don't doubt that;
> But when I pressed her in my arms
> I somehow didn't think about that.
>
> .   .   .   .   .   .
>
> Being common sense, it can't be sin
> To take it as we find it;
> The pleasure to take pleasure in;
> The pain, try not to mind it.   [sc. 5. ll. 110–13, 118–21]

The Spirit's final appeal is the basic notion that youth is a time for sexual experimentation.

> Come, my dear boy, I will not bind you,
> But scruples must be cast behind you.
> All mawkish talking I dislike,
> But when the iron *is* hot, strike!

Good God! to think of youthful bliss
Restricted to a sneaking kiss.   [sc. 9. ll. 100–105]

It seems probable that these assaults should affect Dipsychus's psychic
and sexual integrity. But a redeeming quality of Clough's verse is that he
does not present one-dimensional good and evil struggles even though he
employs the fable structure in his long verse drama. All that the Spirit
says about the temptresses filters down into Dipsychus's subconscious, and
in a remarkable passage, which surely foreshadows the unedited psychic
tapes of Leopold Bloom's daydream walks about Dublin, the hero of
Clough's poem dreams an erotic dream.

I dreamt a dream; till morning light
A bell rang in my head all night,
Tinkling and tinkling first, and then
Tolling; and tinkling; tolling again.

.   .   .   .

Ting, ting, there is no God; ting, ting;
Come dance and play, and merrily sing—
Ting, ting a ding; ting, ting a ding!
O pretty girl who trippest along,
Come to my bed—it isn't wrong,
Uncork the bottle, sing the song!
Ting, ting a ding: dong, dong.   [sc. 6. ll. 7–10, 16–22]

Ultimately, however, the pressures of reason and social convention gain
the upper hand so that Dipsychus resolves to remain pure and to have a
staid Victorian marriage.

The final urban concern of particular interest in *Dipsychus* is the accom-
modation of the sensitive, highly educated soul into the urban throngs
and work force. Here again, the Spirit takes the adversary position of de-
lighting in the cosmopolitan confusion of the city.

Enjoy the minute,
And the substantial blessings in it;
Ices, *par exemple*; evening air;
Company, and this handsome square;
Some pretty faces here and there;
Music! Up, up; it isn't fit
With beggars here on steps to sit.
Up—to the café! Take a chair
And join the wiser idlers there.
Aye! what a crowd! and what a noise!

With all these screaming half-breeched boys.
Partout dogs, boys, and women wander—
And see, a fellow singing yonder.   [sc. 1. ll. 50–62]

But Dipsychus's temperament is a melancholy one which verges on
Wertherian self-absorption.

> The whole great square they fill,
> From the red flaunting streamers on the staffs,
> And that barbaric portal of St. Mark's,
> To where, unnoticed, at the darker end,
> I sit upon my step. One great gay crowd.
> The Campanile to the silent stars
> Goes up, above—its apex lost in air.
> While these—do what?   [sc. 1. ll. 43–50]

Dipsychus's social equation for the city is what Raymond Williams has
defined as the individual (me) versus the masses (everyone else, different
and unknown to me).[30] Dipsychus's conceptions of the urban work forces
are that they suffer daily through "weary workday hours / And from the
long monotony of toil" (sc. 3. ll. 80–81) and that they are "sullied with
polluting smoke" (sc. 4. l. 71). When Dipsychus does not describe the
specifics of the workers' laboring conditions, he sees them as the amor-
phous "masses." Thus, he refers to them as the "herd" (sc. 4. l. 34), "the
ignoble crowd" (sc. 6. l. 82), "the base crowd" and "all ill voices of a
blustering world" (sc. 7. ll. 104–5). For a time, Dipsychus maintains a
Prufrockian distance from the hypocrisy and vanity of city society. He will
refuse

> To herd with people that one owns no care for;
> Friend it with strangers that one sees but once;
> To drain the heart with endless complaisance;
> To warp the unfashioned diction on the lip,
> And twist one's mouth to counterfeit; enforce
> Reluctant looks to falsehood; base-alloy
> The ingenuous golden frankness of the past;
> To calculate and plot; be rough and smooth,
> Forward and silent; deferential, cool,
> Not by one's humour, which is the safe truth,
> But on consideration—   [sc. 4. ll. 34–44]

Gradually, however, because of the Spirit's guiding insistence, Dipsychus
begins to build up a resistance to "these be-maddening discords of the

mind / . . . . And all the vext conundrums of our life" (sc. 10. ll. 15, 17) until he finally resolves "alone" to act and submit.[31] Thus, Dipsychus abandons the fight to maintain his idealism and purity only to join in another struggle; he will accept nineteenth-century city life on its own terms—with all of its competition and corruption. "We ne'er should act at all; and act we must" (sc. 11. l. 160). Alone, Dipsychus consciously resolves to accept his urban fate.

> Welcome, wicked world,
> The hardening heart, the calculating brain
> Narrowing its doors to thought, the lying lips,
> The calm-dissembling eyes; the greedy flesh,
> The world, the Devil—welcome, welcome, welcome!
>
> [sc. 12. ll. 82–86]

Yet in both his dreams and his unconscious realm, Dipsychus continues to be plagued with "a vision" which is the lament of every young man who has recently surrendered a substantial portion of his integrity and individuality to the controlling demands of the nation's economic system.

> O the misery
> That one must truck and practise with the world
> To gain the 'vantage-ground to assail it from;
> To set upon the giant one must first,
> O perfidy! have eat the giant's bread.   [sc. 13. ll. 36–40]

An addendum to the poem, "Dipsychus Continued," reveals that after "an interval of thirty years," the hero has become a courtroom judge. Thus, within the system of Victorian law and convention the sensitive individual can partially exercise his own standards of evaluation and judgment over the forces of competition and corruption evident everywhere. Even as an acute lawyer and an upright judge, however, Dipsychus never gets over his loathing of the "half-foolish, half-greedy" masses. In becoming a judge, Dipsychus takes on a respectable but aloof role. He deals with the city's inhabitants and their problems from a secondhand, elevated position rather than comprehending the urban experience directly. That is why—in this addendum and after the passage of thirty years—he is still haunted by his past now brought to mind by a mysterious female caller. The overwhelming structure of feeling haunting Dipsychus in the addendum is guilt; it is a mental anguish whose roots are unassimilated urban experiences.

Clearly, then, Dipsychus's dilemma is Clough's dilemma. In both the shorter and longer poems that he wrote before his 1853 review, Clough presents the difficult challenge of understanding the urban experience. In fact, Clough himself ended up with the common result evident in the poetry of others who tried to write about the city, a result that he berated in his 1853 review: city poems whose resolutions seemed unable to go beyond either indeterminacy or introspection. In his 1853 review Clough confidently issued a new challenge to other poets; in the poetry that he wrote in the dozen years preceding, however, he left his own call unanswered. He eloquently stated the difficulties of the poet's new function of treating the urban experience, but he was less clear concerning the solutions.

Alexander Smith: The City and the Country

After attempting in *Dipsychus* (1850) to take a stand on urban life, in his 1853 review article Clough called for other poets of the age to write about circumstances of the city. Alexander Smith and Matthew Arnold chose not to follow his advice. Even though Clough praises Smith for his sustained and realistic treatment of the city (primarily Glasgow), a careful examination of Smith's poetry does not substantiate this praise.[32] As G. Robert Stange states, "Alexander Smith . . . never did in his poetry what Clough claimed for him. . . . Smith's poems more often fall back on the stale theme of the desirability of escape from the evils of the city to the purity of the country."[33]

Country and city reverberations are especially important in Smith's first major work, *A Life Drama* (1853). Indeed, it could be argued that the alternation of country and city settings is one of the primary organizing devices of the poem. Smith's conception of the poet's function, and the various voice and character levels in the poem, are significant. Except for the last few scenes of the poem, all of the events are seen through the distancing device of memory and through an invented persona. The hero Walter quotes from the poems of a lost friend and discusses the dramatic events of his life. Toward the end of the poem, the reader learns that Walter has been describing his own story under the name of another person, the poet-friend. This reliance on distancing devices and dual personalities bears a resemblance to the techniques in Clough's *Dipsychus*. In a sense, the poet-friend is a second self of Walter, who in turn is a second self of Smith. What distinguishes Smith's poetry from Clough's, however, is that in *A Life Drama* Smith presents episodes in a narrative style whereas the scenes of Clough's *Dipsychus* are much closer to being transcripts of mental debates and interior struggles. Thus, the quick-paced dramatic action of

Smith's poem captures the excitement and movement both from country to city and within the city more successfully than the subjective dialogues in *Dipsychus*.

In print *A Life Drama* runs over two hundred pages. Approximately three-fourths of the poem presents the frenzied movements of Walter's poet-friend and his fleeting impressions of the country and the city. Rarely is the life or community in either setting rendered in any convincing detail. The city is presented as a place thick with smoke and sin; the country appears as a place of open spaces and balmy breezes. The following few selections convey the flavor.

> From which he drinks such joy as doth a pale
> And dim-eyed worker who escapes, in Spring,
> The thousand-streeted and smoke-smothered town,
> And treads awhile the breezy hills of health. [sc. 2]

> That he grew up 'mong primroses moon-pale
> In the hearts of purple hills; that he o'er-ran
> Green meadows golden in the level sun,
> A bright-haired child; and that, when these he left
> To dwell within a monstrous city's heart. [sc. 2]

> Oft with our souls in our eyes all day we fed
> On summer landscapes, silver-veined with streams,
> O'er which the air hung silent in its joy—
> With a great city lying in its smoke,
> A monster sleeping in its own thick breath.[34] [sc. 4]

Although Clough does not specifically mention any of these passages in his 1853 review, he must have had at least some of them in mind. If that were the case, it is difficult to agree with his judgment that "there is a charm, for example, in finding, as we do, continual images drawn from the busy seats of industry; it seems to satisfy a want that we have long been conscious of, when we see the black streams that welter out of factories, the dreary lengths of urban and suburban dustiness . . . irradiated with a gleam of divine purity."[35]

Only in the last quarter of *A Life Drama* does Smith present urban experience with any direct immediacy and begin to consider the functions of the poet in such a setting. The crucial turn in the poem comes in scene 8 when Walter relates a long tale about a poet who reached the nadir of human experiences while living in the city. By talking about these horrible experiences and degrading events in the city, Walter is able to put them behind him, even as they are recorded in poetry. As a youth the poet was very sensitive and lonely in the crowds. He ultimately convinced himself that it was better to live "With this weak human heart and yearning blood, / Lonely as God, than mate with barren souls" (sc. 8). His best friends were books. He revered the immortal fame of poets, and soon "His own heart / Made him a Poet" (sc. 8). He did not focus on his immediate surroundings but on the past as "alchymist Memory turned his past to gold" and "Imagination opened on his life" (sc. 8). Nature also offered this aspiring poet some inspiration, but economic circumstances allowed him to visit the countryside only on "sabbath-days." In nature the young poet found comfort even as he began to develop a martyr complex.

> These worldly men will kill me with their scorns,
> But Nature never mocks or jeers at me;
> Her dewy soothings of the earth and air
> Do wean me from the thoughts that mad my brain.   [sc. 8]

As the poet returned to the city after his day in the country it was as if he came back to a circle in hell.

> As slow he journeyed home, the wanderer saw
> The labouring fires come out against the dark,
> For with the night the country seemed on flame:
> Innumerable furnaces and pits,
> And gloomy holds, in which that bright slave, Fire,
> Doth pant and toil all day and night for man,
> Threw large and angry lustres on the sky,
> And shifting lights across the long black roads.   [sc. 8]

Perhaps in these lines Smith begins to deserve the praise that Clough suggested for recording the direct experience of an industrialized urban landscape. Yet the poet's efforts go unrewarded as he sinks into the depths of poverty, Wertherism, and oblivion. After these long discussions, which present a romanticized view of the poet, Smith is able to have Walter reevaluate the role of the poet in the city. His cynical friend Edward serves as a voice of challenging opinions. Edward calls the lost poet-friend "a sullen-blooded fool." He proposes that poetry might, among other things, "creep into the lost and ruined hearts / Of sinful women dying in the streets" (sc. 7). Soon after this, Walter meets the pure lady, Violet. He tells her about the most productive poetic endeavors he undertook with his "lost friend"—building a golden city with their imaginative powers.

> Sometimes we sat whole afternoons, and watched
> The sunset build a city frail as dream,

With bridges, streets of splendour, towers; and saw
The fabrics crumble into rosy ruins,
And then grow grey as heath. But our chief joy
Was to draw images from everything;
And images lay thick upon our talk,
As shells on ocean sands. [sc. 9]

This is the most explicit statement in the long work that indicates Smith was indeed attempting to "draw images from everything," to include the "bridges, streets of splendour, towers" of contemporary urban landscape in his poetry. Smith's intention to transform the materials of the city into fit images for poetry cannot be questioned, but his performance in carrying out this task can. The passage just quoted is itself ambiguous in its implications: the poet builds celestial cities from wordly materials, but he destroys them apocalyptically by day's end!

Although Smith did not work as much urban detail into his poetry as Clough would have liked, the last quarter of *A Life Drama* is significant because it presents the city as a place where one almost inevitably encounters atheism and prostitution. These snares would be elaborated more fully by James Thomson, but the responses of Smith's hero, Walter, are worth mentioning. Corruption and competition in the city provide a soil that nurtures the growth of atheism. Only the stars seem to save the hero from its clutches.

In mighty towns; immured in their black hearts,
The stars are nearer to you than the fields.
I'd grow an Atheist in these towns of trade,
Were't not for stars. The smoke puts heaven out;
I meet sin-bloated faces in the streets,
And shrink as from a blow. I hear wild oaths,
And curses spilt from lips that once were sweet,
And sealed for Heaven by a mother's kiss.
I mix with men whose hearts of human flesh,
Beneath the perrifying touch of gold,
Have grown as stony as the trodden ways.
I see no trace of God, till in the night,
While the vast city lies in dreams of gain,
He doth reveal himself to me in heaven.
My heart swells to Him as the sea to the moon;
Therefore it is I love the midnight stars. [sc. 9]

Perhaps the best-known scene of *A Life Drama* is the one in which Walter relives his encounter with the prostitute on a bridge in a city at midnight. "Relives" is not too strong a word to use to describe the dramatic presentation of the event that happened years earlier. The poet Walter distances the hideous encounter—"And now [I] stand in the middle of my life / Looking back through my tears—ne'er to return" (sc. 10). Walter views his consorting with the prostitute as a sin and a disease, "As small-pox passes o'er a lovely face, / Leaving it hideous" (sc. 10). Although Walter, as was typical in popular writing of the time, always links the prostitute with disease, the deepest scars are not physical, but psychological. He has been branded psychologically for life by the degradation of urban perversion of human relationships.

> Woe is me!
> My soul breeds sins as a dead body worms!
> They swarm and feed upon me. Hear me, God!
> Sin met me and embraced me on my way;
> Methought her cheeks were red, her lips had bloom;
> I kissed her bold lips, dallied with her hair:
> She sang me into slumber. I awoke—
> It was a putrid corse that clung to me,
> That *clings* to me like memory to the damned,
> That rots into my being. Father! God!
> I cannot shake it off, it clings, it clings.   [sc. 10]

Scene 10 ends with a hauntingly surrealistic description of the prostitute's white face which haunts the hero's subconscious: "It comes—that face again, that white, white face, / Set in a night of hair; reproachful eyes, / That make me mad." Only by the patient nurturings of the stereotypical angelic Victorian lady, Violet, is Walter restored to some sort of health and psychological balance.

It is fair to say, then, that in *A Life Drama* Smith recognizes the need for the poet to deal with the challenge of the urban experience. However, throughout the long poem he sees the city as the arena of terrible conflicts and temptations. This attitude is especially evident in the climactic scene in which Walter encounters the prostitute on a deserted bridge at midnight. The undesirable aspects of the city, at times graphically presented, never overwhelm Smith because he so easily and so often turns to the country as a desirable place of escape.

Smith continued to explore his attitudes toward city life in his second volume, *City Poems* (1857). In fact, he is one of the earliest nineteenth-century poets to use the word *city* in the title of a volume of poetry. As Mary Jane W. Scott points out, in "Glasgow," one of the volume's six medium-length poems, Smith attained a more mature balance than he had displayed in *A Life Drama*: "Smith at last made the difficult assertion of *acceptance* of the city in all its aspects. . . . Now, he could cry: 'In thee, O City! I discern / Another beauty, sad and stern' (ll. 47–48). . . . 'Glasgow' is a superb illustration of the balance in his poetic vision, of subjective and objective views, good and evil elements which he achieved in *City Poems*. In 'Glasgow' the speaker, clearly Smith himself, proclaims his love-hate relationship with the city, always aware that he belongs to it. . . . Deepest meanings for him are not found in the less-familiar country landscape, but in the city."[36]

In "Horton," "Glasgow," and "A Boy's Poem," the reader finds a mixed attitude conveyed. Realistically, the city has become an inevitable way of life, but survival there often requires a life and death struggle. In "Horton" Smith describes London as a city where one attains fame or languishes in oblivion. He writes

> Of the brave spirits who go up to woo
> That terrible City whose neglect is death,
> Whose smile is fame; the prosperous one who sits
> Sole in the summer sun, the crowd who die
> Unmentioned, as a wave which forms and breaks
> On undiscovered shores.[37]

"Glasgow" is the most sustained tribute to city life in the volume. The speaker sees himself as an urbanite who accepts Glasgow as his ancestors', his own, and his children's home community.

> City! I am true son of thine;
> Ne'er dwelt I where great mornings shine
> Around the bleating pens;
> Ne'er by the rivulets I strayed,
> And ne'er upon my childhood weighed
> The silence of the glens.
> Instead of shores where ocean beats,
> I hear the ebb and flow of streets.   [ll. 9–16]
>
> .   .   .   .
>
> Then wherefore from thee should I range?
> Thou hast my kith and kin:
> My childhood, youth, and manhood brave;
> Thou hast that unforgotten grave
> Within thy central din.
> A sacredness of love and death
> Dwells in thy noise and smoky breath.   [ll. 130–36]

Because of his acceptance based on long-standing communal ties he will make poetry out of the special beauty of the city.

> In thee, O City! I discern
> Another beauty, sad and stern.
> Draw thy fierce streams of blinding ore,
> Smite on a thousand anvils, roar
> Down to the harbour-bars;
> Smoulder in smoky sunsets, flare
> On rainy nights, with street and square
> Lie empty to the stars.
> From terrace proud to alley base
> I know thee as my mother's face.   [ll. 47–56]

This structure of feeling that there is a life and death struggle involved in building the city, together with a recognition of the city's permanence, is also expressed in "A Boy's Poem" in the form of "an impressive conceit of the slow, organic growth of the city."[38]

> Slow the city grew,
> Like coral reef on which the builders die
> Until it stands complete in pain and death.
> Great bridges with their coronets of lamps
> Light the black stream beneath; rude ocean's flock,
> Ships from all climes, are folded in its docks;
> And every heart from its great central dome
> To farthest suburb is a darkened stage
> On which Grief walks alone. A thousand years!
>   [pt. 3. ll. 175–83]

Although the three poems mentioned above are more positive than *A Life Drama* about the city's appearance and energy, they still offer mobility and escape as a means of temporary relief from city life. Granted, the escape is sometimes only psychological and the only movement that takes place is in the imagination of the speaker. In "Horton," for example, a laborer's thoughts on his way to work turn to the countryside.

> Inexorable Labour called me forth;
> And as I hurried through the busy streets,
> There was a sense of envy in my heart
> Of lazy lengths of rivers in the sun,
> Larks soaring up the ever-soaring sky,
> And mild kine couched in fields of uncrushed dew.   [ll. 85–90]

Even in "Glasgow"—the strongest endorsement of the urban landscape in the volume—the urbanized speaker sometimes describes an idealized countryside.

> I love to linger on thy bridge,
> All lonely as a mountain ridge,
> Disturbed but by my foot;
> While the black lazy stream beneath,
> Steals from its far-off wilds of heath. [ll. 76–80]
>
> .   .   .   .
>
> 'Tis only when I greet
> A dropt rose lying in my way,
> A butterfly that flutters gay
> Athwart the noisy street,
> I know the happy Summer smiles
> Around thy suburbs, miles on miles. [ll. 91–96]

Finally, in "A Boy's Poem" (an autobiographical reflection of Smith's early life as a mechanic) the pressures of the city become so intense that other conventional means of escape, such as madness, sleep, death, and a sea voyage, are offered in addition to the escape-to-nature motif. In these passages, Smith is frankly escapist. He not only rejects the realities of urban life, but he allows his imagination to create nonsensical fantasies to satiate his tendencies to wish fulfillment. Thus, the Arcadian idyll takes on picturebook status as "white cottages, half smothered in rose blooms" (pt. 2. l. 50) and "happy hamlets drowned in apple-bloom, / And ivy-muffled churches still with graves" (pt. 3. ll. 118–19) are presented as desirable alternatives to city living. The hymn to Sleep is surely the height of conventional triteness.

> Come, blessed Sleep,
> And with thy fingers of forgetfulness
> Tie up my senses till the day we meet,
> And kill this gap of time. . . . [pt. 2. ll. 90–93]

Likewise, the laborer's lament to end his workday with death verges on melancholic melodrama.

> It is the evening of my day of life,
> I have been working from the early dawn,
> Am sore and weary; let me go to sleep,—
> Let me stretch out my limbs and be at rest
> In the untroubled silence of the grave. [pt. 3. ll. 258–62]

So far, then, the three calls for poets to deal with (and most optimistically, to celebrate) the realities of the contemporary city were consciously answered by Clough and Smith. However, although both poets were willing to recognize the inevitability of city life, usually they only captured the danger and depression of the city and/or contrasted it with the presumably more desirable country way of life. These two attitudes—that city life was inevitable and survival there often required a struggle, and that mobility was still possible despite the city's magnetic attraction—persist in the poetry of Matthew Arnold. What Arnold adds to nineteenth-century poetic attitudes and images about the city is the optimistic sense that, although the city does not seem to fit properly either poetry or human life style in the present, it *may* in the future. Just as the country once provided peace and harmony for mankind, so the city (as Arnold states in several poems) has the potential to attain a similar condition of community, "a solemn peace of its own."

Matthew Arnold: The Promise of Urban Repose in the Future

Even before the appearance of the *Empedocles* volume (1852) and Clough's 1853 review of it, Matthew Arnold was seriously interested in describing the city and the related themes of man's activity in history and his shaping of the natural environment. Like Alexander Smith, who also described the city early in his poetic career, Arnold was often deflected from the arena of the city's hot and cheerless struggle to the scenes of idyllic country life. The special interest of Arnold's poetry, however, is that by the time of the *Empedocles* volume he comes to hope for an equivalent repose *in* the city. Even though Arnold believes that the city will attain a "solemn peace of its own," the agency of that change will be the internal forces of human history and not the workings of magical external forces.

From the time of Clough's 1853 review to the present day, Arnold has not usually been recognized for his ability to write poetry about life in the city. In his 1853 review Clough ranks Alexander Smith's poetry above Arnold's because he feels that Smith's work is more in touch with the actualities and details of urban life, and that his images are drawn firsthand from "the busy seas of industry," "the blank and desolate streets," and "the solitary bridges of the midnight city." [39] Yet it becomes apparent that Clough's main objection to Arnold's poetry is not so much the literal details of the verse, but the mental attitude and social position of the poet who was also his friend. Clough objects to the contemplative attitude, the incipient Wertherism in Arnold's *Tristam* and *Empedocles*: "We listen, indeed, not quite unpleased, to a sort of faint musical mumble, conveying at times a kind of subdued half-sense, or intimating, perhaps, a three-quarters-implied question, Is any thing real?—is love any thing?—what is anything? . . . How is it we find ourselves here, reflecting, pondering, hesitating, musing, complaining, with 'A.'?"[40] Furthermore, Clough suggests that the social background and temperament of Arnold might be a hindrance to writing poetry about the city. He questions whether a temperament that is "highly educated" and possessive of "a keener sense of difficulty in life" is "too delicate for common service."[41] Certainly Clough's critical comments are suggestive and his call for poetry to come nearer to reality in order to take a stand on life in the city is highly important; nonetheless, Clough does not help much in estimating Arnold's attempts in this area because in the review he never discusses the several poems in Arnold's 1852 *Empedocles* volume which are set in London or deal with the place of the city in civilization—"Consolation," "Resignation," "A Summer Night," "The Buried Life," "Lines Written in Kensington Gardens," and "The Future."

Several modern critics have not fully realized the diverse complexity of Arnold's response to the city because they have concentrated their discussions on single city poems. Alan Roper, for example, has high praise for and devotes considerable discussion to "Lines Written in Kensington Gardens," but generally he feels that the city is a minor landscape motif in Arnold's poetry. According to Roper, imaginative intensity was diminished when the poet came in contact with the city and the result was only one significant poem: "By contrast, the plain and its variants in hot or drab cities and brazen prisons seem not to have moved Arnold imaginatively as, say, they moved Dickens. . . . But when Arnold came to express his sense of the active life the urban details he found useful were very few in comparison with his rural scenes. It is of note that Arnold's best 'London' poem is 'Lines Written in Kensington Gardens.'"[42] In a similar manner, G. Robert Stange severely restricts his discussion of Arnold's poetry about the city by focusing on "A Summer Night." Stange hails this poem as "the only English poem of the time which invests the city with the symbolic depth and richness of Baudelaire's Paris" and points to the "realization of the city . . . which makes this poem unique in the canon of even the most urbane of Victorian poets."[43]

Stange's idea of the "realization of the city" is an important one and it provides a clue to a fuller understanding of the variety and dimension of Arnold's response to nineteenth-century urban life. In the several phases of his career, Arnold's thoughts center on the different *possibilities* of the city.

In some early poems Arnold had to work through the problem of what Raymond Williams calls "rural retrospect" in order to realize that man must work upon and often apart from the domain of nature. In another poem and in some of his letters, Arnold considers the possibilities for the poet both as an individual and as a speaker to the growing masses in the city. Finally, Arnold's most extensive musings about the city appear in his 1852 volume and later in his prose writings where he discusses his hopes for man's fulfillment in both the city of the present and of the future.

In three early poems Arnold speaks in a generalized, philosophical way about the realities of man-made towns and cities from the distanced perspective of the countryside, the rural domain of nature. The bardic voice in "Man's Works" (1844) belittles man's puny accomplishments from a typically romantic, Alpine perspective as the poet surveys the movement in the valley below.

> What are man's works
> Whereon he sets most store—his creeping temples,
> His little fretted plots of garden ground,
> His parcelled fields, his gewgaw palaces,
> His puny parks, a play mocking his own state,
> His trees, all their quaint skips and gambols gone,
> Tortured in sullen clumps and modish rows
> From the free use of nature—what are these,
> The mighty Gods of his sweet workmanship,
> Seen from the dizzy summit of an alp?[44]

Two poems in the *Strayed Reveller* volume (1849) express a hope and trust in man's work—including increased activity in cities—even though they are written from the perspective of the countryside. "In Harmony with Nature" (1847) has a Socratic or philosophic tone to its injunctions: "Know, man hath all which Nature hath, but more, / And in that *more* lie all his hopes of good" (ll. 4–6). Indeed, the close of the poem sounds very much like a Carlylean injunction to man to be about his work: "Man must begin, know this, where Nature ends; / Nature and man can never be fast friends. / Fool, if thou canst not pass her, rest her slave!" (ll. 12–14). In "To George Cruikshank: On Seeing, in the Country, His Picture of 'The Bottle'" (1847), Arnold seems at first disturbed that such a starkly graphic depiction of a drunkard's ruination of himself and family should "intrude" by reaching him in the countryside. Almost immediately, however, Arnold counters that a Hardyesque "full look at the Worst" is good because it stresses both the nadir and the pinnacle of the human soul.

Artist, whose hand, with horror winged, hath torn
From the rank life of towns this leaf! and flung
The prodigy of full-blown crime among
Valleys and men to middle fortune born,
Not innocent, indeed, yet not forlorn—
Say, what shall calm us when such guests intrude
Like comets on the heavenly solitude?

.　　.　　.　　.　　.　　.　　.　　.　　.

　　　　　　　　—Not so! The soul
Breasts her own griefs; and, urged too fiercely, says:
'Why tremble? True, the nobleness of man
May be by man effaced; man can control
To pain, to death, the bent of his own days.
Know thou the worst! So much, not more, he *can*.' [ll. 1–7, 9–14]

Increasingly Arnold turned his attention from the more abstract concepts of nature and the human soul to more practical questions. For example, what was the poet's function in the nineteenth-century city and what was the nature of his relationship to its growing number of inhabitants? "Resignation" (1848) is the one poem in the 1849 volume that specifically addresses these questions. The poet should not focus too intensely on his own dilemma, but on the concerns of mankind.

The poet, to whose mighty heart
Heaven doth a quicker pulse impart,
Subdues that energy to scan
Not his own course, but that of man.　　　　　　[ll. 144–47]

But if the poet is not to be self-absorbed, he also must remain somewhat emotionally detached in his observations of the lives of others. Like a modern-day journalist or social worker, he must maintain an emotional distance as he mixes with mankind, and above all he must not "crave" popular fame or attention.

He [the poet] sees, in some great-historied land,
A ruler of the people stand,
Sees his strong thought in fiery flood
Roll through the heaving multitude;
Exults—yet for no moment's space
Envies the all-regarded place.
Beautiful eyes meet his—and he
Bears to admire uncravingly;

> They pass—he, mingled with the crowd,
> Is in their far-off triumphs proud.
> From some high station he looks down,
> At sunset, on a populous town;
> Surveys each happy group which fleets,
> Toil ended, through the shining streets,
> Each with some errand of its own—
> And does not say: *I am alone.*   [ll. 154–69]

In several letters to Clough, Arnold records his further thoughts con-
cerning both the function of the poet in the urban age and the relationship
of himself to the masses. As for the material of poetry, Arnold points out
in a December 1847 letter to Clough that "what you have to say depends
on your age. . . . The poet's matter being the hitherto experience of the
world, and his own, increases with every century." [45] In a more well-
known letter to Clough, written in February 1849, Arnold comments tren-
chantly on the *nature* of the material the poet has to work with in the
nineteenth century: "Reflect too . . . how deeply *unpoetical* the age and all
one's surroundings are. Not unprofound, not ungrand, not unmoving:—
but *unpoetical*" (*Letters to Clough*, p. 99). How then is the nineteenth-
century poet to respond to the challenge and possibilities of this unpoetical
material? A closely related question is what should be the position of the
poet among the growing number of people in this new environment? Ar-
nold tends to be at least as concerned about this problem as he is about the
poet's recalcitrant material. Thus, Arnold lists for Clough the various prob-
lems that trouble him: "My dearest Clough these are damned times—
everything is against one—the height to which knowledge is come, the
spread of luxury, our physical enervation, the absence of great *natures*, the
unavoidable contact with millions of small ones, newspapers, cities, light
profligate friends, moral desperadoes like Carlyle, our own selves, and the
sickening consciousness of our difficulties" (*Letters to Clough*, p. 111). And
finally, Arnold seems to realize and to accept the fact that his fortunes
must inevitably fall as those of the masses rise: "Au reste, a great career is
hardly possible any longer. . . . I am more and more convinced that the
world tends to become more comfortable for the mass, and more uncom-
fortable for those of any natural gift or distinction—and it is as well per-
haps that it should be so" (*Letters to Clough*, p. 122).

The year 1851 marked an important turning point in Arnold's life. By
accepting a position as inspector of schools in April and by marrying Fran-
ces Lucy Wightman in June, Arnold became more deeply engaged in the
actualities of nineteenth-century life and took on the responsibilities of

family life. Lionel Trilling points out that Arnold was "one of the first modern literary men and one of the few eminent Victorians forced to support himself by hard, non-literary work."[46] As a school inspector Arnold traveled extensively and came into intimate contact with the social problems of the day. This new involvement with contemporary social conditions is evident in Arnold's second volume of poetry, *Empedocles on Etna* (1852). Several poems in this volume deal with life in the city, despite what Clough says in his 1853 review. In fact, in some of these poems Arnold reaches the pinnacle of his success in conveying the rich texture of the urban experience, the feeling of being immersed in the city. The author of the 1852 volume is a poet engaged with, involved in, and responsive to the urban environment. Arnold is aware of the possibilities the city holds forth both for himself and for mankind.

In the *Empedocles* volume Arnold exercises his poetic imagination and enlarges upon his own responses to the experience of being and working in the city. With the exception of "The Future," the only city poem written in the collective ("we") voice, all of the poems dealing with the city in the volume are lyric and employ the individual ("I") point of view. By concentrating on his personal responses so exclusively Arnold ignored the advice he gave in his earlier poem "Resignation"; yet, the sheer inevitability of having to work day after day had become a controlling pressure and predominant concern in his life. Now it could be argued that Arnold's poems about the city written in the early 1850s are meant to be representative of the dilemmas faced by other men of the age. But why is it then that Arnold never really presents other people in his city poems, never writes about the city in dramatic monologues or narratives, but instead writes always in the first person "I" lyric form?

In fact, the "I" speaker's mind sometimes appears to wander almost too far into the subjective realms of his own imagination. The poem "Consolation," for example, begins in the foggy setting of Arnold's London lodgings.

> Mist clogs the sunshine
> Smoky dwarf houses
> Hem me round everywhere;
> A vague dejection
> Weighs down my soul. [ll. 1–5]

In this poem Arnold's subjective thoughts wander away to the exotic lands of Asia and Africa. In the cities of Lassa and Rome, as well as "In a lone, sand-hemmed / City of Africa," Arnold's imagination focuses on such scenes of urban suffering as "a blind, led beggar" asking for alms and a crowd of "ten thousand mourners." Roper claims that urban existence causes imaginative dysfunction in the poet; that is, in such a poem as "Consolation," the images are arbitrary and lack imaginative concentration.[47] I would argue, however, that the various urban elements are vital to the poet's imaginative process and that they help to bring him to the conclusion that other urban dwellers have suffered far worse hardships—blindness, poverty, and death—than the momentary dejection he is experiencing in London. His consolation, then, lies in the future. His present "bleak, stern hour" in the city will pass as Time "Brings round to all men / Some undimmed hours" (ll. 74–75).

In "A Summer Night" (1851), the poet begins in a self-absorbed mood by presenting a vivid depiction of his alienation in the streets of the city. Then, in what is almost a classic Arnoldian gesture, the poet's eyes, thoughts, and hopes seem to rise above the present dismal circumstances.

> In the deserted, moon-blanched street,
> How lonely rings the echo of my feet!
> Those windows, which I gaze at, frown,
> Silent and white, unopening down,
> Repellent as the world;—but see,
> A break between the housetops shows
> The moon! and, lost behind her, fading dim
> Into the dewy dark obscurity
> Down at the far horizon's rim,
> Doth a whole tract of heaven disclose!   [ll. 1–10]

But Arnold, unlike some of the romantics, cannot live on moonbeams for very long and so his moon asks a question.

> And the calm moonlight seems to say:
> 'Hast thou then still the old unquiet breast,
> Which neither deadens into rest,
> Nor ever feels the fiery glow
> That whirls the spirit from itself away,
> But fluctuates to and fro,
> Never by passion quite possessed
> And never quite benumbed by the world's sway?'   [ll. 26–33]

The alternative ways of living—to be possessed by passion or to be benumbed by the world's sway—are indeed central concerns to Arnold, a young man familiar with the romantic poets, but also now working amidst the toil and drudgery of city workers. The poem expands the implications of the two life-styles. On the one hand, there are the masses.

> For most men in a brazen prison live,
>   Where, in the sun's hot eye,
>   With heads bent o'er their toil, they languidly
>   Their lives to some unmeaning taskwork give,
>   Dreaming of nought beyond their prison-wall.   [ll. 37–41]

On the other hand, there are the romantic explorers, "a few" who "Escape their prison and depart / On the wide ocean of life anew" (ll. 52–53). These two lines again convey escape in terms of a metaphor of nature. Ultimately, Arnold comes to see the two extreme alternatives in terms of madman versus slave: "Is there no life, but these alone? / Madman or slave, must man be one?" (ll. 74–75). In an important step, Arnold seeks a melioristic compromise position for himself. He concludes the poem on a careful note of hope by saying that yes, life is turbulent and unfulfilled in the city, but that's good because there is then ample opportunity and possibility for improvement.

> But I will rather say that you [Clearness divine!] remain
>   A world above man's head, to let him see
>   How boundless might his soul's horizons be,
>   How vast, yet of what clear transparency!
>   How it were good to abide there, and breathe free;
>   How far a lot to fill
>   Is left to each man still!   [ll. 86–92]

"The Buried Life" (1852) further amplifies the depiction of the city as the arena of "the hot race" that jades, deafens, and saps the energies and sensibilities of its competitors. As in "Dover Beach" (1851), the poet has a faint glimmering of a state of harmonious psychological integration.

> But often, in the world's most crowded streets,
>   But often, in the din of strife,
>   There rises an unspeakable desire
>   After the knowledge of our buried life;
>   A thirst to spend our fire and restless force
>   In tracking out our true, original course.   [ll. 45–50]

Although the longing to tap this subconscious strength comes "often," actual embodiment of the force in expressions of human affection is "rare" indeed. Not only are the moments of saving feeling "rare," but they take the poet out of the city and transport him to country landscapes.

> A man becomes aware of his life's flow,
>   And hears its winding murmur; and he sees
>   The meadows where it glides, the sun, the breeze.   [ll. 88–90]

"Lines Written in Kensington Gardens" (1852) is Arnold's most complex and concentrated city lyric. To Arnold the park is an idyllic retreat from the noisy roar of the city. Historically the park held different implications in the 1850s. There was a lack of public open spaces in many parts of mid-Victorian London. As Francis Sheppard makes clear, the parks were oases for many, and they tended to be crowded: "The royal parks open to wheeled traffic—Kensington Gardens, Hyde Park and Regent's Park—were the most popular, and the Green Park and St James's were convenient for the West End. Many people often came to these oases from a considerable distance, for elsewhere in London many traditional open spaces such as Spa Fields had recently been covered with bricks and mortar, and the municipal authorities had not yet started to establish new parks."[48] These historical facts are important for a full understanding of Arnold's poem. The Kensington Gardens that Arnold presents does not totally correspond to the real park of the age, which was usually crowded with people and closely connected by roads open to traffic to and from the city around it. Rather, it is more like Frederick Olmsted's conception of New York's Central Park. Françoise Choay neatly sums up this conception: "With Olmsted, the urban park will be more thoroughly integrated into the city (which in this case is a metropolis), and at the same time more completely contrasted with it, both as a place of recreation and as a segment of unspoiled nature." Thus, in the terms of such a conception, a stark opposition inevitably arises—"the city becomes more a city and nature, more nature."[49]

Olmsted's principles apply directly to what is going on in Arnold's poem, with one clarification. For the poet, the challenge of the city does not go away easily. In the poem Arnold does not seek escape and he does not merely set up an Olmstedian juxtaposition between city and nature; instead, he seeks an osmotic bond between the two. The poet wishes to transfer to his work-a-day existence in the city some of the calm and peace that he feels in the *rus in urbs* setting. Alan Roper captures this idea exactly when he explains that Arnold "petitions for a sense of peace '*amid* the city's jar,' because he wishes to translate the peace he finds in a glade *surrounded* by the city's jar into a peace when he is *included* in the city's jar."[50]

The park scene that Arnold describes is not an idyll but one which is carefully screened by the poet's selective imagination. Sheep really were kept in Kensington Gardens for the purpose of keeping the grass cropped; and quite likely, nursemaids watched children play among the "blowing daisies" and the "red-boled pine-trees" on any given afternoon. The poet's transforming imagination arranges these details to make a pastoral scene in the midst of the city. The intensity of this heightened scene calls for many lines to end with exclamation marks conveying the feeling of jubilant elevation.

> In this lone, open glade I lie,
> Screened by deep boughs on either hand;
> And at its end, to stay the eye,
> Those black-crowned, red-boled pine-trees stand!
>
> Birds here make song, each bird has his,
> Across the girdling city's hum.
> How green under the boughs it is!
> How thick the tremulous sheep-cries come!
>
> Sometimes a child will cross the glade
> To take his nurse his broken toy;
> Sometimes a thrush flit overhead
> Deep in her unknown day's employ.
>
> Here at my feet what wonders pass,
> What endless, active life is here!
> What blowing daisies, fragrant grass!
> An air-stirred forest, fresh and clear.   [ll. 1–16]

It is not long, however, before the city's reality reasserts itself. Beginning with line 21 the poem becomes clearly autobiographical. The poet grew up in the countryside—"But in my helpless cradle I / Was breathed on by the rural Pan" (ll. 23–24)—and now, as an adult, he finds himself caught up and challenged by the irresistible whirl of metropolitan life.

> I, on men's impious uproar hurled,
> Think often, as I hear them rave,
> That peace has left the upper world
> And now keeps only in the grave.   [ll. 25–28]

Momentarily the poet retreats into the comforting pastoral scene that he had composed from the literal details of Kensington Gardens. This time, however, the "glade" offers not a retreat for strength but a retreat with a painful awareness. The speaker realizes that he is unimportant to the pastoral world of the park because life there would continue without him.

> Yet here is peace for ever new!
> When I who watch them am away,
> Still all things in this glade go through
> The changes of their quiet day.   [ll. 29–32]

The world of the park and the comforting feelings that the poet evoked in its secure seclusion will be valuable only if that feeling of calm can be transferred to the city—the place of man's possibilities, the place where man's activities go on independently, just as nature's activities go on independently in the park. In short, the sensitive individual seeks psychological survival and harmonious integration in the city. If the subjective feeling of calm attained in the park can be recreated imaginatively "amid the city's jar," then the poet's imagination has answered the challenges of both nature and the city.

> Calm soul of all things! make it mine
> To feel, amid the city's jar,
> That there abides a peace of thine,
> Man did not make, and cannot mar.
>
> The will to neither strive nor cry,
> The power to feel with others give!
> Calm, calm me more! nor let me die
> Before I have begun to live. [ll. 37–44]

The final poem about the city to appear in the 1852 *Empedocles* volume is "The Future." The title suggests the poem's prophetic and philosophic implications. Here Arnold speaks not in the individual voice but in the collective voice about the condition of his generation and of generations to come. Of primary concern is the place of cities in the history of civilization. Part of the poem recounts the characteristics of the city as Arnold sees it in his day. He has witnessed the growth of cities at the expense of more open and calm spaces.

> This tract which the river of Time
> Now flows through with us, is the plain.
> Gone is the calm of its earlier shore.
> Bordered by cities and hoarse
> With a thousand cries is its stream.
> And we on its breast, our minds
> Are confused as the cries which we hear,
> Changing and shot as the sights which we see. [ll. 50–57]

Arnold readily admits that one of the "cries" or prophecies of the age foresees the ills brought by an urban industrial society increasing at an exponential rate.

> And we say that repose has fled
> For ever the course of the river of Time.

That cities will crowd to its edge
In a blacker, incessanter line;
That the din will be more on its banks,
Denser the trade on its stream,
Flatter the plain where it flows,
Fiercer the sun overhead.
That never will those on its breast
See an ennobling sight,
Drink of the feeling of quiet again.   [ll. 58–68]

But in the end Arnold dismisses the inevitability of this stifling growth of cities by concluding the poem on a hopeful note with a prayer-prophecy combination which looks forward to a new synthesis, a new possibility which would take some urban industrial factors into account. The outlook is a highly significant one because, though it guarantees no easy road to a new harmony, it does grant that urban existence is a permanent and inevitable stage in mankind's development. One day this stage will attain a separate peace.

Haply, the river of Time—
As it grows, as the towns on its marge
Fling their wavering lights
On a wider, statelier stream—
May acquire, if not the calm
Of its early mountainous shore,
Yet a solemn peace of its own.   [ll. 71–77]

Patrick Brantlinger in his study *The Spirit of Reform* also detects a hopeful and "forward-looking" attitude in Arnold's poem "The Future." He is, however, troubled by the "passive conception of history" implicit in the river metaphor used in the poem and he explains why he feels that "this hope for the future is not very sturdy, partly because the characters in the poem have no control over events. 'We' are adrift on the river of time, and its current determines where we travel and what we pass. Further, we are inert spectators, separated by the river from the scenes of crowded, noisy, vulgar activity that we can feel no part of. History as river works its will on us, rather than we as reformers on it or on the scenes along its banks."[51] In one sense Brantlinger is correct. There were problems in making accurate statements concerning the conditions of the age through the medium and metaphors of poetry. Arnold himself sensed this and that is one reason why he turned his primary energies away from poetry after 1853. When Arnold later returned briefly to the medium of poetry to discuss the city—

in the pair of poems "East London" and "West London" (1863)—conventionality had replaced individuality. Both poems touch only lightly on city misery while looking beyond to a "spirit" or "soul" that "points us to a better time than ours" ("West London," ll. 9, 14). The exclusive reliance on the lyrical individual perspective found in the early poems is gone and instead Arnold introduces narrative and satirical devices. One must agree with Stange that these two short poems "depend for their effects on stock phrases . . . or a stock situation."[52]

But if Arnold's later poetry about the city is not as interesting as that written before 1853, his activities and prose writings over the next thirty years indicate the persistence of his early melioristic hopes for the possibilities of the city. Until his retirement in 1886 Arnold viewed his civil servant position as an inspector of schools as an instrument for serious work, and in his school reports he discussed the greater but more challenging opportunity that an education in the city offered.[53] In *Culture and Anarchy* (1869) Arnold discussed in detail what cultural institutions needed to be preserved in a time of rapid urban and industrial expansion. A decade later, in a passage entitled "Demands on Life" (1880), Arnold contrasted the cities of Paris and London.

> If we consider the beauty and the ever-advancing perfection of Paris,—nay, and the same holds good, in its degree, of all the other great French cities also,—if we consider the theatre there, if we consider the pleasures, recreations, even the eating and drinking, if we consider the whole range of resources for instruction and for delight and for the conveniences of a humane life generally, and if we then think of London, and Liverpool, and Glasgow, and of the life of English towns generally, we shall find that the advantage of France arises from its immense middle class making the same sort of demands upon life which only a comparatively small upper class makes amongst ourselves.[54]

Here, and later in the same passage, Arnold's equations are simple. Many more Frenchmen—"the whole middle class"—make responsible and tasteful demands upon urban life in Paris and this allows the finer possibilities of urban civilization to be realized by many Parisians. Although Arnold is dissatisfied with the present condition of London, the possibilities can be realized if only more Englishmen will acquire a "humane and civilised" taste, and make more demands upon their unrefined urban civilization.[55]

It is important, then, to understand how the trajectory of Arnold's later attitudes recorded in his prose finds its beginning in the poems he wrote about the city before 1853. In those poems written early in his career—before Clough's 1853 review—Arnold most fully recorded his (the poet's) experiences in the city and the hopes he felt urban life held for mankind. The city was indeed a great challenge, a place of possibilities. It could offer the poet a new habitat as well as material for poetry. Generally, Arnold's attitude toward the urban and industrial expansion was melioristic. He felt that his age was at the beginning of a process and that it had a long way to go. The city had potential and prospective value but urban conditions would improve only if man would work on improving them. Early in his career Arnold believed that the poet could help determine the possibilities of the city. In the *Strayed Reveller* volume he affirmed the need to live among people in cities. In several poems in the *Empedocles* volume, he worked through the traditional opposition between the "hot and humid" city and the "peaceful and serene" country. In one poem, "The Future," he recorded a hope that men working with actual circumstances would fulfill a promise and make a life in the city that would one day attain "a solemn peace of its own." In this vision, Arnold shares a perspective on the city that looks back to William Blake and forward to D. H. Lawrence.

Walker and Buchanan: Groping and Coping in the City

Although Clough, Arnold, and Smith recognized that the city could offer the poet a new habitat as well as new material for poetry, there was an implicit assumption in the statements of all three poets that the challenge of the city would be great and perhaps even overwhelming. The final poet whose works and experiences fall within the compass of Clough's 1853 review is William Sidney Walker. To Clough's mind, Walker serves as an example of the poet whose mental balance is overturned by the city.

Circumstances forced Walker to spend the last sixteen years of his life (1830–1846) alone in "miserable lodgings in some court in the neighbourhood of St. James's."[56] The city was for him, as it sometimes was depicted in the poetry of Clough, Arnold, and Smith, a place where one had to struggle constantly in order to maintain individual integrity and psychological integration. Whereas Clough and Arnold secured other employment as a means to livelihood, Walker insisted on making a living strictly as a poet in the city. Fate and the public response had different plans for him. His deteriorating condition is well documented by his biographer: "It is painful to dwell on the recollection of his later years. During the course of them the author of this memoir had repeated opportunities of visiting him in London, and at each succeeding visit found his condition, both in mind and body, deteriorated, his lodgings more squalid, and his person more neglected."[57] Walker was indeed afflicted both in mind and body. Physically he suffered from "the stone" which caused "ravages on his constitution," and "his sense of hearing had become so morbidly acute that even when in the country, and much more in London, he was fain to stop his ears with cotton, and finding even that insufficient, with kneaded crumbs of bread." Walker also suffered mentally. He had hallucinations partly induced by the noise and commotion of the city: "On one occasion he called up a medical friend at two in the morning, with a pitiable complaint that his head had been crushed flat by the wheels of a waggon."[58] Finally, having come from a country background, he suffered from the absence of community in the city: "But as his mental disease increased, his visits to his few remaining friends [in Cambridge] were gradually discontinued; and though his longing for the society and sympathy of congenial minds was so intense as not a little to aggravate his mental sufferings, his life became daily more and more solitary."[59]

Walker recorded his deteriorating condition in his poetry. Both mentally and physically, Walker became a grotesque distortion. His mind served as a prism, capturing the extreme distortions of life in the city for a poet. Walker falls into the tradition (which goes back to the eighteenth-century poet Thomas Chatterton) of the romantic legend of the starving poet in the urban jungle. In his poetry Walker vividly presents the sheer physical and mental stress of the city so that in reading him, one has the sense that he is a poet who anticipates the intensity of urban loneliness and madness depicted in Thomson's *The City of Dreadful Night*. As the following selections from Walker's canon indicate, his view of the city is direct and affecting—even though its roots lie in isolation and madness.

> For I am vext
> With many thoughts: the kindly spirit of hope
> Is sick within me: fretting care, and strife
> With my own heart, have ta'en from solitude
> Its natural calm; while in the intercourse
> Of daily life, and by the household hearth,
> The silence of the unapproving eye
> Falls on my heart;   ["Peace to the Far Away," ll. 14–21]

> They go, and I remain. Their steps are free
> To tread the halls and groves, in thought alone
> To me accessible, my home erewhile
> Heart-loved, and in their summer quiet still

As beautiful, as when of old, return'd
From London's never-ebbing multitude
And everlasting cataract of sound,
'Midst the broad, silent courts of Trinity
I stood and paus'd; so strange, and strangely sweet
The night-like stillness of that noontide scene
Sank on my startled ear.   ["They Go, I Remain," ll. 1–11]

'Tis utter night; over all Nature's works
Silence and rest are spread; yet still the tramp
Of busy feet, the roll of wheels, the hum
Of passing tongues,—one endless din confused
Of sounds, that have no meaning for the heart,—
Marring the beauty of the tranquil hour,
Press on my sleepless ear. Sole genial voice,
The restless flame, that flickers on the hearth
Heard indistinctly through the tumult, soothes
My soul with its companionable sound,
And tales of other days.[60]   [" 'Tis Utter Night," ll. 1–11]

The city is not just a place of struggle, but a merciless consumer of hopes and a spoiler of all promises of peace. An "everlasting cataract of sound" and an "endless din" of confusion, the city oppresses human life. The poet lives in solitary anguish and sees only "censure and disbelief" in the faces of his fellow citizens. The city is a hostile landscape that has no meaning for the poet who, traditionally, deals in the truths of the human heart: "one endless din confused / Of sounds, that have no meaning for the heart." Certainly Walker's "lunacy" does not render his view of the city irrelevant; indeed, the disturbing report that he gives of the city causes Clough—and his theories about poetry's relation to the city—much consternation in his 1853 review of the unfortunate poet's volume.

Juxtaposed with all the mental and physical horror in Walker's verse is a strong yearning to return to happier, rural days of close community; hence, the recurrence of the words *remembrance* and *memory* throughout the volume. At times this longing for a peaceful bower verges on embryonic regression, as in the line "my weary sense for refuge; as a child" (" 'Tis Utter Night," l. 12). Walker's tendencies toward "rural retrospect" are familiar in nineteenth-century British poetry; to this regression he adds a realistic depiction of misery in the city. This combination of idyllic memory and realistic description is elaborated and refined in the poetry that Robert Buchanan wrote in the 1860s.

There has been a tendency to assume that all mid-Victorian poets met urban problems with the attitude of evasion and regression evident in Walker's works. Robert Buchanan's poetry resists the application of such a simplistic formula.

In an essay entitled "Nature and the Victorian City: The Ambivalent Attitude of Robert Buchanan," R. A. Forsyth argues that although "Buchanan struggles towards a new structure of feeling based on a conscious turning from the countryside to the city as the real centre of current life," he nonetheless has a "continued ambivalence towards both."[61] Yet Forsyth grants that "it seems valid to regard ambivalence not as evasive, but rather as an adjustment device, giving the participant some small area for psychic manoeuvre and accommodation."[62]

Because Buchanan's attitude toward the city can be regarded, in Forsyth's words, as "ambivalence [and] not as evasive," his poetry should be treated as an important coda to the responses evident in Clough, Arnold, and Smith. True, Clough's review was written almost ten years before Buchanan ever came down to London. Yet attitudes and issues posed by Clough in his review article are dealt with in the poetry that Buchanan wrote over a decade after Clough's review. In many ways Buchanan answers Clough's call for a poet in and of the city. In other respects, however, his struggles with the city are as problematic and contradictory as those waged by Clough, Arnold, and Smith. Forsyth concisely sums up his estimation of the strategy of Buchanan's urban poetry.

> Although the real source of these poems, as suggested, is moral outrage at the hellish city—thereby invoking its shadowy counterpart of heavenly ruralism—it seems to me neither satisfactory nor sufficient merely to dismiss them as escapism, or the lurid titillation of one wishing to expose the "shame of the city." For what we have here, rather, is an ambivalence of attitude where the complexity and strain of a chosen role—the poet of the "unsung city streets"—is so imaginatively demanding that Buchanan, almost unconsciously, uses the defensive strategy of reviling the subject while continuing to play the role.[63]

Forsyth's concluding estimation is suggestive of a way to schematize Buchanan's urban poetry; primarily, his response involves an interplay of form and content, the how and the what. The modes and themes of Buchanan's poems about the city tend to fall into two broad categories: lyric poems about the role of the poet in the city and about the constant lure of the countryside from which he came; and poems, often in the dramatic monologue or narrative form, about realistic social conditions and relationships among the unfortunate in London. Both of these categories present a distinctly different voice and make for a mixture in the volume *London Poems* (1866). Sentimentality and realism, and subjectivity and objectivity stand side by side in the volume. Buchanan engages the Victorian city consistently and amply. Compared to Walker and Smith, Buchanan exhibits a tough sensibility in the face of urban existence. Yet, more often than not, he found it necessary to color raw urban details with pathos and melodrama in order both to soften and to emphasize grim events for his audiences.

The question of "a chosen role of the poet," to borrow Forsyth's phrase, is a central theme in the life and poetry of Buchanan. At the age of nineteen, his father's complete financial failure brought a crisis to his life. In early May 1860 he and David Gray, another young Scottish poet, went to London to seek their literary fortunes. Indeed, in a later memoir of Gray, Buchanan recalled that they resolved to take "the literary fortress by storm."[64] In fact, Buchanan's arrival in London was "less than auspicious." He and Gray somehow got on separate trains, and they did not find each other until several weeks later. Also, on the train ride down, he lost his ticket and his baggage was impounded at the station for a week. Several of Buchanan's father's socialist friends in London came to his rescue with food, shelter, and small sums of money. At least he fared better than Gray, who slept that first night in Hyde Park, where he contracted a bad cold, and in December 1861 died from rapidly deteriorating health.[65]

Despite Buchanan's "less than auspicious" arrival in London, over the next ten years he recorded his impressions of his newly adopted urban environment and he devoted considerable thought to the nature of his role as a poet in an urban setting. In the prose dedication to W. H. Dixon at the beginning of *London Poems* (1866), he wrote that the volume was "the last of what I may term my 'poems of probation,'—wherein I have fairly hinted what I am trying to assimilate in life and thought." In an essay on poetry published in 1868, Buchanan maintains that he tried to show that actual contemporary life affords much better material for the poet than does material from the past: "The further the poet finds it necessary to recede from his own time, the less trustworthy is his imagination, the more constrained his sympathy, and the smaller his chance of creating true and durable types for human contemplation." He then adds a comment about his audience: "The success of my writings with the simple people may be no sign of their possessing durable poetic worth, but it at least implies that I have been labouring in the right direction."[66] In the poetry itself, other revealing reflections on the urban poet's role are evident.

"Bexhill, 1866," the first poem in *London Poems*, presents Buchanan's vacillation between the opposing environments of the country and the city. As the poet tries to create verse while at his seaside retreat, impressions of the city haunt him.

> Now, on this sweet still gloaming of the spring,
> Within my cottage by the sea, I sit,
> Thinking of yonder city where I dwelt,
> Wherein I sicken'd, and whereof I learn'
> So much that dwells like music on my brain.
> A melancholy happiness is mine![67]

Although pettiness and fierce competition are the rule in the city, there is the realistic recognition that with adequate preparation and awareness, the poet can sustain himself there.

> The good days dead, the well-belovèd gone
> Before me, lonely I abode amid
> The buying, and the selling, and the strife
> Of little natures; yet there still remain'd
> Something to thank the Lord for.—I could live!   [ll. 19–23]

Although Buchanan accepts the fact that he can live in the city, he nevertheless conveys a frank awareness that whenever he tries to focus his poetic talents directly on city conditions, he hears a deflective call that would have him write what Raymond Williams has described as the poetry of "rural retrospect or retreat," that melancholy longing for an Arcadian rural community, that "use of the country, of 'nature,' as a retreat and solace from human society."[68]

Certainly Buchanan was aware of the attractiveness of rural community, but he also knew that the more the poet turned to memory and the country, the less competently he would be able to treat the actualities of the city. The tension persists, however, and it turns strikingly on the pivotal word *yet*.

> Thereto, not seldom, did I seek to make
> The busy life of London musical,
> And phrase in modern song the troubled lives
> Of dwellers in the sunless lanes and streets.
> Yet ever I was haunted from afar,
> While singing; and the presence of the mountains
> Was on me; and the murmur of the sea
> Deepen'd my mood. . . .   [ll. 54–61]

The poet finds another problem in writing realistic poetry about the city: the city's "Truth [is] hard to phrase and render musical." All around he sees only indifferent crowds on the city's streets.

> But easier far the task to sing of kings,
> Or weave weird ballads where the moon-dew glistens,
> Than body forth this life in beauteous sound.
> The crowd had voices, but each living man
> Within the crowd seem'd silence-smit and hard:
> They only felt the dimness in their eyes,
> And now and then turn'd startled, when they saw
> Some weary one fling up his arms and drop,
> Clay-cold, among them,—and they scarcely grieved,
> But hush'd their hearts a time, and hurried on. [ll. 80–90]

In the final analysis Buchanan's youthful resiliency is irrepressible, and after a brief rural retreat, he resolves anew to make poetry of the city— "Wherefore in brighter mood I sought again / To make the life of London musical" (ll. 125–26). He immediately adds, however, that melancholy and melodrama will be important ingredients in his poetry because such harsh and horrifying reality as he will present must be absorbed or softened with the cleansing device of tears.

> And if I list to sing of sad things oft,
> It is that sad things in this life of breath
> Are truest, sweetest, deepest. Tears bring forth
> The richness of our natures, as the rain
> Sweetens the smelling brier; and I, thank God,
> Have anguish'd here in no ignoble tears— [ll. 132–37]

At least three other poems, as well as the concluding poem in the volume, deal fundamentally with the function of the poet and poetry in the city. In "The Lark's Flight," the conventional romantic symbol of the lark is brought to the city. The poet invests the bird with further meanings so that it becomes a messenger to report urban woes to God. Clearly the lark represents no fragile bird, but Buchanan's poetry.

> O Lark! O Lark!
> Up! for thy wings are strong;
> While the Day is breaking,
> And the City is waking,
> Sing a song of wrong—
>
> .   .   .   .   .

> Rise up to God! rise up, rise up, to God!
> Tell Him these things!   [ll. 158–62, 188–89]

"Summer Song in the City" is a similar invocation to poetry to stay in the city and fulfill its urgent mission.

> Poesy, O Poesy,
> Stay in London lanes with me!
>
> .   .   .   .   .   .
>
> O Poesy! here lies thy duty,
> In darker days and fouler air—
> Poesy, O Poesy!
> Fold thy wings and do not flee![69]

Personal thoughts on the role of the urban poet as seer are expressed in "London, 1864," a poem that no doubt is derived from Wordsworth's "Ode: Intimations of Immortality." In its sectional divisions and emphasis on past joy, present grief, and glimpsed consolation, it is similar to Wordsworth's ode. After four years of living in London, Buchanan wonders if the city has corrupted his sensibilities. Although he realizes that the grandeur of nature still exists, the misery he has seen and experienced in the city has tarnished his naive glory in his humanity.

> While the spirit of boyhood hath faded,
> And never again can be,
> And the singing seemeth degraded,
> Since the glory hath gone from me,—
> Though the glory around me and under,
> And the earth and the air and the sea,
> And the manifold music and wonder,
> Are grand as they used to be!   [ll. 47–54]

The next two sections of the poem ask what consolation there is "for the joy that comes never again" and where is there "a refuge from pain?" The sections are not hollow imitations of Wordsworth, but are fleshed with the specifics of the disturbing urban landscape.

> For the sound of the city is weary,
> As the people pass to and fro,
> And the friendless faces are dreary,
> As they come, and thrill through us, and go
>
> .   .   .   .   .   .
>
> And the weariness will not be spoken,
> And the bitterness dare not be said,

The silence of souls is unbroken,
And we hide ourselves from our Dead!
And what, then, secures us from madness?   [ll. 63–66, 71–75]

The emotional effect of the cumulative "and" is striking; the sequence of *and*s underscores the temporal misery of city life but also indicates the poet's acceptance of the apparent spatial endlessness of the urban environment. The final line—"And what, then, secures us from madness?"—is Walker's question; it is the question of the speaker in Tennyson's *Maud*; it would be the question of James Thomson and many others in the years to come. For a moment, Buchanan believed he had an answer—at least for himself. As a poet he was in touch with artistic impulses and he could send his voice and soul up above it all.

And there dawneth a time to the Poet,
When the bitterness passes away,
With none but his God to know it,
He kneels in the dark to pray;
And the prayer is turn'd into singing,
And the singing findeth a tongue,
And Art, with her cold hands clinging,
Comforts the soul she has stung.

.   .   .   .

And the Poet, with pale lips asunder,
Stricken, and smitten, and bow'd,
Starteth at times from his wonder,
And sendeth his Soul up aloud!   [ll. 79–86, 97–100]

If "London, 1864" sounds Wordsworthian in tone and structure, "L'Envoi to London Poems," the final poem to treat the question of the role of the poet in the city, sounds Whitmanesque in its tone and outlook. It opens with the bardic proclamation that "I do not sing for Maidens . . . [or] School-boys," but instead "I sing for Dives and the Devil too" (ll. 1, 7, 16). Four poems in the volume deal with fallen women, and one deals with a dishonest lawyer. Yet in this final poem Buchanan lets abstractions carry him away and he fails to support them with convincingly concrete characters from the urban scene; hence he seems more like a youth imagining the terrors of hell on a Sunday morning.

I sing of the stain'd outcast at Love's feet,—
Love with his wild eyes on the evening light;
I sing of sad lives trampled down like wheat
Under the heel of Lust, in Love's despite;

> I glean behind those wretched shapes ye see
> In the cold harvest-fields of Infamy.   [ll. 19–24]

The second major concern that Buchanan presents in poems written in the individual lyric voice is the deflective call of the countryside. Nearly all of the poems on this subject begin in the city; sometimes the poet forces his mind to return to the city in order to draw a contrasting conclusion, or sometimes the city never reappears. "Langley Lane: A Love Poem" is the most sentimentally indulgent invocation of a pastoral setting— with a suburban address—to be set against London.

> In all the land, range up, range down,
> Is there ever a place so pleasant and sweet,
> As Langley Lane, in London town,
> Just out of the bustle of square and street?
> Little white cottages, all in a row,
> Gardens, where bachelors'-buttons grow. .   [ll. 1–6]

Likewise, "Spring Song in the City" deals more with a song than with the city. The poet does not stop to listen for a reply to the question posed in the opening lines—"Who remains in London, / In the streets with me?"—because he rushes on to indulge in wish fulfillment.

> Oh, to be a-roaming
> In an English dell!
> Every nook is wealthy,
> All the world looks well. . . .   [ll. 57–60]

In the lyric "The Blind Linnet," Buchanan imaginatively projects his own feelings onto a poor sempstress he sees through a window. In an arch-romantic transformational moment, the poet presumes that when the sempstress's life gets too unbearable in the city, she can close her eyes and become a bird piping in the free and open spaces of the countryside.

> But the sempstress can see
> How dark things be;
> How black through the town
> The stream is flowing;
>
> .   .   .   .   .
>
> So at times she tries,
> When her trouble is stirr'd
> To close her eyes,
> And be blind like the bird.
> And *then*, for a minute,

. . . she feels on her brow
The sunlight glowing, . . . [and hears]

A broad and beautiful river,
Washing fields of corn,
Flowing for ever
Through the woods where she was born—

[ll. 47–50, 53–57, 61–62, 65–68]

In the poetry of Buchanan discussed so far, it seems apparent that while he recognized that the poet might perform an important function in the city (an answer to Clough's call), he also tended to be deflected in his resolve to treat the city directly by the same forces that tempted Clough, Smith, and Arnold—a subjective plaint about the poet's sensibility in a troubled time and place, and memories of and retreats to the country or the pastoral past. In some of his poems, however, Buchanan manages to go beyond his predecessors to work out an individual and partially successful way of treating the city with its variegated stories and types, and its exciting and frightening energies. The treatment of the sempstress in the lyric "The Blind Linnet" serves well as an effective anticipation of and transition to another major category of poems in Buchanan's *London Poems* volume—poems that realistically treat urban inhabitants' social conditions and relationships. These poems are either dramatic monologues or narratives that use some of the devices of the novel to treat the realities of the city. Although nearly all of the characters in these poems are lower-class figures, they find themselves in a variety of situations. Buchanan is weakest at presenting male characters. The opportunist in "Attorney Sneak" is a conventional caricature of the greedy barrister "sucking the blood of people here in London" (l. 112). In presenting the dilemmas of fallen or destitute women Buchanan is at his best; these poems show insight into the social conditions and relationships associated with urban industrial life. "The Little Milliner; or, Love in an Attic" presents a young girl with simple hopes who is "good and pure amid the [city's] strife." In a sense, it is the first poem about London apartment or "flat" life, where one sees and hears his neighbors but never gets to know them, except imaginatively. Here the male speaker's fantasy approaches lechery.

And every night, when in from work she tript,
Red to the ears I from my chamber slipt,
That I might hear upon the narrow stair
Her low 'Good evening,' as she pass'd me there.

Realism Versus Escapism, 1850–1870

> And when her door was closed, below sat I,
> And hearken'd stilly as she stirr'd on high,—
> Watch'd the red firelight shadows in the room,
> Fashion'd her face before me in the gloom,
> And heard her close the window, lock the door,
> Moving about more lightly than before,
> And thought, 'She is undressing now!' and oh!
> My cheeks were hot, my heart was in a glow!
> And I made pictures of her,—standing bright
> Before the looking-glass in bed-gown white.   [ll. 37–50]

"Liz" and "Jane Lewson" present the plight of two fallen women. They are not professional prostitutes, but both have given birth to children out of wedlock. In the poetry of Clough and Smith, written a decade before Buchanan's, such figures were branded as wicked women and diseased pariahs. As Cassidy points out, in the poetry of Buchanan such a judgment "was gradually giving away to the concept that she was at least partially an unfortunate victim of social and economic maladjustments. . . . Buchanan presents sexual irregularity as an almost inevitable outgrowth of London slum life."[70] In "Liz" the young girl is dying after the birth of her illegitimate son. She tells the story of her hard life to a clergyman who has come to comfort her in her dingy tenement room. The dramatic monologue evokes the reader's sympathy for her. She was born in the city and is one with the urban environment.

> It does not seem that I was born. I woke,
> One day, long, long ago, in a dark room,
> And saw the housetops round me in the smoke,
> And, leaning out, look'd down into the gloom,
> Saw deep black pits, blank walls, and broken panes;
> And eyes, behind the panes, that flash'd at me,
> And heard an awful roaring, from the lanes,
> Of folk I could not see.   [ll. 54–61]

She can recall only one day when she felt a yearning to escape, when she "took a sudden fancy in [her] head / To try the country" (ll. 234–35). But at the end of the day, she is convinced that the stillness of country life is unsustaining to her temperament.

> Well, I was more afraid than ever, then
> And felt that I should die in such a place,—
> So back to London town I turn'd my face,

And crept into the great black streets again;
And when I breathed the smoke and heard the roar,
Why, I was better, for in London here
My heart was busy, and I felt no fear.
I never saw the country any more.
And I have stay'd in London, well or ill—
I would not stay out yonder if I could.
For one feels dead, and all looks pure and good—
I could not bear a life so bright and still.   [ll. 283–94]

In London, she followed the example of her street-vendor friends and
found a tolerable man of the slums with whom to live. Poverty put mar-
riage out of the question. Yet she loves Joe Purvis and wonders how he
and the child will get along after her death.

There's Joe! I hear his foot upon the stairs!—
He must be wet, poor lad!
He will be angry, like enough, to find
Another little life to clothe and keep.   [ll. 311–14]

The young woman in "Jane Lewson" is driven to the streets and a life of
sin more by the strict Calvinism of her two older unwed sisters than by
social or economic oppression. Yet Buchanan presents her tale in such a
way that the reader's sympathy is always with Jane, the abandoned woman
shunned by conventional society. In this way Buchanan is both observing
social conditions and asserting his moral indignation about them. It is the
drab, strict life in her urban home and the desire for motherhood that lead
Jane to seek a lover.

                    Coldly she heard
The daily tale of human sin and wrong,
And the small thunders of the Sunday nights
In chapel. All around her were the streets,
And frightful sounds, and gloomy sunless faces,
And thus with tacit dolour she resign'd
Her nature to the hue upon the cheeks
Of her cold sisters. Yet she could not pray
As they pray'd, could not wholly feel and know
The blackness of mankind, her own heart's sin;
But when she tried to get to God, and yearn'd
For help not human, she could only cry,
Feeling a loveless and a useless thing,

> Thinking of those sweet places in the fields,
> Those homes whereon the sun shone pleasantly,
> And happy mothers sat at cottage doors
> Among their children.   [ll. 93–109]

Jane hoped to be married and thus put an end to the community's gossip and shocking stares. After the baby girl came, however, she grew ill and awoke one day to hear that her lover had fled across the seas. The community only heaped more shame on Jane. After many years pass, Buchanan shows his basic sympathy for the unfortunate by having "God" grant Jane a proper place in a suburban dream house that is owned by her daughter Margaret, who has married a prosperous husband. Although this reward is a clear example of Buchanan's favorite use of restrained melancholy in order to evoke compassion, the twentieth-century reader is likely to view the happy "cottage close to town" as Dickensian sentimental suburbanism, but without the Dickensian gusto.

> And they dwelt together,—leaving
> The dismal dwelling in the smoky square,
> To dwell within a cottage close to town;
> But Jane lived with them only for a year;
> And then, because the heart that had been used
> To suffering so long could not endure
> To be so happy, died; worn out and tired,
> Kissing her child; and as her dying thoughts
> Went back along the years, the suffering seem'd
> Not such a thankless suffering after all.   [ll. 694–703]

In "Jane Lewson" Buchanan comes close to imitating the narratives found in the popular fiction of the day. In "Nell" he develops this narrative style even more effectively as he touches the pulse of the frightening energies in the city. "Nell" is a melodramatic and suspenseful narrative of a destitute woman who wanders through the streets of London before the scheduled execution of her husband. Again, social and economic oppressions are evident since the condemned man has experienced the desperate stages of unemployment, intemperance, and murder. But what is memorable about the poem is the wife's graphic rendering of the moods, sights, and sounds of London. Through Nell's senses the reader experiences the reality of being in the vast city.

> How clear I feel it still!
> The streets grew light, but rain began to fall;

I stopp'd and had some coffee at a stall,
Because I felt so chill;
A cock crew somewhere, and it seem'd a call
To wake the folk who kill!
The man who sold the coffee stared at me!
I must have been a sorry sight to see!
More people pass'd—a country cart with hay
Stopp'd close beside the stall,—and two or three
Talk'd about *it*! I moan'd, and crept away!   [ll. 134–144]

Nell's recollections express some of Buchanan's most subtle responses to the urban scene. The word *still* resonates with the twofold ambiguity of meaning both "quiet" and "again." The drizzling rain mixed with breaking light reminds the reader of the seventh lyric in Tennyson's *In Memoriam*. Nell conveys her longing for inner warmth by drinking hot coffee at a stall; yet it is a stall outside because she has no cozy hearth. The cock crowing is, of course, a traditional symbol of betrayal. The blank, but terrifying indifference of the city's inhabitants is captured in the stare of the coffee vendor. The country cart with hay is another significant image because it represents the harvest of the countryside now cut down—a sign of death—and boxed up—a sign of captivity—in a cart. The people presumably are talking about the murder, but the pronoun *it* is sufficiently ambiguous to suggest other sensational stories of violent night crimes in London.

After 1870 the poems that Buchanan wrote about the city have little to do with reality. In "The Earthquake; or, Six Days and a Sabbath" (1885), an earthquake drives many people out of London. "The City of Dream" (1888) and "The Wandering Jew" (1893) are religious epics that "show only too clearly that the city was filled with nightmarish shapes and shadows and that the real Wandering Jew was the tortured theological vagrant, Robert Buchanan."[71] However, the ground that Buchanan pioneered so deliberately as a city poet in the *London Poems* between 1866 and 1870 was to be explored again in the works of poets for years to come. Traces of the ambivalent tension between country and city and the escapism of "rural retrospect" can be found in the works of poets laureate as far forward as Robert Bridges ("London Snow" and "Indolence") and John Masefield ("London Town"). Likewise, the introduction of narrative and dramatic monologue devices to treat and to present real characters in the urban environment flourished later in the poetry of T. S. Eliot, though the subject matter and situations altered as London's sociohistorical circumstances changed and developed. In the next two decades poets would continue to respond to the realities of London life and they would use some of the dramatic and narrative devices that Buchanan pioneered; however, hysteria became the dominant tone as social upheaval came to the city's streets. In his own time, Buchanan alone went further than any of the poets who were mentioned in or who wrote immediately after Clough's 1853 review in answering the specifications of Clough's call for a poet to be in and of the city.

Chapter Three
The Urban Volcano, 1870–1890

Society's Equilibrium Challenged by
Depression and Riots

Although the twenty years between 1870 and 1890 were bracketed by violence, changes occurred at a steady and peaceful pace throughout the two decades. Progress was made in the political sphere as British society moved toward democracy during the period. Successive Reform Acts added substantial numbers to the electorate. The 1832 act increased the electorate by 500,000, the 1867 act by nearly one million, and the 1884 act by two million. More members of society prospered as real wages rose at a steady pace throughout the twenty-year period. Yet there was discontent during this period, especially among the middle class. An economic depression resulted as industrial capital wore out and prices generally began to fall. The middle class's uneasy sense of economic instability was coupled with a growing sense of political instability and an increasing consciousness of social unrest.

Even though most of the 1870s and early 1880s were free of violent demonstrations and disruptions, dramatic events like the Paris Commune, the Hyde Park Riots, Bloody Sunday in London, and various mass murders and strikes made lasting impressions on the public. These violent events at the beginning and end of the twenty-year period symbolized for many people the threat of great changes to come. Depending on one's perspective, the city thrust forward various problems which demanded solutions or encapsulated the more self-satisfied inhabitants' worst fears. In the summer of 1866, for example, London's Hyde Park was the scene of violent demonstrations and confrontations that resulted in the arming of special police with truncheons. Only a few years later, many Britons followed with great interest the alarming and sometimes absurd violence that troubled Paris during its siege by Prussian forces (1870) and the subsequent proclamation of the Paris Commune (1871). The events in Paris were of special significance to Londoners, and numerous articles concerning the plight of Paris and the possible implications for English society

93

appeared in *Fraser's* and other popular journals of the day. The two sieges of Paris represented not only the most extreme example of the separation of a great city from its surrounding and supporting countryside but also the most bitter and revolutionary class conflict yet in the urban streets. Tremendous energies concentrated and intensified in the metropolis so that Paris seemed to take on a life of its own. As one observer put it: "When you know Paris, she is not a town, she is an animated being, a natural person, who has her moments of fury, madness, stupidity, enthusiasm."[1] Once more, the Paris Commune of 1871 with its waving red flags, violent demonstrations, and destruction of the Vendôme Column had strong overtones of class conflict and revolution. Although patriotic as well as sociopolitical issues were involved, the Commune "was a combination of the proletariat and the lower middle classes against the upper classes with their rural allies."[2]

Fifteen years after the Paris Commune, it seemed to many that the violent turmoil had found its new home in London. The period from 1886 to 1889 came to be remembered as the "Four Violent Years." Whipped up by speeches in Trafalgar Square, 2,000 unemployed Londoners marched through the West End in February 1886. They carried red flags, cudgels, and stones. On their way to Hyde Park, the mob smashed the windows of the Conservative Club and looted shops on Pall Mall. The most organized rally occurred on November 13, 1887, when 100,000 demonstrators marched on Trafalgar Square. Mounted guards were called out to disperse the crowd. The day came to be called "Bloody Sunday" because police and demonstrators suffered considerable casualties and two civilians died in the fray. A year later, in the autumn of 1888, the "Jack the Ripper" murders added to urban terror when the cries of newsboys interrupted the solemnity of the new Lord Mayor's procession. London once again became a tense and violent battleground in August 1889 when the famous dock strike paralyzed Thames River shipping. Over 60,000 dock workers rallied and won over popular sympathy through the carefully organized propaganda of John Burns.

While British society was moving peacefully and effectively through democratic sociopolitical reforms between 1870 and 1890, the attention of many members of the middle class was continuously being drawn to the segment of the population immersed in poverty, disheartened by unemployment, or attracted to the idea of revolution. Poverty and unemployment certainly plagued London throughout the nineteenth century and before. What occurred between the years 1870 and 1890 was a growing concern over the overcrowded and forbidding sections in the squalid East End of London. Blanchard Jerrold captured this new note of awareness in the text that accompanies Gustave Doré's *London: A Pilgrimage* (1872): "We travel East, and at once come upon speculators of another world, merchants for whom nothing is too small, or mean, or repulsive. The violent contrasts of London life struck Addison—as still they strike every close observer. But in his day the contrasts were not so crowded together as they are now; and the poor were not in such imposing legions. . . . The West End Londoner is as completely in a strange land as any traveller from the Continent."[3]

Clearly, East London was different and dangerous. According to G. M. Young, the mortality rate was "twice as great in the East End as in the West. In adjacent streets it [life expectancy] varied from 38 to 12."[4] Although the concentrated misery and squalor to be found in the East End of London was great, the area had a certain vitality and diversity that attracted a number of observers who recorded what they saw in various studies that drew increasing attention to the plight and problems of the area. The titles of some of the published accounts are revealing: Andrew Mearns's *The Bitter Cry of Outcast London* (1883) and Salvation Army General William Booth's *In Darkest England and the Way Out* (1890). The most patiently researched and statistically accurate report according to the standards of modern sociologists was Charles Booth's seventeen volumes on *The Life and Labour of the People in London* (1889–1903). These studies as well as a wealth of articles concerning the problems of poverty and unemployment were read by a substantial number of serious middle-class Victorian readers.

It was little or no comfort that the East End of London represented and even dramatized destitution in a localized area. The middle and upper classes of the West End became increasingly aware of the gulf between themselves and "the other half" of the metropolis. But greater awareness brought only greater anxiety as the more privileged members of society feared infection or insurrection from the underprivileged. As B. I. Coleman points out, the East End's destitution seemed "beyond the reach of traditional paternalism" and suffering came to be associated with political disaffection, class conflict, irreligion, and public health problems. "The condition of the urban poor attracted less attention during the mid-Victorian phase of economic optimism, but in the 1880s the revelation of the gulf between the rising standards of society at large and the condition of the slum population shattered much of the complacency."[5] The expansionary energies of the 1850s and 1860s not only had erected new buildings and a transportation system but also had removed the wealthy to the suburbs and brought dislocation and overcrowding to the poor left behind in the central city. Now in the last quarter of the nineteenth century, many viewed the city as a nest of problems—mass poverty, unemployment, physical and moral degeneracy, overcrowding, and economic exploitation. To the many Victorians who had believed in the self-help approach to poverty and in an organic society to which all contributed, the idea that the capitalistic system should now create idle and useless members of society was particularly disturbing. Yet the grim facts were that in the years 1879, 1886, and 1894, unemployment rates were alarmingly high. It was in this late nineteenth-century period that the terms "unemployed and idle . . . developed their modern senses of being 'out of paid employment' or of being 'in employment but not working.'"[6]

In the 1880s, then, there was a growing concern about the masses even though no dangerous movement was really growing amongst them. Raymond Williams has done much to help our generation come to a fuller understanding of the true state of the masses in Victorian times. Above all, he insists on seeing Victorian working classes as people, men and women who were really helpless and could never finally help themselves. Repeatedly, he castigates positions which view the working classes as monstrous, brutal, and semiconscious because "this way of seeing the working people is not from fact and observation but from the pressures of feeling exiled: other people are seen as an undifferentiated mass beyond one, the 'monstrous' figure."[7]

The most detailed and important socioeconomic study which elaborates Williams's call for a reassessment of the Victorian working class is Gareth Stedman Jones's *Outcast London: A Study in the Relationship Between Classes in Victorian Society*. With a wealth of support drawn from figures and observational studies of the time, Jones argues that it is now time to do what the upper and middle classes of Victorian England did not do—"draw a clearer distinction between the 'true' working classes on the one hand, and the casual 'residuum' on the other."[8] Jones admits that there were both geographical and economic pressures which tended to concentrate the poorer classes of society together.

> Even more serious was the suggestion that the growing housing shortage was pushing the respectable working class into the same living quarters as the disreputable poor. Thus, while the geographical separation of rich and poor was becoming ever more complete, the poor themselves were becoming more closely crammed together regardless of status or character. In this situation, the onset of cyclical depression was particularly disturbing. For, as the depression deepened, signs of distress began to appear in the ranks of the respectable working class. "Agitators" were already beginning to blur

the distinction between the respectable working class and the "re-siduum" by appealing to both under the slogan of "relief to the unemployed." The dangerous possibility existed that the respectable working class, under the stress of prolonged unemployment, might throw in its lot with the casual poor.[9]

Thus, what Jones calls for is found only rarely in Victorian writings: the awareness that there was a working class that often was diligent and did its best to contribute to society, that there were many unemployed who were only seasonably laid off, and that the vicious and semicriminal element made up less than two percent of the population of East London. The suffering and disgrace of the poor in the East End had the potential of engendering danger to the middle-class way of life. However, the pattern of feeling which saw East London as a jungle filled with idle, thriftless, violent, and outrageous primitives was a response unsupported by the facts.

Yet the structure of feeling that most thoroughly and consistently pervades late-Victorian social commentary is the one that sees the masses as the most undifferentiated and dangerous element of urban society. The city's concentration of unprecedented numbers of people made it appear as a frightening place full of change, disorder, and even desolation. Carlyle in "Shooting Niagara: and After?" (1867) felt that by passing the Second Reform Bill England had taken "the Niagara leap of completed Democracy . . . towards the Bottomless or into it," and that the end of all things good and sound had arrived.

Matthew Arnold also became alarmed at the popular disturbances over the Second Reform Bill and expounded upon the urban propensity to disorder in *Culture and Anarchy* (1867–1868). His view of the masses or "the Populace" or "residuum" is almost paradoxical. On the one hand, he sees them as physically degenerated, "eaten up with disease, half-sized, half-fed, half-clothed," but on the other hand, he sees a disturbing and growing vitality in them—they are "swarming," "festering," "perpetually swelling." Arnold's perspective on the working classes is always that of a middle-class man. At times he will use the masses as a mediated symbol to expose and chide the hollow complacency of his fellow citizens by casually referring his readers to their fellow urban inhabitants who are as numerous as they are frightening—"Those vast, miserable, unmanageable masses of sunken people." At other times, Arnold addresses himself more specifically to the problem of the half-developed but emerging working class: "But that vast portion, lastly, of the working class which, raw and half-developed, has long lain half-hidden amidst its poverty and squalor, and is now issuing from its hiding-place to assert an Englishman's heaven-born privilege of doing as he likes, and is beginning to perplex us by marching where it likes, meeting where it likes, bawling what it likes, breaking what it likes,—to this vast residuum we may with great propriety give the name of *Populace*." Arnold wants to include the working classes in the general community of Englishmen and he urges his readers to conceive of "no perfection as being real which is not a *general* perfection, embracing all our fellow men with whom we have to do. . . . So all our fellow men, in the East End of London and elsewhere we must take along with us in the progress towards perfection." Yet the conclusion to Arnold's work leaves the reader with the impression that the specters of change and democratic progress still haunt Arnold's mind. A rioter is a "playful giant," who is rough and raw; a mob can only be "bent on mischief." Then, too, there is the famous reference to his father's advice that the Romans used to "flog the rank and file, and fling the ring-leaders from the Tarpeian Rock!" No good can come of riotous anarchy and "the lovers of culture may prize and employ fire and strength" against it.[10]

So even though social and political reforms were being peacefully realized between 1870 and 1890, the most prevalent feeling in the minds of English writers was that the urban masses were dangerous and to be feared. Wilfrid Ward comments on a quotation from an 1871 letter of Cardinal Newman's: "'The lowest class, which is most numerous, and is infidel, will rise up from the depths of the modern cities, and will be the new scourges of God.' This great prophecy, as it may be called, is first fulfilled in Paris."[11] As late as 1889, when violent trouble had reached London, writers were invoking the specter of the incendiary skies caused by the Paris Commune uprising of 1871. Thus, G. R. Sims warned in *How the Poor Live* (1889) that mass poverty "has now got into a condition in which it cannot be left. This mighty mob of famished, diseased and filthy helots is getting dangerous, physically, morally, politically dangerous. The barriers which have kept it back are rotten and giving way, and it may do the state a mischief if it be not looked to in time. Its fevers and its filth may spread to the homes of the wealthy; its lawless armies may sally forth and give us the taste of the lesson the mob has tried to teach now and again in Paris, when long years of neglect have done their work."[12]

The response of poets to the tribulations and sporadic turmoil of the 1870s and 1880s was very similar to the common response expressed by other writers of the period. All the poets discussed in this chapter had an idea of the city that was very much influenced by their idea of the masses or residuum. This largely unknown but ever increasing element of urban society served as the origin of fear and panic (for Gerard Manley Hopkins and Coventry Patmore), the reason for hope (for Roden Noel and William Morris), or the grounds of despair (for James Thomson).

The intensity of their utterances makes Hopkins and Patmore two of the most sensational examples of the nineteenth-century norm of poetic response to the city that G. Robert Stange outlines in his essay "The Frightened Poets." For these two orthodox Catholic poets, the urban residuum—which both of them had observed firsthand—engendered only panic and disdain. In the late 1870s and early 1880s Hopkins had worked for three years in slum neighborhoods, but it was not until the disturbance of "Bloody Sunday" that his violent reaction to the swift pace of change showed up in his poetry. In the poem "Tom's Garland: Upon the Unemployed" (1887), Hopkins was forced, under the stress of socio-economic reality, to question his faith in the basic justice of God's "natural order" for society. The poem represents a unique confrontation of Hopkins's religious and aesthetic ideas with the grim social conditions that had become part of his experience. The stress of social problems broke rather than revealed an "inscape," and Hopkins immediately decided to eschew further social commentary. Patmore was even more vitriolic when he commented in the two poems "1867" and "A London Fête" on what he thought to be disturbing and chaotic social changes of the day.

Poets like Roden Noel and William Morris, however, introduced new poetic forms as well as hopes for social reform in their versions of the city. Noel looked at the city with its teeming masses and believed that surely something must come *into* the situation to justify and stabilize what he saw. In such poems as "The Red Flag" (1872) and "A Lay of Civilisation" (1885), Noel seems the most direct and objective of the various poetic commentators of the age. There is a journalistic immediacy to the form and content of his poems, and they tend toward narrative poetry and fiction as they tell a story by employing caricature and partially developed characters. Noel is so intensely and immediately attracted by the present turbulent situation and the stark juxtapositions of rich and poor that he rarely steps back to pillory the masses with vitriolic or hysterical rhetoric. The fact that he is removed from the people, however, leads him to summon help from such outside sources as God and divine justice.

William Morris also looked at the city's teeming masses but he resolutely believed that something grand would come *out of* the situation only through and after a violent revolution swept away the ugly dross and oppressive inequities. Besides the short songs inspiring revolution in *Chants for Socialists*, Morris turned back to the events of the Paris Commune uprising in *The Pilgrims of Hope* (1887). The passage of years allowed him to examine more fully the historical facts and characters involved in the turmoil. Whereas Noel describes the events, Morris narrates them and thus gives them fuller historical and revolutionary significance.

James Thomson shared Morris's steadfast belief in a new society. Thomson's unrelenting attitude permeates "The City of Dreadful Night" (1874), but it is the antithetical attitude of pessimistic despair based on frustration and skepticism. Thomson looked at the city's teeming masses and despaired that *nothing* would come, from within or without, to change the undesirable urban situation. Darkness and death pervade Thomson's city, and it is not the darkness and death just before the dawning of resurrection or redemption. All is enervated, run-down, and diminished in the atheistic Thomson's vision. His enormous melancholy even numbs the hysterical fears found later in other writers of the period who recorded their anxieties after Thomson wrote his nightmare vision.

Hopkins and Patmore: The Active Crater

The ideas in Hopkins's "Tom's Garland: Upon the Unemployed" (1887) date back to 1871, and the work cannot be appreciated fully without some understanding of the pattern of the poet's engagement and subsequent disengagement with social and political concerns in the course of his career. Hopkins's most controversial political statement was made in an 1871 letter to Robert Bridges.

> I am afraid some great revolution is not far off. Horrible to say, in a manner I am a Communist. . . . It is a dreadful thing for the greatest and most necessary part of a very rich nation to live a hard life without dignity, knowledge, comforts, delight, or hopes in the midst of plenty—which plenty they make. They profess that they do not care what they wreck and burn, the old civilisation and order must be destroyed. This is a dreadful look out but what has the old civilisation done for them? . . . England has grown hugely wealthy but this wealth has not reached the working classes; I expect it has made their condition worse.[13]

This letter must be seen in perspective, since it would be a mistake to conclude that this was Hopkins's political stance throughout his life or at the time he wrote "Tom's Garland." The "Red-letter" was written only four years after Hopkins graduated from Oxford and at a time when he was exploring all sorts of new ideas in his philosophical studies at St. Mary's Hall, Stonyhurst. In 1871 the revolutionary government established in Paris, the Commune, would have been in the news. Hopkins may have been merely exploring an idea in this letter. Not until the period between 1878 and 1881 was he to have a direct interest in the working classes as a preacher in London and Liverpool. Hopkins's political statements after the "Red-letter" are never so bold. When Hopkins writes again to Bridges, after a lapse of over two years, he still feels that the working classes are not being treated fairly, but he repudiates communism as a solution to the problem: "I have little reason to be red: it was the red Commune that murdered five of our Fathers lately—whether before or after I wrote I do not remember. So far as I know I said nothing that might not fairly be said" (*Letters*, 1: 29).

Having rejected communism as a social panacea, and perhaps even having rejected any social or secular solution at all, Hopkins sought justification for the hard work and grim plight of the urban working classes in scriptural texts. From his pulpit Hopkins repeatedly praised the work ethic and endorsed the prevailing social class structure. He believed that there was worth in every human activity and for those who worked hard and suffered greatly here on earth, there would be great rewards in heaven.[14] He advocated that every man must accept the prevailing class structure and do his duty by it: "There are then, as you know, in commonwealths ranks or (as they say) *estates*; for instance in our own are three, the crown, the peers, the commons. . . . But THE COMMON GOOD IS TO BE REALISED, it is to be brought about, BY ALL the citizens or members and estates of the commonwealth DOING THEIR DUTY" (*Note-books*, pp. 271–72).

But as comforting as scriptural endorsement of social complacency may have been to some, the conditions and victims of late nineteenth-century England continued both to sadden and to anger him: "I remarked for the thousandth time with sorrow and loathing the base and bespotted figures and features of the Liverpool crowd" (*Letters*, 1: 127). Elsewhere, Hopkins condemned the degrading effects of industrialism: "My Liverpool and Glasgow experience laid upon my mind a conviction, a truly crushing conviction, of the misery of town life to the poor and more than to the poor, of the misery of the poor in general, of the degradation even of our race, of the hollowness of this century's civilisation: it made even life a burden to me to have daily thrust upon me the things I saw," (*Letters*, 2: 97); and, "What I most dislike in towns and in London in particular is the misery of the poor; the dirt, squalor, and the ill-shapen degraded physical (putting aside moral) type of so many of the people, with the deeply dejecting, unbearable thought that by degrees almost all our population will become a town population and a puny and unhealthy and cowardly one" (*Letters*, 3: 291). Hopkins was so disturbed by the living conditions of the day laborers in the Liverpool slums that his creative output as a writer was threatened. "But I never could write; time and spirits were wanting; one is so fagged, so harried and gallied up and down. And the drunkards go on drinking, the filthy, as the scripture says, are filthy still: human nature is so inveterate. Would that I had seen the last of it" (*Letters*, 1: 110). And so it was that when Hopkins came to write "Tom's Garland" in the fall of 1887, a unique set of circumstances came together which led him to make a poetic statement about social concerns that had been bothering him for years. The poem was written in Ireland from the position of both a spiritual and national exile described in the terrible sonnet "To seem the stranger lies my lot" and against the backdrop of weekly riots and upheavals in the streets.[15]

Interestingly enough, there is another seed for "Tom's Garland" besides the details drawn from Hopkins's own social experiences—the influence of a very early entry (1865) in one of his notebooks, a sonnet entitled "Work" by Ford Madox Brown.

> Work! which beads the brow and tans the flesh
> Of lusty manhood, casting out its devils;
> By whose weird art transmuting poor men's evils
> Their bed seems down, their one dish ever fresh;
> Ah me, for want of it what ills in leash
> Hold us; its want the pale mechanic levels
> To workhouse depths, while master spendthrift revels:
> For want of work the fiends him soon enmesh.
> Ah, beauteous tripping dame with bell-like skirts,
> Intent on thy small scarlet-coated hound,
> Are ragged wayside babes not lovesome too?
> Untrained their state reflects on thy deserts,
> Or they grow noisome beggars to abound
> Or dreaded midnight robbers breaking through.[16]

A close comparison of the two poems reveals that Hopkins carefully avoided placing the blame for the grim working conditions he had seen on the wealthier members of British society. With this important difference, the similarities in structure and subject matter between Brown's poem and "Tom's Garland" are unmistakable. In his first four lines, Brown praises the power and "weird art" of work to "transmute poor men's evils"; in his first eleven lines, Hopkins presents workmen at the end of a rewarding day claiming their just rewards of food and sleep.[17] Then Brown turns to the "ills in leash," the cruel, leveling effects of unemployment which send the mechanic to the "workhouse depths" and even the parsimonious to the "fiends." A similar shift occurs in Hopkins's poem as he describes in lines 12 to 18 the physical and spiritual woes of the unemployed. Just before the end of the two poems, however, the marked difference occurs; whereas Brown devotes lines 9 to 12 to an exposure of the indifferent and hypocritical attitude of the "beauteous tripping dame with bell-like skirts," Hopkins aims no such questioning remarks at the British upper classes. Curiously enough, Brown's and Hopkins's outlooks do converge once again in the final two lines of their poems as Brown fears that the unemployed will turn into "noisome beggars" and "dreaded midnight robbers" and Hopkins intensely fears that the two-headed monster of unemployment—"Hangdog dull" and "Manwolf, worse"—will "infest the age." [18]

As useful as the backdrops of sources and cultural history are for an understanding of "Tom's Garland," most striking is the dramatic explosion of the structure of feeling within the poem itself. The poet had always met his fellow human beings with joy and enthusiasm. The first twelve lines of "Tom's Garland" are no exception; an easy familiarity and rapport are established as Hopkins greets Tom Navvy at the end of a full day's work. Tom commands the poet's absolute attention; his name is repeated seven times in the first six lines. An incipient mockery develops as Hopkins dwells on the warmth of Tom's meal and bed and the smug opinions and snide "heart-at-ease" that it produces. Abruptly, perhaps even automatically, Hopkins thinks of the obverse of Tom's condition—the unemployed who are idle, not because they are resting after a full day's work, but because they have no opportunity to do their duty for God and country. The attitude of affirmative joy is eclipsed by a specter of sadness, distress, and negativism. Such an attitude causes Hopkins to revert to the diction of the "terrible sonnets." In lines 12 to 16, for instance, the words *no* and *nor* appear seven times. Hopkins deeply sympathizes with the unemployed who are alienated outcasts, "stranger[s] . . . / Among strangers" ("To seem the stranger lies my lot" [ll. 1–2]). Hopkins almost recognizes the distinctions that Gareth Stedman Jones's study insists upon—a clearer distinction between the working classes (Tom and Sturdy Dick) and the casual unemployed. What is so typically nineteenth-century about Hopkins, however, is that irrational intensity and disgust soon overwhelm any serious consideration of the plight of the unemployed sector of society. For Hopkins, the society that breeds lives with no function, that provides no opportunity to serve in God's scheme of things, is a tense and unstable society. The intense awareness of such an ugly social landscape can inspire neither joy, harmony, nor inscape. For this reason, the last two lines of the poem can only sound a harsh declamatory note and starkly expose the disease festering on the body politic of Victorian society: "This, by Despair, bred Hangdog dull; by Rage, / Manwolf, worse; and their packs infest the age." By the end of "Tom's Garland" the structure of feeling explodes outward into chaotic fragments.

When Hopkins's limited audience of two, Bridges and Dixon, could not understand the syntax and meaning of "Tom's Garland," further fears and uncertainties were nurtured in the poet's mind. On December 22, 1887, he admitted to Dixon that "perhaps 'Tom's Garland' approaches bluster and will remind you of Mr. Podsnap with his back to the fire" (*Letters*, 2: 153).[19] When Hopkins again tried to explain the meaning of "Tom's Garland" to Bridges on February 10, 1888, the frustration of not being able to find viable solutions for the segment of humanity that was increasingly excluded from God's benevolent social order caused him to reinforce the doubts and tensions of the closing lines of the poem with further vitriolic name-calling: "And this state of things, I say, is the origin of Loafers, Tramps, Cornerboys, Roughs, Socialists, and other pests of society" (*Letters*, 1: 274). In the same letter, Hopkins told Bridges of the ultimate implications of the sonnet's artistic and intellectual failure: "It is plain I must go no further on this road" (*Letters*, 1: 272). Hopkins was a severe critic of himself and he eschewed further social commentary because he realized that his social vision had reached a chaotic outer limit that could not be accommodated in his poetry. The shock of the explosion of the structure of feeling at the end of "Tom's Garland" was so profound that Hopkins attempted no further inscapes of Victorian society before his death, two years later.

In two of his short poems another Catholic poet of the age, Coventry Patmore, expressed a somewhat similar attitude toward the urban masses and democratic changes of the day. Until 1868 hangings of condemned Newgate prisoners were public affairs and attracted large crowds of spectators. Such an assembly is the subject of Patmore's "A London Fête" (1854). This poem's structure and movement are particularly striking. The first eighteen lines describe the beastly individual figures who assemble at such an event; in lines 19 to 39, individuals merge and Patmore exposes the brutality of the assembled mob; in lines 40 to 47, the focus is again on individual figures who now are shown to have become even more beastly for having participated in the horrendous community "celebration." The individuals assembling for the public hanging are a varied lot: "Mothers {who} held up their babes to see," "a girl {who} from her vesture tore / A rag to wave with, and join'd the roar," "a yelling man," and a "bawling sot."[20] The individuals gathering in the street are less than reputable and they are like the thunderous noise before a storm as they frantically "blasphemed and fought for places." As the dramatic moment of anticipation approaches, there is a disquieting intensity to the fixed but unified stare of the mob.

> The rabble's lips no longer curst,
> But stood agape with horrid thirst;
> Thousands of breasts beat horrid hope;
> Thousands of eyeballs, lit with hell,
> Burnt one way all, to see the rope
> Unslacken as the platform fell.   [ll. 21–26]

As the rope tightens around the condemned man's neck, an atavistic roar "confused and affrighting" is heard. To the Patmorian bystander, the London mob takes on the dimensions of the Satanic throng. Indeed, for the individuals in the crowd, witnessing a public display of the imposition of capital punishment has no cathartic or deterrent effect. The crowd disperses into individual figures who leave the scene one by one to commit crimes of their own.

> The show complete, the pleasure past,
> The solid masses loosen'd fast:
> A thief slunk off, with ample spoil,
> To ply elsewhere his daily toil;
> A baby strung its doll to a stick;
> A mother praised the pretty trick;
> Two children caught and hang'd a cat;
> Two friends walk'd on, in lively chat;
> And two, who had disputed places,
> Went forth to fight, with murderous faces.   [ll. 38–47]

In a later poem entitled simply "1867" (1877), Patmore makes a shrill political statement. In early editions a footnote to the title read, "In this year the middle and upper classes were disfranchised by the Tory Government"; in later editions the footnote read, "In this year the middle and upper classes were disfranchised by Mr. Disraeli's Government, and the final destruction of the liberties of England by the Act of 1884 rendered inevitable." The tone of the poem is an odd combination of an alternation between a strong, prophetic Old Testament voice and a weak lament that poetry cannot possibly matter anymore.

> In the year of the great crime,
> When the false English Nobles and their Jew,

By God demented, slew
The Trust they stood twice pledged to keep from wrong,
One said, Take up thy Song,
That breathes the mild and almost mythic time
Of England's prime!
But I, Ah, me,
The freedom of the few
That, in our free Land, were indeed the free,
Can song renew?
Ill singing 'tis with blotting prison-bars,
How high soe'er, betwixt us and the stars;
Ill singing 'tis when there are none to hear.   [ll. 1–14]

Patmore sees the expanded popular voice as a plague or a flood visited upon England by a wrathful God: "A term of God's indignant mood" (l. 61). Biblical and industrial metaphors are mixed together as Patmore refers to the lumpen masses rising and swelling: "the fever'd steam / That rises from the plain" (ll. 33–34), "the orgies of the multitude, / Which now begin" (ll. 62–63), and "the swelling tide / Of that presumptuous sea" (ll. 67–68). The poem ends in near hysteria as Patmore sees the work of civilization threatened everywhere.

And, now, because the dark comes on apace
When none can work for fear,
And Liberty in every Land lies slain,

  .   .   .   .

Restrain'd no more by faithful prayer or tear,
And the dread baptism of blood seems near.   [ll. 73–75, 80–81]

Although Hopkins and Patmore represent the extreme limits of the strain of fearful or reactionary response evident in nineteenth-century poetry, there are clear differences even in their similar outlooks. Both poets reacted with alarm against the anarchy, poverty, and "bestiality" of the residuum of the city. Hopkins's attitude, however, is one of failed or impeded sympathy for the masses while Patmore's is much closer to disdain and disgust. After working directly with human weakness and misery, Hopkins is baffled in his sympathy and he fears that Tom may join the ranks of the disgruntled unemployed. The reasons for Hopkins's fear and rejection are clear; something terrible will occur in the city because no one can redeem or work effectively with the good that is in a precarious state. Hopkins's fear is similar to that found in social reformers like Charles Booth—it is a gesture that begins in sympathy and turns to fear out of the sheer helplessness (even hopelessness) of such sympathy before the immensity of the task of reform. Patmore's attitude, however, is more reactionary. He feels disdain and disgust for the masses. When he describes the dispersing crowd in "A London Fête," he conveys a disturbing version of society in which the people *are* beasts (as opposed to having been made into beasts by oppression and injustice).

Noel and Morris: From Observation to Revolution

In both form and content, the poetic devices and outlooks of Roden Noel and William Morris were more variegated and open than those found in the poetry of Hopkins and Patmore. Hopkins and Patmore expressed their opinions on the sociopolitical developments of the day in relatively short poems (the ode or extended sonnet form); Noel and Morris needed more lines to work out their commentaries. Hopkins and Patmore seemed to be driven into a narrow corner of fear and panic in the isolated instances of their responses to the anarchy and poverty in the residuum of the city; Noel and Morris were more open to discovering different sources of hope for the city.

The similarities in background and the differences in final outlook between Noel and Morris are striking. Although Noel, the son of the first Earl of Gainsborough, was aristocratic and widely traveled, he developed a sympathetic concern for the plight of the urban poor in both London and Paris. The contrasts between wealth and poverty within these cities are central to the content and structure of his two long poems, "The Red Flag" (1872) and "A Lay of Civilisation, or London" (1885). Morris also came from a comfortable, albeit middle-class background. He spent his childhood in the fashionable London suburbs and was educated at Marlborough and Oxford. After a decade of indulgence in medieval and Norse escapism, Morris's hatred of capitalism and the effects of the industrial revolution led him to look forward in both his writings and his life to the revolution that would bring, after widespread destruction, hope and promise for all. *The Pilgrims of Hope* (1887) deals with the historical action of the Paris Commune of 1871 and records the price of individual sacrifice for the cause of the revolution. *Chants for Socialists* (1885–1893) looks forward to the promise of the future and incites revolutionary action in the present.

To some extent, the subject of Noel's "The Red Flag" and Morris's *The Pilgrims of Hope* are the same: the uprising of the masses in Paris in 1871 and the corresponding implications for London. The poets differ most in the techniques of their expressions. Here the major Lukácsian standards for judging art can be usefully applied because they render insight into the forms and purposes of the two poems. In his essay, "Narrate or Describe?" Georg Lukács maintains that the best art is that which strives to achieve a "comprehensive exposition of the social milieu," "a rich, comprehensive, many-sided and dynamic artistic reflection of objective reality," or "an adequate and comprehensive artistic reflection of reality." [21] Mere description of character and events inhibits this aim because it lacks a stance or perspective which tends to let subjective distortion get in the way. Lukács's axiomatic distinctions are polar and uncompromisable: "In Zola the race is *described* from the standpoint of an observer; in Tolstoy it is *narrated* from the standpoint of a participant. . . ." "Narration establishes proportions, description merely levels. . . ." "Description contemporizes everything. Narration recounts the past. . . ." "The descriptive method results in compositional monotony, while narration not only permits but even promotes infinite variety in composition." [22] In treating the same sequence of events, the Paris uprisings of 1870–1871, Noel and Morris demonstrate respectively the implications of employing contrasting literary techniques: that description tends to be flattening, static, and immediate while narration tends to be dynamic and historical.

The structure of Noel's "The Red Flag" (1872) is divided into two nearly equal parts: an on-the-scene report of contemporary conditions in Paris and London, and a series of satirical caricatures that expose the tenuous hypocrisy of upper- and middle-class Londoners toward the future course of society in both Paris and London. On the whole, reviewers found much more to praise in the first part of the poem than in the second part. In the eyes of J. A. Symonds, Noel almost seems to answer (twenty years later) Clough's call for a poet who records the city's reality. Symonds praises Noel for his "intense and realistic treatment," his "enthusiasm for actual life and contemporary history," his ability to capture the "freshness of the present, the pulses of common humanity" and thereby proving "that the poet need not return upon the past for material." [23] More specifically, Symonds writes:

> The situation is finely conceived and powerfully presented. The sincerity of the poet, his intense feeling for the terrible, the realism with which he has wrought every detail of his picture, and his passionate sympathy with the oppressed, make the general effect of this poem very impressive. As a satire, "The Red Flag" is by no means so powerful as it is when regarded as a highly realistic picture. Mr. Noel has neither the Juvenalian fluency of invective nor

the Popian trick of satiric epigram. The force of his attack consists in the vehement intensity of his grasp on actual facts and possible consequences. In reading his poem, we seem to breathe the stagnant atmosphere which precedes a tempest.[24]

That Noel has an "intense feeling for the terrible" is immediately evident in the poem as the human carnage of the Paris Commune is vividly described.

> There is peace in London!
> Not here, as yonder, men blaspheming loud,
> Begrimed with slaughter, cruelty aflame,
> Drag some dishevelled woman through the crowd
> To shoot her with a blundering blind aim:
> She with her hopeless hunted face of fear
> Grovelling falls, and to her dying ear
> Pierce her foul fellows with inhuman jeer.
> There, all along the fair arcaded street
> Where they are murdering, in sacks lie thrown
> Dead men and women; where the dainty feet
> Were wont to loiter; there the brilliants shown
> Lured eyes that vied in lustre with their own.
> But these are ghastly, whence the warm life-flood
> Oozing hath stained the flags with human blood![25]

Yet only a few of the lines of the poem dwell on the chaotic situation in Paris, and only briefly does Noel draw back from the immediate scene to show an awareness of the larger implications of the events in the history of the world.

> Priests, women, soldiers, children, all afire;
> Paris around them roars a funeral pyre,
> Screaming, blaspheming; are the corpses dumb?
> Verily here is Pandemonium!
>
> So fills itself another crimson page
> Of human story; so from age to age
> Men reap the fruit of hate and wrath and Death
> From the red seed they sowed, and with mad breath
> Cherished for harvest: still they strew the same,
> Mutual rancour, fear, and scorn, and shame;
> And still it breaks to fury and to flame.

> Liberty watereth with many a tear
> The growth maturing; still she hopes to rear
> Her own frail flower, but ever hides her eyes
> When she beholds the infernal blade arise—
> Ever a gory growth, a venomous thing,
> Now named Mob-rule, now Slavery to a King.   [ll. 79–95]

After describing the carnage in Paris, the scene shifts as the directing voice of the poem records, in the passive manner of a tourist, the disturbing contradictions throughout London. In the first half of the poem, the reader is given a series of descriptive tableaux which repeatedly emphasize the stark contrast of poverty and wealth appearing in close proximity on London's streets. The turn in the stationary observer's perceptions ("I lately stood before. . . .") usually comes at a colon or semicolon division.

> There is peace in London.
> And in this peace I lately stood before
> A mean brick housefront at a dingy door
> In a foul street: the place was very near
> Where wealthy folk inhabit half the year.
>
> .   .   .   .
>
> Nay, but this woman cowering in the gloom,
> Dark, speechless, ghastly, starving, haunts the room
> With horror—lowest sunken in the fate
> That slowly whelms her kindred desolate!
> She lurks a silent corpse, and yet alive:
> About her all her fainting family strive
> With bony fingers tightening their hold;
> While near them lords and ladies drain the gold
> That sparkles with exhilarating pleasure,
> Fair, in fine raiment, wantoning at leisure.
> To starve in London! on the stones where wealth
> Indifferent saunters, dull with food and health!
>
>   [ll. 96–100, 209–20]

Although Noel looks upon the hopeless human suffering in London from the standpoint of a stationary and stunned observer, it would be a mistake to conclude that he was unmoved by the misery. Like the many quasi-sociological investigations of this period, Noel chose to view London with his pen in hand so that he could quicken the social consciousness of his readers. The precision of his detailed descriptions surely carries some force.

> Are not this London's million ordured courts
> Verily curst ineffable resorts
> Of ghouls more horrible than Easterns feign?
> Do ye not note them yonder at the pane
> Mopping and mowing, spectres foul yet dim
> In subtle blue miasma mists that swim,
> There at the dingy pane, with dull dead eyes,
> Faces wormfretted, lank, with livid dyes,
> And loathly trunk slow revelling in slime
> Under the window—brood of folly and crime!
> Ye fearful Hydras, Cholera and Fever,
> Batten on starving huddled slaves for ever!   [ll. 281–92]

Perhaps sensing that—to borrow Luckács's words—"the descriptive method results in compositional monotony," Noel has his narrator abandon the stationary observer's role and take on that of the ambulatory auditor who eavesdrops in the second part of the poem.

> Yet very nigh there often pace the street
> Casual farers with indifferent feet:
> And when the craftsman goes to breathe awhile
> Upon the stair, he sees the cheery smile,
> Hears happy snatches of a careless talk
> From comfortable strangers in their walk. . . .
>
> . . . Now 'tis a Dean, who as he ambles by
> Raises a question of church-millinery;
> Or in allusion to the squalid street
> Observes that, howsoever God may mete
> The lot of each, all should be docile, which
> One may name 'Gospel according to the rich.'   [ll. 326–37]

Various caricature figures come forth to express their hypocritical, but representative social philosophies. The speakers are separated by a pause in which an ominous refrain builds to a disturbing echo.

> The lonely toiler, gasping for some air,
> Listens in shadowy poison of the stair,
> Listens, a wounded beast within his lair. . . .
> . . . And there is *Peace* in London!   [ll. 371–74]

The silly, aloof comments are overheard as "the beautiful tripping dame with bell-like skirts" from Ford Madox Brown's sonnet "Work" makes a brief angelic appearance.

> Now trips a dame who lifts her skirt for fear
> Of many a foul contamination here,
> Revealing delicate ankles to the friend,
> Who (to assist) his manly arm may lend.
> 'Think what a desperate misery may slink
> In these low neighbourhoods from whence we shrink?'
> In silver tones she whispers: 'Look! there prowl
> Two terrible ragged ruffians with a scowl.'   [ll. 375–82]

A dandy standing nearby quickly joins the woman in conversation so that the aristocratic view of the urban masses in both Paris and London is presented in a lively satirical exchange.

> 'Near our town-houses! who could fancy it?'
> Drawls out the dandy with more birth than wit.
> She, with a slight quick shiver, half a sigh:
> 'One's heart aches even to *dream* such poverty!'
> (It jarred her nervous sensibility.)
> 'And yet, as Mister Glozeman said in church,
> To make the vessel of the State to lurch,
> To shake our ancient Order is the worst
> Crime: it deserves the torture, 'tis accurst
> Of God and man—he meant the Communist
> Canaille in Paris. . . .'
> Then, as if breeding were a little at fault
> In that last ardour of her friend's assault
> Even on hereditary foes, the mob,
> On swarms unclean, who sweat and starve and rob,
> She waved aside the subject she had lent
> Her glance in passing, drawling as she went,
> 'They say the poor are so improvident!'
> Half absently she spoke, to weightier themes
> Turning anon—to cunning, lordly schemes. . . .
>   [ll. 383–93, 398–406]

It is the capturing of this world-weary, nonchalant attitude of the calm before the storm, coupled with the constant repetition of the deceptively calming refrain "And there is *Peace* in London!" which lends subtlety to Noel's political and poetical statement. Oddly enough, the auditor does not recreate the two gentlemen's conversations he overhears next, but instead rails at what he believes them to stand for—a religion of opiate quackery to be used as a social control device on the masses and a socioeconomic system based on the latest theories of social Darwinism. Here Noel moves from mere observation to concerned condemnation as he berates religion that is "relegated to the lower orders, / A panacea for popular disorders, / A pap for babes and women" (ll. 511–13). The new code of the day is the "plethoric gospel of the well-to-do" which demands that

> Ye war with all your fellows for existence,
> And when you've thrown them, still with fierce insistence,
> Grind them beneath you, crush them all to death,
> That you may breathe a more luxurious breath.   [ll. 551–54]

After the supposedly neutral auditor has thoroughly damned what the two gentlemen stand for, he then records their own words, which turn out to be even more reprehensible and extreme. Noel insists that his auditor is an unbiased, objective recorder of the social scene whose seemingly unbelievable report can be verified readily with his sources.

> How these two friends congenial conversed
> Here, as the listener heard it, is rehearsed,
> As from his slightly varied point of view
> It might have sounded to the speakers too.   [ll. 562–65]

And so, the two gentlemen recite all the current conservative social theories as they attempt to work out verbally a Podsnappian solution to poverty.

> 'If many starve to swell our opulence,
> That's an arrangement due to providence.
> Who prates of wealth's more equal distribution,
> Or generous masters, means the revolution.'
>
> .   .   .   .
>
> 'How frail is human nature! how will pity
> Confuse a fool's heart in a crowded city!'
>
> .   .   .   .
>
> 'The State! what call has that to interfere?
> Are we not free-born Britons living here?
> If these like not their scrofulous dens, you know,
> They're free to change their quarters; let them go.
> Why one of these may struggle uppermost!'
>
> .   .   .   .
>
> 'Ah! pestilent 'education'—*that's* the cause,
> Which *makes* them carp at our existing laws
> The dogs are always yelping for a bone:

Fling them to bite a weighty moral stone!'

.   .   .   .

'A man must grab whatever he can get;
We human creatures are not angels yet.'
[ll. 568–71, 585–86, 632–36, 665–68, 669–70]

The commentaries seem to become more irrational as the conversation becomes more lively. Yet the excerpts mirror social theories held at the time and reflect the fear of many upper- and middle-class Victorians that social schemes of control over the urban masses were crumbling. As a poet who is himself a gentleman, Noel tries to warn his gentlemen readers that such extreme positions will not be able to stand up to the rapid changes taking place in late nineteenth-century urban society. A more flexible and hopeful attitude toward social change is needed or else catastrophe will ensue.

Rumbling clouds of a cataclysmic storm gather throughout the poem and finally come together in the last few pages as the speaker has a nightmare vision of the destruction of London. This destructive vision emphasizes again that stubborn resistance to social change will only bring disaster. In the vision, the havoc of Paris descends on London.

> Fire ruddies all the city! toward Thames
> Rolls like the Seine, a tide of eddying flames;
> Vessel, and wharf, and every striding arch
> Glows in the fire-fiend's victorious march.
> Hark! to the huge bell, whose portentous boom
> Ponderous falling fills the soul with doom.
> Lo! surging human seas arise and fall
> Around the lurid grandeur of St. Paul.
> Torches illume their wild convulsive toils,
> Windily flaring; all around there boils
> Vile human refuse, for the dainty spoils
> They have wrung from others wrangling fierce and hoarse. . . .
> . . . Then must avenging butchery begin:
> Their sin we strangle with our stronger sin.
> England must join the anarchic devil's dance,
> That wilders and exhausts delirious France!

[ll. 711–22, 728–31]

The refrain has become a shrill battle cry now: "There is *War* in London!" For only the second time in the poem, Noel momentarily steps in to consider the larger historical implications of the imagined civil war. He wants to make sure that history assigns the blame to the hypocritical social theories of the rich.

Who declared war? for ye shall bear the blame!
History seeks your insignificant name
To pillory with everlasting shame!
Who declared war? The man who dared to teach
That men are natural enemies each to each;
Set in uncompromising battle array
Labour and wealth: the fruit you eat to-day
Glares very crimson, scribbling Galifet! . . .
Bring forth your mitrailleuse! but, hypocrite,
Yea, you may shoot them; you may drown the people
In their own life-blood. . . .   [ll. 732–39, 754–57]

Noel's honest realism is far more effective than his harshly contrived satire in the poem. "The Red Flag" ends on an apocalyptic note with a nightmare vision of the destruction of London. Thus, Noel urges his point on his readers: indifference or resistance to social change will only bring cataclysmic disaster to England. If urban suffering is not alleviated soon, only a divine miracle can possibly save London.

G. Robert Stange briefly mentions Roden Noel in his pioneer article "The Frightened Poets" because he feels that Noel is "an interesting representative of the explicit fusion of the endemic fear of revolution and unrestraint (the French disease) and the anti-metropolitan bias of the rural gentry, the class from which he and so many other English poets came. Noel's view of the city was both first-hand and, in its sympathies, radical; but it did not cease to be also Tory and pastoral."[26] Along the lines of Stange's two categories, "The Red Flag" (1872) was Noel's political statement. It focused immediately on the revolutionary tensions and glaring contrasts between rich and poor in the city of London (always with the inflammatory skies of Paris in the background). On the other hand, "A Lay of Civilisation, or London" (1885) is a more widely philosophical statement which expands the terms of the contrast to compare the crime and evil of the city with the innocence and good of the countryside. Although "The Red Flag" employed many satirical devices and descriptions, satire is rarely used in "A Lay of Civilisation." In a sense, satire is a very immediate propagandistic device. In the crisis of a tumultuous political situation, it assumes that there is still a small amount of time left for men to correct abuses. In "The Red Flag," Noel's satire against the wealthy social theories of the day was intense and indignant. By the time Noel wrote "A Lay of Civilisation," thirteen years had passed and he now expresses his view that the evil of the cities must inevitably be accepted. Yet he refuses to despair completely. The poem first appeared in the volume *Songs of the Heights and Deeps* (1885). The title of the volume indicates the poet's intention to balance, perhaps even reconcile, good and bad aspects of contemporary life. Noel sees his function as a poet to be an honest but elevating task; he will be aware of the worst, but will also put up against wrongs the finer values of life in order to help raise the unredeemed elements of human nature and the environment to a higher level. In "The Red Flag" Noel employed a brash and vehement satire to condemn the rich and clerical authorities; however, in "A Lay of Civilization" he both presents the plight of the city and offers the hope of moderation and redeeming faith through nature and human goodness. Thus, the repeated refrain of the latter poem is the image of "Happy birds fluting in the leafy woods, / And children playing by the rivulet" (ll. 117–18). Like Hopkins, Noel was shocked by the degradation, doubt, and despair that he saw in urban slums. Somehow Noel managed to keep a basic faith that what he saw would one day be redeemed, but his religion and poetry were both shaken and shaped by the harsh social conditions. Witness this extract from one of his letters.

> I am not the poet of free-will as Browning was. So far, I may be less a moral poet. . . . My Calvinism is much what it was, but it is now turned into Pantheism, with the additional idea of ultimate restoration for all, and establishment of each in the function proper to him as integral factor and unit (or cell) of the universal organism, through the experience, good or evil, he has gone through. . . . I am not prepared to say that many may not find this an immoral doctrine. I cannot help it. Only so can I keep faith at all, in view of the frightful moral and physical evils I see around me.[27]

Noel's ability to keep "a strong faith" in *Songs of the Heights and Deeps* won the praise of an *Academy* reviewer. The reviewer's comments show insight into "A Lay of Civilisation" and reflect the widespread distaste for the despairing response to the city found in the poetry of James Thomson.

> The mist of hopelessness which clings to so many latter-day prophets, and deprives their utterances of all solace and encouragement, does not cloud the poems of Mr. Noel. The faith which dissipates it is indeed vague as a wind, but it is steady and invigorating. Although he by no means dwells upon the sunny side of things, but takes a wide sweep of them, comprehending all the joy and grandeur of the natural universe, all the sin and squalor of civilisation, he never despairs. . . . In the first poem, "A Lay of Civilisation or London," pictures of misery and wrong, of social and spiritual disease, succeed each other like terrible phantoms. . . . Yet, notwith-

standing the contrast of all this crime and ugliness with the beauty of nature and the purity of innocent children, the poet is able to conclude his dreadful survey with lines of noble comfort. . . . So the evil in this world does not appear to Mr. Noel triumphant, as it appeared to the late James Thomson; nor is he satisfied with both good and evil, as Walt Whitman is; but, not so much a Pantheist as a Pan-Christian, his survey of existence breeds in him a strong faith in the ultimate conquest of the good, or the blending of good and evil into something more divine than can be grasped by the finite intellect.[28]

In "A Lay of Civilisation, or London," then, Noel continues to juxtapose the glaring contrasts of wealth and poverty, but he relents in his indignant satiric attacks on the rich. Instead, he presents a grim and exclusive picture of metropolitan degradation and poverty; the poor are unrelentingly brutalized and bestialized more by the impersonal fact of "the city" than by "the wealthy." His descriptions of London read like entries in a guidebook to the circles of Dante's *Inferno*.

But over all a brown Plutonian gloom
Of murk air dismal and defiled, the breath
Of our so monstrous town—her visible sin,
And weight of wan woe, blotting out sweet heaven!   [ll. 84–87]

This huge black whirlpool of the city sucks,
And swallows, and encroaches evermore
On vernal field, pure air, and wholesome heaven—
A vast dim province, ever under cloud,
O'er whose immeasurable unloveliness
His own foul breath broods sinister, like Fate.   [ll. 313–18]

But most are weary in this Babylon,
Whether men idle, or contend for bubbles;
The happiest are they who minister.
Beyond these regions, reaches of dim street,
A sullen labyrinth of ill-omened hovels:
Ah! dull, grey, grovelling populations, yet
That are rank human soil, wherein we force
Our poor pale virtues, and our venomous sins
Of gorgeous growth, our proxy-piety,
Official food, that yields no sustenance,
But chokes with outworn fantasy free life,
What hope, O people? . . .   [ll. 625–36]

These descriptions present a nightmare vision of a Babylon gone wrong. Yet only once in the poem does Noel touch upon political philosophy. In answer to the question "What hope, O people?" Noel states emphatically his belief that "red convulsive strife" would simply bring about "moaning silence under other lords" (ll. 636, 638). The poet's basic Tory conservatism appears only once.

> And yet methinks more health is in the old,
> Renewing youth from fountains of the new,
> Than in rash overthrow of all men built,
> With salt of insolence sown in holy places.   [ll. 673–76]

Noel's basic outlook in the poem—that the city is unnatural, a crime against nature—is evident in the sweeping condemnatory descriptions previously quoted and in the minute contemporary detail wherein Noel denounces the first public electric lighting, which had appeared in London just three years before the poem was completed.

> But on the vasty parapet above
> Those Titan tunnels, ghastlier for the glare
> Of our electric mockery of moons.   [ll. 707–9]

Whereas the poets of the 1890s celebrated the artificial, glowing lights of the cities, Noel in 1885 chose to indict the new street lighting because it only added to the grotesqueness of the city's atmosphere. Against all the unnaturalness of the metropolis, Noel arrayed lengthy descriptions of pastoral landscapes in his song of the city. Nevertheless, the speaker moves inevitably from these long dreamlike trances set in the Arcadian Isles to an awareness of the horrifying town. Although many lines are spent reminding the reader of the attractiveness of the state of nature, Noel is realistic enough to admit that the happy countryside days are fading.

> Down a green dale I heard some children roam,
> Merrily laughing by a rivulet;
> Then a hawk hovered, and sweet songs were hushed
> In the grove under.   All the scene grew dim,
> Appeared to melt before mine eyes, and change.
> I heard, and heard not, for the land dissolved,
> And clouding slowly, lo! another sound,
> Akin to the sea-sound, was in mine ears,
> Resembling some huge roar of a far furnace,
> Whose sullen flare through wallowing mists impure

Burned like the fire-flush from those realms of Dis
In that deep-mouthed verse of the Mantuan.
Huge murmur from the throat of Babylon!
Illimitable leagues of piles confused. . . .   [ll. 57–70]

Such shifts occur several times in the poem, and always Noel employs
transitional devices such as "The happy vision faded. . . . I hear / Again
the troubled surge of London town" or "I am on the country-side again;
but ah! / Nor here may I escape" (ll. 548, 551–52, 757–58).[29]

Yet childlike innocence and redemptive virtue are found not only in the
idyllic countryside settings of Noel's poem; there are some examples evi-
dent in the heart of the city itself. Noel attempts to underline the realism of
two incidents by granting footnote recognition to his newspaper sources—
"I am indebted for this incident to a writer in the *Daily Telegraph*" (p.
501). Both of the incidents relate the compassion shown by or to children
brutalized by the city. The first case relates how a "seven-year-old cripple;
in a cot, / That seemed an orange-case disused" (ll. 362–63) is ministered
to by his grandmother, who uses various scraps about the tenement to
construct a model of a rural landscape for his pleasure.

And she hath helped him order on the floor
A mimic park with turfs from a lark's cage,
Wherein are planted perpendicular
Thin sticks of deal, their foliage woolly shreds
From old frayed borders of the grandame's gown;
A baking-dish contains the mimic lake,
And, swimming there, a dinted bird, once white.   [ll. 381–87]

The second case concerns a boy "suffering in hospital, / His members
crushed and mangled by a wain, / Whose wheels passed o'er him playing
in the street" (ll. 408–10). The sight of the mangled child on his death-
bed moves the boy's father to agree to abide by the boy's last wish: "Prom-
ise thou never wilt ill-use, or strike, / Or be unkind to mother when I'm
gone!" (ll. 423–24). Other tales involving widows and orphans are also
recounted. Here again the concept of the poet as interpretative observer is
important since Noel sees various scenes and tells the reader from a posi-
tion *outside* of the events described how to interpret their significance.
Furthermore, Noel sees his function as poet to be an elevating mission;
against the brutality of the city he sets instances of human compassion and
love. He also sets against the urban industrial landscape the remembered
ideal of a more harmonious and idyllic life in the countryside. It is for
these reasons that in the final fourteen lines of "A Lay of Civilisation" Noel

reaffirms his basic faith that his mission as a poet is to supplicate understanding, comfort, uplift, inspire, and redeem the metropolitan masses.

> Therefore, dear birds, in leafy woods ye warble,
> And you, my children, by the rivulet
> Play, laughing merrily, because the world
> Is sound at heart, howe'er it seems to ail.
> God-fronted, dragon-trained, 'tis but a marred
> Image in souls, who travail yet ungrown,
> Who, ruffled, slowly waver into rest.
> And why we arise or fall, no mortal knows,
> Save that by change alone the unchanged abides;
> Love breathes amid the ruin of red wrong.
> For a moment only of our infinite life
> With one wild wing-pulse cleaving earth's rent air,
> Oh! lift we one another from this hell
> Of blindly-battling ignorance to God! [ll. 839–52]

Walter Bagehot once remarked that Dickens's especial genius in the delineation of city life was due partly to his realizing that "London is like a newspaper. Everything is there, and everything is disconnected. There is every kind of person in some houses; but there is no more connection between the houses than between the neighbours in the lists of 'births, marriages, and deaths.'"[30] Roden Noel was probably the last poet of the city to believe that connections could be made on a grand scale, across class lines. He hoped that his poetry could help to redeem the city and he tried to expand the awareness of London's inhabitants. What Noel sees in the city is important but even more significant is his perspective on the urban situation; in both of the long poems examined, he stands outside the action and summons help from beyond the social resources of the city. The form of Noel's poems reveals the character of his response to the city. Fundamentally, he is not a full participant in the everyday realities of the city and has the detached consciousness of an observer who knows all about God and the rural past. But God and the rural past are a wholly different set of values and possibilities, and when that structure of feeling comes in direct contact with the realities of the nineteenth-century city, Noel— like Hopkins and Patmore—is shocked by the difference. But unlike Hopkins and Patmore, Noel is unwilling to give up in the face of what appear to be overwhelming odds because he holds on to a basic faith that if he can only describe what he sees from the outside, he can also prescribe a cure that will borrow elements from the traditional values that he has held in the past. In the final analysis, however, the poetic format in which Noel is an observer who has a solution and yet is not an actor in the poems tends to weaken the plausibility of the solution.

William Morris, in the course of his political and poetical career, came to the conclusion that what was there in the city was beyond connection and redemption and that it must therefore be destroyed, cataclysmically swept aside. Only by starting anew could the cause of establishing an order of radically new and entirely different societal connections be ushered in triumphantly. From the time of his joining the Social Democratic Federation (1883) until his death in 1896, Morris was completely convinced that a posture of militant socialism was the only viable response to the squalor in the cities that industrial capitalism continued to foster; the London he saw and heard had to be destroyed completely and a revolutionary new social order had to take its place. No urban sensual thrill, no cultural treasure, nothing could justify the sparing of London as it existed. Given this political philosophy, the idea of creating art for the museum of immortal artifacts is totally foreign to Morris's thinking. Only art that stirred indignation at the workers' oppressions, only art that gleamed with the light of the promise of the new social order was worth making. And it indeed had to be made quickly; no Paterian degrees of exquisite refining could be tolerated, given the exigencies of the time. In an 1883 letter to Mrs. Burne-Jones, Morris expressed just such sentiments, maintaining that poetry "has now become unreal: the arts have got to die, what is left of them, before they can be born again."[31] Poetry, if it was to justify itself at all, must be immediately affecting, readily comprehensible (even by those who were illiterate); there was no need for it to be either highly polished or overly complicated in plot or character development. If poetry was to be truly "common property," metaphoric and philosophical complexity as well as attempts to discover original images to convey the experience of the city had to be avoided.

Thus, the short poems that became Morris's *Chants for Socialists* were read or sung at socialist meetings and were disseminated through various socialist journals and pamphlets. His lyrics welcoming the new day of social equality and liberty for all rely on such conventional romantic imagery as blossoming springtime, rising sun, thundering storm, radiating light, embracing ocean, and prophesying wind. Rarely are specific urban industrial conditions elaborated; the few times the city is mentioned, such conventional adjectives as *wicked* or *hateful* are attached. In these songs there is an urgent call for the popular and complete actualization of the revolutionary vision of the new social order.

"The Day Is Coming" (1884), a series of couplets in the popular street-ballad tradition, comments on both the present and future state of the workingman. Even though the poem does not use workingman's diction, a worker attending a meeting or reading a journal at night after a long day at work might very likely assent to both the depiction of his present lot and the visionary hope for a better future.

> For then, laugh not, but listen to this strange tale of mine,
> All folk that are in England shall be better lodged than swine.
>
> Then a man shall work and bethink him, and rejoice in the deeds
>   of his hand,
> Nor yet come home in the even too faint and weary to stand.
>
> Men in that time a-coming shall work and have no fear
> For to-morrow's lack of earning and the hunger-wolf anear.[32]

Morris then proceeds to catalogue *what* will be shared by all men in the future, and he definitely wishes to include "the lovely city, and the little house on the hill, / And the wastes and the woodland beauty, and the happy fields we till" (ll. 23–24). At the same time, Morris reminds his listeners and readers that the economic and social structure of the contemporary city is the workingman's deadly enemy because it daily saps his strength and will to fight back.

> O why and for what are we waiting? while our brothers droop and
>   die,
> And on every wind of the heavens a wasted life goes by.
>
> How long shall they reproach us where crowd on crowd they dwell,
> Poor ghosts of the wicked city, the gold-crushed hungry hell?
> .   .   .   .
> It is we must answer and hasten, and open wide the door
> For the rich man's hurrying terror, and the slow-foot hope of the
>   poor.
>
> Yea, the voiceless wrath of the wretched, and their unlearned
>   discontent,
> We must give it voice and wisdom till the waiting-tide be spent.
>   [vol. 9. ll. 35–38, 43–46]

The contrast between Morris's attitudes and those of Hopkins and Patmore is evident here. Hopkins feared that the urban masses would become more violently vocal even as they became hungrier and more discontented. Patmore bitterly lamented that the Second and Third Reform Bills had transferred the political voice from the aristocracy to the illiterate masses. Morris here expresses the sentiment that the urban masses are really helpless as well as voiceless and that when they assume their rightful place and power, peace and not anarchy will result. He sees the mission of his poetry in educative terms; he will spread the gospel of the Socialist movement among the poor, who are ignorant and apathetic not because they are beastly but because they are being abused daily and kept down by the captains of industry.

The fundamental structure of "The Voice of Toil" (1884) is also based on contrasting the misery and apathy of the oppressed workers against the militant power they could wield if they acted collectively. As wage slaves, the working classes are but undirected and unsuspecting sheep to be fleeced.

> Where fast and faster our iron master,
> The thing we made, for ever drives,
> Bids us grind treasure and fashion pleasure
> For other hopes and other lives.   [vol. 9. ll. 13–16]

As dedicated workers for the Cause (the new social order), the workers are above all else, men, and beyond that the producers of help, hope, and joy.

> Come, shoulder to shoulder ere the world grows older!
> Help lies in nought but thee and me;
> Hope is before us, the long years that bore us
> Bore leaders more than men may be.
>
> Let dead hearts tarry and trade and marry,
> And trembling nurse their dreams of mirth,
> While we the living our lives are giving
> To bring the bright new world to birth.   [vol. 9. ll. 29–36]

"All for the Cause" (1884) reiterates the necessity for violent destruction and personal oblivion—"When the Cause shall call upon us, some to live, and some to die!" (vol. 9. l. 2). Ultimately, however, the new social order must transcend all personal values: "There amidst the world new-builded shall our earthly deeds abide, / Though our names be all forgotten, and the tale of how we died" (vol. 9. ll. 29–30).

That Morris's socialist songs did affect contemporaries is attested to by F. W. Jowett, who recalled singing "The March of the Workers" (1885).

> Sometimes in summer-time the joint forces of Leeds and Bradford
> Socialism tramped together to spread the gospel by printed and
> spoken word in neighbouring villages. And at eventide, on the way
> home, as we walked in country lanes or on river bank, we sang—
>
> 'What is this, the sound and rumour? What is this that all men
>   hear,

> Like the wind in hollow valleys when the storm is drawing near,
> Like the rolling on of ocean in the eventide of fear? 'Tis the people
>   marching on . . .'

And we believed they were![33]

But even though Morris's songs helped foster the Socialist movement,
they rarely, and then inadequately, record specific events in late-nine-
teenth-century London. "A Death Song" (1887), for instance, was written
as a direct tribute to Alfred Linnell, who was killed by London police in
the melée in Trafalgar Square on "Bloody Sunday," 1887. Morris uses the
occasion to make a clear-cut call for proletarian solidarity, but he never
captures the specifics of the scene in the poem as fully as he did in his
letters and speeches. The dead man becomes a hero, an embarrassing re-
minder to the dullard rich, while the specifics of the historical event fade
away. Morris's memorial song, however, conveys his firm belief that the
gulf between the rich and the poor—the "us-them" dichotomy—was as
wide as the mouth of a volcanic crater and as potentially eruptive.

> We asked them for a life of toilsome earning,
> They bade us bide their leisure for our bread;
> We craved to speak to tell our woeful learning:
> We come back speechless, bearing back our dead.
> *Not one, not one, nor thousands must they slay,*
> *But one and all if they would dusk the day.*   [vol. 9. ll. 7–12]

In a larger sense, it is unwise to expect detailed, on-the-scene descrip-
tions of historical events like "Bloody Sunday" in Morris's short socialist
songs because that was not their intended purpose. (Morris is simply try-
ing to construct a popular or collective poetry.) Nor will the reader who is
seeking extensive literal transcriptions of such crucial historical events as
the Paris Commune, "Bloody Sunday," the dock strike, and other tur-
bulent demonstrations of the period find them in Morris's long poem, *The
Pilgrims of Hope*, or even in his prose romance *News from Nowhere*. In
Lukácsian terms, Morris simply is not in the business of "description,"
but is interested in purposeful historical "narration." As outlined earlier,
Lukács maintained that narration provides "the necessary distance," "per-
mits the selection of the essential after the action," "establishes propor-
tions," and allows events to be "*narrated* from the standpoint of a partici-
pant." All of these principles help to explain Morris's intent and execution
in *The Pilgrims of Hope* (1885–1886). In Morris's utopian romance, *News
from Nowhere* (1890), "Bloody Sunday" becomes transformed in the narra-
tor/participant's memory into the single event that touched off "the whole

revolution. . . . That massacre of Trafalgar Square began the civil war, though, like all such events, it gathered head slowly, and people scarcely knew what a crisis they were acting in" (vol. 16. p. 117). *News from Nowhere* is futuristic fantasy, a brand of fiction. Although *The Pilgrims of Hope* was written in 1885–1886 about historical events that took place fifteen or more years earlier, in this later work Morris's essential intent and practice are very similar. He compresses events and tells them from the point of view of participants in their private as well as public histories in order to show what the historical forces of his time are leading toward.

The three most striking features of *The Pilgrims of Hope* are the backdating of events, the inadequacy of poetry to describe events, and the proletarian perception of events. The poem was written in thirteen installments between April 1885 and July 1886. If it has one central theme, it is the start of the Socialist movement. Over three-quarters of the poem is set in the London of the 1860s, and the remaining quarter describes the events of the Paris Commune of 1870–1871. The Socialist movement as Morris knew it, however, did not begin in Britain in the 1860s but in the 1880s. There was no Socialist movement in middle-class circles (apart from the Christian socialism of 1848–1854) until the 1880s, even though Marx had followers among the working class from at least 1848 on. This casting of events back in time allows Morris to distance problems and doubts he was experiencing in working with the movement in the present; furthermore, it provides a climactic and cathartic event for the dissension, apathy, and near despair that he knew in the Socialist movement of the 1880s and depicts in his poem about the 1860s.

From Morris's own comments about and within *The Pilgrims of Hope*, it is evident that in the later portion of his career he had reservations about the adequacy of poetry to treat and affect events. From the outset, the plot structure of the poem seemed to him vague and confusing. In March 1885 Morris wrote to his daughter May: "I am pounding away at a continuation of my March poem ["The Message of the March Wind," published earlier as a short socialist song]: I want to make a sort of lyrical romance of it: next time I shall try my hand at a versified Socialist meeting. But what shall I do with my couple in the long run?"[34] In 1886, after the final installment had been published, he was contemplating "getting my *Pilgrims of Hope* in order, so as to make a book of it: I shall add and alter a good deal though."[35] Later Morris grudgingly granted his friend Buxton Forman permission to reprint the poem for private circulation, but he warned that the work needed further revision and added that he did not have the time to do that. Most important is May Morris's description of the strained circumstances under which the poem was composed—clearly indicating that

The Urban Volcano, 1870–1890

Morris was responding to his immediate experiences in the 1880s: "Piece by piece it was written, after he had returned home—he wrote late usually—from poor quarters full of sights and stories which had wrung his heart by their sordidness and dull endurance: it was written in sorrow and anger, in revolt at the things he saw and the things he divined, and the slight, effective sketches of the narrative bring home to many of us who have lived on into the time of tragedy and violence of the Twentieth Century, the meetings and street-corner gatherings of those days of scarcely articulate unrest and discomfort" (vol. 24. p. xxxii). In this same volume the narrator of the poem at several points expresses his opinion that poetry, words even, are inadequate to capture the essence of historical events.

> But all was nothing to this, the London holiday throng.
> Dull and with hang-dog gait they stood or shuffled along,
> While the stench from the lairs they had lain in last night went up
>   in the wind,
> And poisoned the sun-lit spring: no story men can find
> Is fit for the tale of their lives; no word that man hath made
> Can tell the hue of their faces, or their rags by filth o'er-laid.
>
> > [sec. 3. ll. 27–32]

> O fool, what words are these? Thou hast a sorrow to nurse,
> And thou hast been bold and happy; but these, if they utter a
>   curse,
> No sting it has and no meaning—it is empty sound on the air.
> Thy life is full of mourning, and theirs so empty and bare
> That they have no words of complaining; nor so happy have they
>   been
> That they may measure sorrow or tell what grief may mean.
> And thou, thou hast deeds to do, and toil to meet thee soon;
> Depart and ponder on these through the sun-worn afternoon.
>
> > [sec. 8. ll. 77–84]

> And then what I needs must tell of as a great blank; but indeed
> No words to tell of its horror hath language for my need:
> As a map is to a picture, so is all that my words can say.
>
> > [sec. 13. ll. 49–51]

Clearly in such passages as these, the early Morris—the "idle singer of an empty day" enchanting his readers to "forget six counties over-hung with smoke"—is beginning to be superseded by a later Morris who looks to new concerns. As a poet, he is still wondering if he can do any good. The difference now is the new subject matter about which he chooses to write.

Yet a difference in subject matter was immediately accompanied by the difficulty of finding a form for that material and, unfortunately, the urgent press of events would not allow him the time to develop a poetic form to match the pace of the proletarian revolution. Then too, Morris was not really interested in being a formally or technically innovative poet.

At the beginning of the nineteenth century Blake called for a complete spiritual, mental, and emotional revolution in London. At the end of the nineteenth century Morris called for a thoroughgoing social, political, and economic revolution in that same metropolis. The new perception of the city that Morris records in *The Pilgrims of Hope* is the proletarian outlook. Morris was not the first to point out that the amount of money one had in his pocket could influence his perception of the city—the Spirit had made that point thirty years earlier in the café scene of Clough's *Dipsychus*. But Morris's poem was undoubtedly the first to present extensively what it felt like to descend the economic scale of the city. The hero of *The Pilgrims of Hope* starts out in his urban employment as a skilled craftsman (a joiner) with the extra income of a legacy from his father. As the poem unfolds, he loses the legacy, his job, and finally his freedom when he is imprisoned for agitating on street corners. The full feel of what this worsening economic situation means to the physical and spiritual existence of the hero and his family is graphically depicted. In *Culture and Society* Raymond Williams argues that Morris's uniqueness consists in this presentation of and identification with the growing working class: "This was a just recognition that the real issues were always immediate and contemporary, and that the establishment of a new kind of society had to begin in conditions of the old anarchy which it sought to replace. . . . The significance of Morris in this tradition is that he sought to attach its general values to an actual and growing social force: that of the organized working class. This was the most remarkable attempt that had so far been made to break the general deadlock."[36]

Although Morris saw oppression and squalor as the present lot of London's working class, he did not respond to these conditions with Hopkins's fear or Patmore's anger or with Thomson's pessimism and despair, but with fervent hope and confidence that his work might "extend a real socialist consciousness among working men" so that they would soon realize that they would be the chief architects and elements of the new order of society.[37] In seeing sources for hope in the city, Morris is closest to Roden Noel. But whereas Noel's hope for change in the city was based on the half-certainties of unknown factors, Morris's hopes for social change were wholehearted because they were based on a confidence in active historical forces. Thus, to understand the events that befall the hero Richard in *The Pilgrims of Hope* is to recognize the wave of hope for the society of the future.

From the outset Richard is depicted as a special and independent person. As his mother relates in section 4, "Mother and Son," Richard was the product of her illicit relationship with a rich man. The union was a beautiful, redeemed moment, however, because it occurred in the idyllic countryside.

> When the river of love o'erflowed and drowned all doubt and fear,
> And we two were alone in the world, and once, if never again,
> We knew of the secret of earth and the tale of its labour and pain
>
> [vol. 24, sec. 4. ll. 8–10]

This information concerning the locale of the hero's conception is important because the mother wants her son to know that he is not one of "the dregs of the city sty." The mother then describes marriage in London as a kind of prostitution or state of degradation.

> Many a child of woman to-night is born in the town,
> The desert of folly and wrong; and of what and whence are they
>   grown?
> Many and many an one of wont and use is born;
> For a husband is taken to bed as a hat or a ribbon is worn.
> Prudence begets her thousands: 'Good is a housekeeper's life,
> So shall I sell my body that I may be matron and wife.'
> 'And I shall endure foul wedlock and bear the children of need.'
> Some are there born of hate—many the children of greed.
>
> [vol. 24, sec. 4. ll. 81–88]

Although the hero is allowed to pass his formative years in the serenity of the countryside, the attraction of the metropolitan center becomes irresistible as the young man reaches maturity. The old country inn is sedately quaint, but he realizes that the hope of the future lies with the urban masses in the great city.

> So the hope of the people now buddeth and groweth—
> Rest fadeth before it, and blindness and fear;
>
> .   .   .   .
>
> For it beareth the message: 'Rise up on the morrow
> And go on your ways toward the doubt and the strife;
>
> .   .   .   .

But lo, the old inn, and the lights and the fire,
And the fiddler's old tune and the shuffling of feet;
Soon for us shall be quiet and rest and desire,
And to-morrow's uprising to deeds shall be sweet.

[vol. 24, sec. 1. ll. 61–62, 65–66, 69–72]

Richard's first impression of the city is typical. He is not unique in re-cording the dual responses of the Wordsworthian "confusion" and the Arnoldian "prison."

Was all nought but confusion? What man and what master
Had each of these people that hastened along?
Like a flood flowed the faces, and faster and faster
Went the drift of the feet of the hurrying throng.

.   .   .   .

They passed, and day grew, and with pitiless faces
The dull houses stared on the prey they had trapped;
'Twas as though they had slain all the fair morning places
Where in love and in leisure our joyance had happed.

My heart sank; I murmured, "What's this we are doing
In this grim net of London, this prison built stark
With the greed of the ages, our young lives pursuing
A phantom that leads but to death in the dark?"

[vol. 24, sec. 2. ll. 9–12, 33–40]

Similarly in section 3, "Sending to the War," Morris seems merely to re-peat in the fashion of Roden Noel an awareness of the startling juxta-positions of wealth and poverty in his descriptions of London during the chauvinist/imperialist wars of the 1860s.

But here were the streets of London—strife stalking wide in the
   world;
And the flag of an ancient people to the battle-breeze unfurled.
And who was helping or heeding? The gaudy shops displayed
The toys of rich men's folly, by blinded labour made;
And still from nought to nothing the bright-skinned horses drew
Dull men and sleek-faced women with never a deed to do;
While all about and around them the street-flood ebbed and
   flowed,
Worn feet, grey anxious faces, grey backs bowed 'neath the load.

[vol. 24, sec. 3. ll. 11–18]

But Morris's response to London does not rely on conventional structures of feeling for very long. By the end of section 3, the narrator/participant has his first vision of the socialist future to come. Richard is not a mere daydreamer but an idealist with firm and practical conviction; he looks forward to the day when the duped city crowds before him will make up the vital element of the new order.

> And the crowd was swaying and swaying, and somehow, I knew
> not why,
> A dream came into my heart of deliverance drawing anigh.
>
> Sun and wind in the street, familiar things made clear,
> Made strange by the breathless waiting for the deeds that are
> drawing anear.
> For woe had grown into will, and wrath was bared of its sheath,
> And stark in the streets of London stood the crop of the dragon's
> teeth.
> Where then in my dream were the poor and the wall of faces wan?
> Here and here by my side, shoulder to shoulder of man,
> Hope in the simple folk, hope in the hearts of the wise.
>
> [vol. 24, sec. 3. ll. 57–58, 75–81]

To the narrator/participant, the masses in the streets, when exposed to agitation, education, and organization, will become his welcome human comrades in the future, and there can be no peace in London until that goal is attained: "Peace at home!—what peace, while the rich man's mill is strife, / And the poor is the grist that he grindeth, and life devoureth life?" (vol. 24, sec. 3. ll. 87–88).

Sections 5 to 7 of *The Pilgrims of Hope* trace the hero's deteriorating economic misery, which is relieved only by his conversion to the socialist cause. Although the hero seems comfortably secure in his "joiner's craft" position, he feels that there is no sense of community, no social purpose to his existence in the city. By chance, a workmate invites Richard to attend a radical socialist meeting one evening.

> So we went, and the street was as dull and as common as aught you
> could see;
> Dull and dirty the room. Just over the chairman's chair
> Was a bust, a Quaker's face with nose cocked up in the air;
> There were common prints on the wall of the heads of the party
> fray,
> And Mazzini dark and lean amidst them gone astray.

Some thirty men we were of the kind that I knew full well,
Listless, rubbed down to the type of our easy-going hell.
My heart sank down as I entered, and wearily there I sat
While the chairman strove to end his maunder of this and of that.

[vol. 24, sec. 5. ll. 78–86]

As this description indicates, Morris held no illusions about the simple, even squalid settings in which the seeds of revolution would thrive. Nor did Morris entertain any optimistic notion that the working classes would immediately embrace the revolution with open arms. Although Richard quickly converts to the socialist cause, he sees dissension and apathy on the faces of others present in the small room.

He ceased, and I thought the hearers would rise up with one cry,
And bid him straight enroll them; but they, they applauded
  indeed,
For the man was grown full eager, and had made them hearken and
  heed:
But they sat and made no sign, and two of the glibber kind
Stood up to jeer and to carp, his fiery words to blind.

.   .   .   .

But my hope full well he answered, and when he called again
On men to band together lest they live and die in vain,
In fear lest he should escape me, I rose ere the meeting was done,
And gave him my name and my faith—and I was the only one.

[vol. 24, sec. 5. ll. 104–8, 113–16]

Soon after Richard's conversion, he loses the extra-income legacy from his father and he becomes a full-fledged member of the working class: "So I who have worked for my pleasure now work for utter need: / In 'the noble army of labour' I now am a soldier indeed" (vol. 24, sec. 6. ll. 31–32). But if Richard's new position entitles him to a genuine proletarian badge, it also brings him work dissatisfaction, fear, and an unwanted move to the Soho slum district. Again, to Morris, economic status governs physical and mental existence in the city.

but now that to work I must stick,
Or fall into utter ruin, there's something gone, I find;
The work goes, cleared is the job, but there's something left
  behind;
I take up fear with my chisel, fear lies 'twixt me and my plane,
And I wake in the merry morning to a new unwonted pain.

> That's fear: I shall live it down—and many a thing besides
> Till I win the poor dulled heart which the workman's jacket hides.
> .   .   .   .
>   and to-morrow must we go
> To a room near my master's shop, in the purlieus of Soho.
> No words of its shabby meanness! But that is our prison-cell
> In the jail of weary London.   {vol. 24, sec. 6. ll. 40–46, 67–70}

The plight of Richard and his family continues to worsen in sections 6 and 7 as Richard first loses his job and then his freedom because he is a frequent political speaker at streetcorner meetings. Certainly the purpose of Morris's tale is not to protract melodramatic miseries but to show that both employers and judges, indeed all those in authority in Victorian society, are committed to stifling the voice of workingmen. To be sure, they have careful social philosophies worked out which they readily preach. Thus, the voice of the employer:

> 'Now I'll give you a word of warning: stay in it as long as you can,
> This working lot that you like so: you're pretty well off as you are.
> So take another warning: I have thought you went too far,
> And now I am quite sure of it; so make an end of your talk
> At once and for ever henceforth, or out of my shop you walk.'
>   {vol. 24, sec. 6. ll. 112–16}

And the voice of the judge:

> 'What have you got to do to preach such perilous stuff?
> To take some care of yourself should find you work enough.
> If you needs must preach or lecture, then hire a chapel or hall;
> Though indeed if you take my advice you'll just preach nothing at
> all.'   {vol. 24, sec. 7. ll. 85–88}

These lines sound like Noel's overhearing of conversations. But here again the Lukácsian distinction between observer and participant as it applies to the poetry of Noel and Morris is useful. The difference in Morris's poem is that the reader sees and hears these pronouncements through his identification with Richard, a man of declining fortune.

Since any effective action on Richard's or the movement's part seems at present in London to be blocked on all sides, in the remaining sections of the poem Morris transfers the urban scene to the Paris Commune uprising. In the Paris Commune, Morris found the one historical event in recent memory that could serve as a rallying cry to demonstrate that socialist dreams could be transformed into real deeds. Yet again Morris's harsh brand of realism appears; the struggle requires tremendous individual sacrifices, including the loss of wives and best friends. Morris's choosing the Paris Commune uprising as the symbolic and climactic struggle of the poem leaves no doubt that his brand of socialism is revolutionary and not evolutionary. Section 11, "A Glimpse of the Coming Day," provides a brief vision of the ideal egalitarian social order to come. For a short time the city of Paris becomes a city of hope and joy. The "day of deeds" has ushered in the "day of deliverance."

> So at last from a grey stone building we saw a great flag fly,
> One colour, red and solemn 'gainst the blue of the spring-tide sky,
> And we stopped and turned to each other, and as each at each did
>   we gaze,
> The city's hope enwrapped us with joy and great amaze
>
> .   .   .   .
>
> There was now no foe and no fool in the city, and Paris was free;
> And e'en as she is this morning, to-morrow all France will be.
> We heard, and our hearts were saying, 'In a little while all the
>   earth—'   [vol. 24, sec 11. ll. 37–40, 47–49]

The final sections of the poem, 12 and 13, describe respectively the universal and personal consequences of the defeat of the Paris Commune. The narrator/participant, now looking back at the tragic happenings, views himself as but "an atom of the strife." He then proceeds to deliver a forty-line cosmic eulogy to the "Earth" and mankind. Although Richard has witnessed the workings of the "brutal" and "ruthless" bourgeois war-machine, he has also had the rare privilege of serving with the army of the people, the army of the future: "Yea and we were a part of it all, the beginning of the end, / That first fight of the uttermost battle whither all the nations wend" (vol. 24, sec. 12. ll. 33–34). The narrator/participant describes his grief over the death of his wife (who remains nameless) and his friend Arthur in the Paris street fighting. But just as the future hope for the socialist cause has sustained him throughout the poem, he refuses to let himself be overwhelmed by his deeply personal losses. Instead, he embraces his son and resolves to continue the struggle with the young boy by his side.

> I came not here [England] to be bidding my happiness farewell,
> And to nurse my grief and to win me the gain of a wounded life,
> That because of the bygone sorrow may hide away from the strife.
> I came to look to my son, and myself to get stout and strong,
> That two men there might be hereafter to battle against the wrong;

And I cling to the love of the past and the love of the day to be,
And the present, it is but the building of the man to be strong in
   me.   [vol. 24, sec. 13. ll. 83–89]

The Pilgrims of Hope is unique in Morris's poetic canon for its realistic descriptions of city employment, city crowds, and early socialist meetings. For contemporary details of the ugly conditions in late-nineteenth-century England, only Morris's essays and the prose romance *News from Nowhere* can rival it. In the 1880s Morris was one of very few writers who saw the city with a particular literalism, and who also saw hope for the city after a brief period of violent destruction. He was able to envision—especially through the example of the Commune—the city as a battleground for the violent class warfare that was necessary to establish the peaceful utopian society of the future. His own productive and propagandistic activity in this period demonstrated that political action and imaginative vitality could interact and even reinforce each other. And yet even for Morris the interaction was never sure. Certainly he surpassed Noel in terms of urban involvement by going beyond Noel's distanced descriptions and by assuming the narrative stance of an active participant with solutions. But even though Morris's form and subject matter were different, he was never convinced of the adequacy of poetry in general or of his own poetic forms to capture or affect contemporary historical events. Morris and Noel, then, are poets who looked at the city and saw sources of hope in it. Although they differed in their stances or perspectives on the city and had their doubts about the effect that their poetry might have on the contemporary scene, they never succumbed to the profound pessimism of James Thomson, who looked on and was defeated by the contemporary urban scene. In Thomson's view, there was and could be *no* hope from either inside or outside the city.

James Thomson: The City as Wasteland

William Morris and James Thomson stand together in opposition to Hopkins, Patmore, and Noel because as their careers developed they both severed more and more ties with the established social, political, and religious order of the late-Victorian period. All five poets saw a fearsome concentration of power in the dense growth of the masses in metropolitan areas. But it is exactly on this point that their differing attitudes can be sorted out more clearly. To Hopkins and Patmore, the masses represented a clear threat to the established order of society and indirectly to the controlling mores of organized religion. To Noel, the stark juxtaposition of wealth and poverty seemed to indicate an unstable and unnatural state of affairs that would quickly readjust to some new as yet unknown order. For Morris, the urban masses would soon lead the way through the destruction of the old order to the new and just society of the future. Thomson saw the masses as stony figures in a perverse drama of urban and cosmic despair; the figures in Thomson's city are dreadful not because of their numbers but because of their enervation.

Of all the poets discussed, it is in the development of James Thomson's poetic response to the city that the complete negation of Blake's optimistic hope of building London into the New Jerusalem is most devastatingly evident. Several critics, including R. A. Foakes, William D. Schaefer, and others, have outlined Thomson's move from an early romanticism to a disturbing realism. Indeed, Thomson often extends Clough's 1853 call for a new, realistic treatment of the city to one for a surrealistic approach. Certainly there are some personal reasons that contributed to Thomson's pessimism: the early deaths of his parents and of his girlfriend Matilda Weller; the decline of religious faith; the debilitating effects of alcohol; and the misery and oppression that he experienced for the majority of the years he lived in London.[38] But the essential issue here is the development of Thomson's intensely personal nightmare vision in his poems that focus most directly on the urban environment.

In 1855 Thomson visited London and described his impressions of a classic London landmark, St. Paul's Cathedral. In the poem "The Approach to St. Paul's," the city's exciting freshness and awesome majesty appeal to Thomson, but he is disturbed by the materialistic impiety of the city's masses, whose lives are "sordid" and "restless" without religion.

> Eastwards through busy streets I lingered on;
> Jostled by anxious crowds, who, heart and brain,
> Were so absorbed in dreams of Mammon-gain,
> That they could spare no time to look upon
> The sunset's gold and crimson fires, which shone
> Blessing keen eyes and wrinkled brows in vain.
> Right in my path stood out that solemn Fane
> Whose soaring cupola of stern grey stone
> Lifteth for awful beacon to the sky
> The burning Cross: silent and sole amid
> That ceaseless uproar, as a pyramid
> Isled in its desert. The great throngs pressed by
> Heedless and urgent: thus Religion towers
> Above this sordid, restless life of ours.[39]

The Urban Volcano, 1870–1890

In the 1850s, Thomson's admiration and reverence for both God and the romantic poets remained as yet undiminished. He thought that imaginative transcendence and escape were still possible in poetry, and that at least part of a poet's role involved the delivery of prophetic messages. Evidently the problem of widespread impiety among urban dwellers (which he had just barely presented in "The Approach to St. Paul's") weighed on his mind. As a result, he wrote the long allegorical poem "The Doom of a City: A Fantasia," which urges those who have been frozen into stone by their materialistic greed to repent or be destroyed.

"The Doom of a City" (1857) opens with a deliberate dismissal of the world of material reality

> From out the house I crept,
> The house which long had caged my homeless life:
> The mighty City in vast silence slept,
> Dreaming away its tumult, toil, and strife:
> But sleep and sleep's rich dreams were not for me,
> For me, accurst, whom terror and the pain
> Of baffled longings, and starved misery,
> And such remorse as sears the breast,
> And hopeless doubt which gnaws the brain
> Till wildest action blind and vain
> Would be more welcome than supine unrest,
> Drove forth as one possest
> To leave my kind and dare the desert sea;
> To drift alone and far   [pt. 1. ll. 1–14]

But with Thomson, the flight to romantic transcendence is not instantaneous; the poet "works up" to his vision by walking at night around the deserted streets of the metropolis.

> I paced through desert streets, beneath the gleam
> Of lamps that lit my trembling life alone;
> Like lamps sepulchral which had slowly burned
> Through sunless ages, deep and undiscerned,
> Within a buried City's maze of stone;
> Whose peopling corpses, while they ever dream
> Of birth and death—of complicated life
> Whose days and months and years
> Are wild with laughters, groans, and tears,
> As with themselves and Doom
> They wage, with loss or gain, incessant strife,
> Indeed, lie motionless within their tomb.   [pt. 1. ll. 26–37]

In time, such romantic symbols as the floating boat ("My boat lay waiting there, / Upon the moonless river" [pt. 1. ll. 42–43]) occupy the poet's imagination so that the reality of the city fades away like the images in a dream.

> So slowly faded back from sight,
> As doth a dream insensibly
> Fade backward on the ebbing tide of sleep,
> That city which had home nor hope for me,
> That stifling tomb from which I now was free.   [pt. 1. ll. 51–55]

For the remainder of part 1 of the poem, the "Romantic assertion" that the gifts of inspiration and transcendence are unique to the visionary poet is made in line after line of rich description. Often the steady flow of luxuriant images is reminiscent of Keats's early poetry. But as happened so often in the later poetry of Keats, by the end of part 1 it becomes apparent that the content of the vision may bring disappointing knowledge.[40]

> I knew, but would not know,
> I knew too well, but knowledge was despair,
> It came on vast and slow,
> And dipt those baleful meteors in the brine;
> Whence soon it lifted them with hideous cries
> That flung strange horror through the shuddering air.
>   [pt. 1. ll. 259–64]

The interest of Thomson's poetic response involves the nature and content of his imaginative vision. Second generation romantics like Keats and Shelley explored visionary heights, only to retrieve disturbing knowledge. Thomson was working in the same vein, but unlike most romantic poets he began with the city. He wrote like a visionary poet whose transcendent vision brought dark and disturbing truth and this happened when his subject was the city, which he saw in a visionary mode as tomblike and frightening.

Part 2 of "The Doom of a City" is entitled "The City" and in it transmogrified urban details are used to inform the vision. The city that Thomson has reached by way of his imagination is a stony and silent place.

> What found I in the City, then, which turned
> My deep and solemn hope to wild despair?
> What mystery of horror lay inurned
> Within the royal City great and fair?
> What found I? Dead stone sentries stony-eyed,
>
> .   .   .   .

> Stone statues all throughout the streets and squares,
> Grouped as in social converse or alone;
> Dim stony merchants holding forth rich wares
> To catch the choice of purchasers of stone.
>
> > [pt. 2. ll. 189–93, 197–200]

It is as though the entire turbulent restlessness of a large metropolis had instantaneously been caught in the grip of some gigantic life-negating force.

> The whole vast sea of life about me lay,
> The passionate, heaving, restless, sounding life,
> With all its tides and billows, foam and spray,
> Arrested in full tumult of its strife
> Frozen into a nightmare's ghastly death,
> Struck silent from its laughter and its moan;
> The vigorous heart and brain and blood and breath
> Stark, strangled, coffined in eternal stone.   [pt. 2. ll. 209–16]

In part 3, "The Judgements," the poet is allowed to approach the very gates of Heaven and witness the terrible destruction of Cosmopolis, the Mausolean City. The city is apocalyptically destroyed by fire, storm, and the arrival of beasts. "Of the City's vast palatial pride / Of all the works of Man on every side" there "remained no vestige" and "erasure had been scarcely more complete" (pt. 3. ll. 215–16, 219, 228). The solitary stone people are consumed in the disaster.

    The poem would simply go down in literary history as a fanciful nightmare vision if it ended here. In part 4, however, Thomson shows his more serious intent by taking on the role of the poet who will bring back warnings of the misfortunes of others so that he can save his society. In part 4, "The Return," the poet feels disgust and apprehension on viewing the dense storm cloud that hangs over his city.

> Before me, in the drowsy night outspread,
> The City whence in anguish I had fled
> A vast dark Shadow loomed:
> So still, so black it gloomed,
>
> .   .   .   .   .   .
>
> Its awful mass of life oppressed my soul:
> The very air appeared no longer free,
> But dense and sultry in the close control
> Of such a mighty cloud of human breath.
> The shapeless houses and the monstrous ships

> Were brooding thunderclouds that could eclipse
> The burning sun of day.   [pt. 4. ll. 43–46, 53–59]

In this surcharged atmosphere, the poet feels ambivalence toward the mighty city akin to that found in some of Buchanan's poetic statements. The city evokes both feelings of fear and pity.

> And while I gazed upon the sleeping City,
> And pondered its unnumbered destinies,
> A flood of awe and fear, and love and pity
> Swelled in my heart and overflowed my eyes
> With unexpected tears.
> The burden of the message I had brought
> From that great City far across the Sea
> Lay heavy on my soul. . . .   [pt. 4. ll. 67–74]

At this point in his career, Thomson felt that repentance and redemption could still be achieved by the city's inhabitants. Like Buchanan, he admitted that there are good as well as evil characteristics about the city. Unlike Buchanan, Thomson does not list in his own voice the advantages and disadvantages of the city, but instead has a "Spirit" speak the message to the city through the poet.

>   when suddenly
> That Spirit which will never be withstood
> Came down, and shook and seized and lifted me,—
> As men uplift a passive instrument
> Through which to breathe whatever fits their mood.
>   [pt. 4. ll. 86–90]

The Spirit grants that the poet's city is "rich and strong . . . wise and good and free" but also points out that there is much evil, guilt, and social injustice present (pt. 4. ll. 125–32). The Spirit's complaint about urban prostitution is voiced as strongly as it was in the poetry of Smith and Buchanan (pt. 4. ll. 147–52). Thomson's final message—as delivered to him by the Spirit—to the potentially doomed city in 1857 was "Repent, reform, or perish!" (pt. 4. l. 119).

    By 1865 Thomson was beginning to move away from this romanticism of transforming vision and prophecy to a new but not yet bleak realism. In "Sunday at Hampstead" (1863–1865) the machinery of transcendental thrusts, so dominant in "The Doom of a City," has been abandoned and the most that a weary workingman from the city can hope for is an enjoyable picnic in the country on Sunday. The city can thus be escaped physically and temporarily, yet its psychological oppression looms ever

present. The limits and nature of escape are defined in the very title—
"Sunday at Hampstead: An Idle Idyll by a Very Humble Member of the
Great and Noble London Mob." Yet even in "an idle idyll," there is room
for manipulation, room for the scrambling of fact and dream. And so it is
that even though "monstrous grimy London lay beneath," the pleasant
country perspective of Hampstead Heath momentarily encourages the
dreamy blurring of the city's harsh reality.

> Here will we sit, my darling,
> And dream an hour away:
> The donkeys are hurried and worried,
> But we are not donkeys to-day.
>
> Though all the weary week, dear,
> We toil in the murk down there,
> Tied to a desk and a counter,
> A patient stupid pair!   [pt. 1. ll. 9–16]

In the poem, the laborer comes to question the reality of his work and it
fades into a dreamy state of unreality. This dismissal of the city's mundane
reality in turn spills over into a heightened enjoyment of a vital coun-
tryside. There is, however, an edge of melancholy to this pleasant scene
because Thomson calls it a "sad sweet calm."

> Day after day of this azure May
> The blood of the Spring has swelled in my veins;
> Night after night of broad moonlight
> A mystical dream has dazzled my brains.
>
> A seething might, a fierce delight,
> The blood of the Spring is the wine of the world;
> My veins run fire and thrill desire,
> Every leaf of my heart's red rose uncurled.
>
> A sad sweet calm, a tearful balm,
> The light of the Moon is the trance of the world;
> My brain is fraught with yearning thought,
> And the rose is pale and its leaves are furled.   [pt. 11. ll. 1–12]

Thomson's "Sunday Up the River" (1865) is the second of the Sunday
idyllic tributes to the countryside. This poem is unabashedly lighthearted
and optimistic. The poem demonstrates that the romanticism of his early
career had not yet completely lost its attraction. In terms of vision, the
poem offers no prophetic insight or message; here the poet is content

to rely completely on objective, passive observation and distanced, even dreamy description of a rural setting. The first stanza conveys the romantic flavor of the poem.

> I looked out into the morning,
> I looked out into the west:
> The soft blue eye of the quiet sky
> Still drooped in dreamy rest.   [pt. 1. ll. 1–4]

What is especially interesting about "Sunday Up the River" is that it won some attention from critics and editors. It was published in *Fraser's Magazine*, Thomson's "only reputable appearance in respectable literary society," and Froude, the editor of *Fraser's*, "was so struck with the merit of the poem that he asked Charles Kingsley's opinion upon it, which was warmly in its favour."[41] Clearly the conventional poetic taste of the 1860s preferred poetry about landscapes out of the city to frightening and doom-filled descriptions of the city itself.

Although the critical opinion of "Sunday Up the River" was favorable, Thomson returned in his most interesting poetry to visions like those of "The Doom of a City." In an April 1882 letter to his sister-in-law, he warned her not to read his later poems "The City of Dreadful Night," "In the Room," and "To Our Ladies of Death" because they had been "written under the evil inspiration of the Melancholy of Insomnia."[42] In the twentieth century, critics like Ridler and Walker seem to agree that "In the Room" (1867–1868) and "The City of Dreadful Night" (1870–1873) are among Thomson's most outstanding poems, the epitome of the "unromantic pessimism of his maturity."[43] These poems attract the attention of the twentieth-century critic because they explore the terrifying realm of the individual human mind. The two poems are case studies of mental alienation from the surrounding world and they exhibit the darkest side of melancholy by moving beyond compassionate sadness and partial dejection to numbing depression and complete enervation of spirit.

In the poem "In the Room" one sees not just a person sadly separated from his neighbors in a tenement dwelling (as in Buchanan's poem "The Little Milliner") but a suicide who is mourned only by his paltry collection of furniture. Here the loneliness of solitude is macabre; the tenant of the room cannot speak because he is lying dead on the bed. Therefore, in a *tour de force*, the furniture pieces must present the dingy details of the setting of the deceased's life. Walker gives an excellent synopsis of the poem:

> In a drab chamber with a "chilly hearth and naked floor," the pieces of furniture converse about him. The cupboard complains that it

gets no more than a pinch of meal and a crust all the week long; and the mirror grumbles that the Man is not so gay and happy as the previous tenant, Lucy, and that last night he was pale, his eyes were too bright, and he muttered bad words. The table sighs that it grows weary of his weight as he writes endlessly, and the grate responds peevishly that his labor is all futile since he burns everything he writes. The mirror again grumbles: ". . . with this dullard, glum and sour, / Not one of all his fellow-men / Has ever passed a social hour." The bed then startles them with the quiet announcement that the Man lies dead upon it; and the vial adds that he had drunk its contents of poison.[44]

Although Walker and Ridler admire the tormented terrors of the individual mind as presented in "In the Room" and in some sections of "The City of Dreadful Night" because these lines "speak directly to us" as twentieth-century readers, critics like Raymond Williams and William D. Schaefer have insisted that the Victorian and social aspects of Thomson's poetry, especially "The City of Dreadful Night," should be stressed more than they have been. For example, concerning Thomson's place in the canon of literature about the city, Williams has written: "But what is distinct in Thomson . . . is that his city is projected and is significantly total: it is a symbolic vision of the city as *the* condition of human life."[45] The two adjectives "projected" and "total" capture exactly the duality of Thomson's long poem, his most complete and thoughtful view of the city and mankind. In one sense, Thomson's vision in "The City" is constrictive because he conveys, as in the much shorter poem "In the Room," his own private mental and emotional impression that his individual misery and misfortune are all there is to life; yet in another sense, his vision is social, connective, and "total," because he comes to believe that with the ever-increasing size and density of the urban environment, *all* mankind shares in and will be subjected to the same fate of misery. Furthermore, with careful manuscript documentation, Schaefer in "The Two Cities of Dreadful Night" demonstrates that Thomson wrote the poem in two stages, one in 1870 and the other in 1873. Schaefer argues that by treating the two drafts separately it can be seen that "the 1870 'City' and the 1873 'City' are unquestionably two very different poems in concept and intention."[46] The first seven sections as well as sections 10, 11, 18, and 20 were written in 1870; the rest were written in 1873. According to Schaefer, the basic differences between the two drafts are:

All six of the narrative passages written in 1870 had been fantastic, supernatural, highly allegorical, but there is not the faintest suggestion of allegory in this narrative section [sec. 8], nor will allegory be discovered in any of the sections written after this, for it seems clear that Thomson was simply not continuing the same poem. In the 1870 "City of Dreadful Night" men who like Thomson had seen Faith or Love or Hope die, suddenly found themselves trapped in the dreadful city, driven insane through personal grief. But the 1873 city is no longer symbolic of a state of mind, a realm of personal grief, of individual suffering which cannot communicate; the poem now deals with a universal situation that concerns all mankind, for here "Fate" has become the villain condemning all men to a meaningless life. This 1873 "City of Dreadful Night" has become, in fact, a sort of pessimist's manifesto; the inhabitants of the city are not, as in 1870, joined by accident through emotional suffering, but are actually members of a secret fraternity banded together in the city because they have intellectually arrived at the realization . . . that all life is fraudulent and meaningless.[47]

The two central fears in the poem are the focus of the two distinct drafts of the poem. In the 1870 "City," Thomson explored the unrelieved terrors of his highly imaginative mind; in the 1873 "City," he was able to walk outside of his *individual* self-absorption, but amidst the new *social* community of suffering he again found only loss of purpose in everything, for everyone. In the 1870 "City," all of the derogatory metaphors of the city in the nineteenth century—as prison, hell, and hot plain—are condensed to a new emblem of what Schaefer calls "a nightmare city of the mind, a personal hell suffered by the isolated individual."[48]

> The City is of Night, but not of Sleep;
> There sweet sleep is not for the weary brain;
> The pitiless hours like years and ages creep,
> A night seems termless hell. This dreadful strain
> Of thought and consciousness which never ceases,
> Or which some moments' stupor but increases,
> This, worse than woe, makes wretches there insane.
>
> [sec. 1. ll. 71–77]

The intensity of this melancholy complaint marks Thomson's departure from nineteenth-century poetry about the city. In the 1870 draft he is not whimpering about his uncomfortable lot in the city, but about his inability to tolerate the throbbing mental stimulation that he experiences nightly walking the streets of the city. He cannot cope with the unrelenting barrage of mental images that are projected from *inside* his head out onto the silent night of the sleeping city ("I have seen phantoms there that were as men / And men that were as phantoms flit and roam" [sec. 7. ll. 15–16]).

Yet to Thomson, the poet trying to complete the draft of the poem, the consuming terror of the individual mind appeared to be an unrelieved and hopeless topic for poetry. The 1870 "City" was really going nowhere; the lines were merely spinning around in a Wertherian whirlpool. Thomson put the poem aside by the end of October 1870. The modern side of Thomson that looked forward to the twentieth-century psychological dilemma—the side praised by Walker and Ridler—had reached a dead end. In April 1872 Thomson left London for the American West as secretary of the Champion Gold and Silver Mines Company. He remained in Central City, Colorado, until the mining venture failed and he was recalled to London in December 1872. He resumed work on the 1873 "City" in June, but was interrupted from July to September because he was sent by the *New York World* to cover a revolution against the monarchy in Spain. He finally finished the poem in late October 1873, three years after he had left off with the final section of the 1870 "City." The 1873 "City" leaves behind the personal hell in his mind and strikes an essentially Victorian note by asking whether

> Our isolated units could be brought
> To act together for some common end?
> For one by one, each silent with his thought,
> I marked a long loose line approach and wend
> Athwart the great cathedral's cloistered square,
> And slowly vanish from the moonlit air.
>
> Then I would follow in among the last:
> And in the porch a shrouded figure stood,
> Who challenged each one pausing ere he passed,
> With deep eyes burning through a blank white hood:
> Whence come you in the world of life and light
> To this our City of Tremendous Night?—   [sec. 12. ll. 1–12]

Although this gospel is disappointing news, at least a fraction of the poet's task of disseminating the most essential messages to mankind is again realized. The anguished congregation gathers together to hear with resounding clarity the religion of "Necessity Supreme" proclaimed by the thunderous antipreacher.

> O melancholy Brothers, dark, dark, dark!
> O battling in black floods without an ark!

O spectral wanderers of unholy Night!
My soul hath bled for you these sunless years,
With bitter blood-drops running down like tears:
Oh, dark, dark, dark, withdrawn from joy and light!

My heart is sick with anguish for your bale;
Your woe hath been my anguish; yea, I quail
And perish in your perishing unblest.
And I have searched the highths and depths, the scope
Of all our universe, with desperate hope
To find some solace for your wild unrest.

And now at last authentic word I bring,
Witnessed by every dead and living thing;
Good tidings of great joy for you, for all:
There is no God; no Fiend with names divine
Made us and tortures us; if we must pine,
It is to satiate no Being's gall.   [sec. 14. ll. 25–42]

Thomson muses over the words of the antipreacher and concludes that there is some comfort to be derived from meeting Truth honestly and completely.

My Brother, my poor Brothers, it is thus;
This life itself holds nothing good for us,
But it ends soon and nevermore can be;
And we knew nothing of it ere our birth,
And shall know nothing when consigned to earth:
I ponder these thoughts and they comfort me.   [sec. 16. ll. 49–54]

By extending the terms of the antipreacher's vision, the city becomes for the narrator the present embodiment of the "renewed assurance / And confirmation of the old despair" (sec. 21. ll. 83–84). The poet even goes so far as to indulge in the ancient art of prophesying the future when he projects beyond the present emblem of the city to see no hope in utopian fantasies located in outer space. Looking beyond the city to the stars and planets, the grim message for mankind is that

If we could near them with the flight unflown,
We should but find them worlds as sad as this,
Or suns all self-consuming like our own
Enringed by planet worlds as much amiss.   [sec. 17, ll. 22–25]

The two parts of "The City of Dreadful Night" are thus important for understanding Thomson's development. Part 1 is an anthology of familiar nineteenth-century images of the city as a personal hell, with a notable difference being the surreal, "modern" intensity that Thomson achieves by marking his vision so clearly as a projection of a particular psychology or consciousness. But part 2 is something new altogether; it is no longer, really, a response to the city but rather a use of the city as an emblem of a social, indeed a universal condition. Neither fear nor hope is felt any longer from the city because its features of crowd and incoherent hurry are not peculiar—they are the signs of how it always is everywhere. Nothing different is going to happen anywhere because there is nothing outside the city. Thomson sees that the city is the emblem of everything and that there is certainly nothing (including its citizens) in his city to save it. Life in the city depicted in Thomson's later poetry means unrelieved enduring of misery and despair, a state whose only relief is the courage of facing up to a knowledge of the real condition of humanity, and the release of death.

This chapter touches the extreme ends of the spectrum as far as various poets' hopes and fears for the city are concerned. Even though Noel and Morris differed from Hopkins and Patmore in that their responses to the city were hope or panic, respectively, all four figures felt that one day another, better possibility for the city, or at least for humans who might escape or transform the city, might be realized. Thomson alone disagrees. For him, the city is all, all is the city. Thomson's achievement is, first of all, to behave like an ambitious romantic poet—to draw a moral from the city, to see it as a vision of terror, to escape from it to nature—but then, second of all, to convert it to emblems of personal and then universal conditions. From Thomson's atheistic position, the dimension of the flawed universal plan is cosmic. His fears were essentially philosophical and spiritual rather than social or political. In this sense, he stands isolated in his troubled despair from the other poets discussed in this chapter.

Chapter Four
The Poetry of the Nineties

New Ways to Write Poetry about the City

The question as to whether the 1890s marked "a beginning, an end, or a transition" in literary forms and outlooks has been raised and only partially answered in an essay by Helmut E. Gerber.[1] In the sense that poets continued to write about the city of London throughout the nineties, the decade represents a transition period of continuity with the years that precede and follow it. In another sense, however, forms and topics of the nineties poets exhibited some important beginnings. Yet the decade also represents a clearly discernible endpoint in the sense that many of their accomplishments were later severely criticized as being inadequate for the dimensions of the city and many of their poetic innovations were consequently dropped or extensively modified at the turn of the century.

What appears with varying fervor throughout the nineties is a confidence that the poet could and ought to make poetic statements regarding the people, spirit, and conditions of London. In 1891 W. E. Henley responded with excitement to a letter from his friend Charles Whibley who had recorded his approval of the first part of the *London Voluntaries*: "I'm glad you think I've pulled it off. It's a new game, as you say; and I seem to discern in it some possibilities of London as material for verse that may have some chance of living."[2] Several years earlier, Walter Pater had touched on the potential for fascination with the city in *Marius the Epicurean* (1885): "Life in modern London . . . is stuff sufficient for the fresh imagination of a youth to build its 'palace of art' of."[3] Arthur Symons was a disciple of Pater's and a leading poet and critic throughout the nineties. Almost immediately after the appearance of Henley's *London Voluntaries*, Symons expressed his enthusiastic praise: "Here, at last, is a poet who can so enlarge the limits of his verse as to take in London. And I think that might be the test of poetry which professes to be modern—its capacity for dealing with London, with what one sees or might see there, indoors and out."[4] Symons unabashedly expressed his boredom with the countryside and proclaimed that the best environment for poets and poetry was the city.

> I lived in London for five years, and I do not think there was a day during those five years in which I did not find a conscious delight in the mere fact of being in London. When I found myself alone, and in the midst of a crowd, I began to be astonishingly happy. I needed so little, at the beginning of that time. I have never been able to stay long under a roof without restlessness, and I used to go out into the streets, many times a day, for the pleasure of finding myself in the open air and in the streets. I had never cared greatly for the open air in the country, the real open air, because everything in the country, except the sea, bored me; but here, in the 'motley' Strand, among these hurrying people, under the smoky sky, I could walk and yet watch.[5]

In response to a reviewer who had called the poems in Symons's early volume *Silhouettes* "unwholesome" because they had "a faint smell of patchouli about them," the poet defended strongly both the individuality of his poetry and the integrity of its urban contents.

> Patchouli! Well, why not Patchouli? Is there any "reason in nature" why we should write exclusively about the natural blush, if the delicately acquired blush of rouge has any attraction for us? . . . If you prefer your "newmown hay" in the hayfield, and I, it may be, in a scent-bottle, why may not my individual caprice be allowed to find expression as well as yours? . . . I am always charmed to read beautiful poems about nature in the country. Only, personally, I prefer town to country; and in the town we have to find for ourselves, as best we may, the decor which is the town equivalent of the great natural decor of fields and hills.[6]

In 1876 the poet Austin Dobson seemed hesitant about accepting the city as the new territory for poetry—"Mine is an urban Muse, and bound / By some strange law to paven ground." In the nineties, however, poets welcomed and even celebrated the "strangeness" of London in their poetry. One of Richard Le Gallienne's poems opens with the line "Ah, London! London! our delight" and in "London Town" Lionel Johnson echoes Symons in proclaiming his allegiance to the city:

> Let others chaunt a country praise,
> Fair river walks and meadow ways;
> Dearer to me my sounding days
> Is *London Town*:

> To me the tumult of the street
> Is no less music, than the sweet
> Surge of the wind among the wheat,
> By dale or down.[7]

The titles of several volumes of poetry confirm the increasing concentration of poets on aspects of the urban environment as interesting and proper topics for poetry: Frederick Locker-Lampson's *London Lyrics* (1857–1893), W. E. Henley's *London Voluntaries* (1893) and *London Types* (1898), John Davidson's *Fleet Street Eclogues* (1893), Ernest Rhys's *A London Rose* (1894), Arthur Symons's *London Nights* (1895), and Laurence Binyon's *London Visions* (1896). Also characteristic of the period were gift books such as W. E. Henley's *A London Garland* (1895) and Wilfred Whitten's *London in Song* (1898).

Forms and Types of Poetry about London

But whether or not a particular poet of the nineties used "London" in the title of his volume to underscore the legitimacy of the city as a proper topic of poetry, he was more likely to use a variety of shorter poetic forms—ode, eclogue, ballad, lyric, sonnet—to record his individual impressions of the city. The only generalization that consistently applies to the poets of the nineties is their preference for shorter poetic forms over longer narrative or epic expressions; however, this choice to write in shorter poetic forms about the sweeping grandeur of the city was criticized at the end of the decade.

In an 1898 review entitled "The Poetry of London," an anonymous critic for the *Spectator* mentioned recent gift book collections of verse such as Wilfred Whitten's *London in Song*, and went on to complain that these anthologies and the poets who contributed to them had not yet gone far enough to capture "the vastness of London." No poet had in either form or content treated London as a world of its own: "And yet there is no poetry of London as a whole. The marvellous Metropolis whose parishes are great cities, and whose people is one of the wealthiest of nations, whose fall would mean drought in the spring of charity throughout three-quarters of the globe, who is at once banker, almoner, and reporter for all mankind, has as yet found no *sacer vates*, perhaps never will find one. For no one celebrates in verse the world as a world, and London is not a microcosm, but a world."[8] In a short essay, "A Defence of Detective Stories," written for a popular newspaper, G. K. Chesterton expounded upon "the roman-

tic possibilities of the modern city" and "the poetry of London." The po-
etry that Chesterton had in mind was not verse at all but rather the
detective story as "a perfectly legitimate form of art" with the detective as
"the agent of social justice . . . the original and poetic figure." Note how
Chesterton validates the city as a storehouse of epic imagery that deserves
literary preservation and yet implicitly prefers to take the urban material
out of the hands of poets in order to place it into those of their new descen-
dants, the writers of detective stories.

> The first essential value of the detective story lies in this, that it
> is the earliest and only form of popular literature in which is ex-
> pressed some sense of the poetry of modern life. Men lived among
> mighty mountains and eternal forests for ages before they realised
> that they were poetical; it may reasonably be inferred that some of
> our descendants may see the chimney-pots as rich a purple as the
> mountain-peaks, and find the lamp-posts as old and natural as the
> trees. Of this realisation of a great city itself as something wild and
> obvious the detective story is certainly the *Iliad*.
>
> This realisation of the poetry of London is not a small thing. A
> city is, properly speaking, more poetic even than a countryside, for
> while nature is a chaos of unconscious forces, a city is a chaos of
> conscious ones. The crest of the flower or the pattern of the lichen
> may or may not be significant symbols. But there is no stone in the
> street and no brick in the wall that is not actually a deliberate
> symbol—a message from some man, as if it were a telegram or a
> post card.[9]

A third writer who felt that the materials of the city should be fash-
ioned into a poetry of epic proportion was William Dean Howells. As an
observer from the United States, Howells was impressed enough with the
sights and sounds of London's streets to call for an epic poet to preserve the
excitement of what he experienced.

> Of all the sights of London streets, this procession of the omnibuses
> is the most impressive, and the common herd of Londoners of both
> sexes which it bears aloft seems to suffer a change into something
> almost as rich as strange. They are no longer ordinary or less than
> ordinary men and women bent on the shabby businesses that pre-
> occupy the most of us; they are conquering princes, making a
> progress in a long triumph, and looking down upon a lower order
> of human beings from their wobbling steeps. It enhances their ap-
> parent dignity that they whom they look down upon are not merely

the drivers of trucks and wagons of low degree, but often ladies of title in their family carriages, under the care of the august family coachman and footman, or gentlemen driving in their own traps or carts, or fares in the hansoms that steal their swift course through and by these ranks; the omnibuses are always the most monumental fact of the scene. . . . If ever London has her epic poet, I think he will sing the omnibus; but the poet who sings the hansom must be of a lyrical note.[10]

Although some critics called for epic poetry about London, the nineties poets chose to write on "a lyrical note" about urban materials and moods. This is not to say that any two poets writing in the 1890s took exactly the same approach to the city. In fact, three strains predominated in poetry at this time: (1) the eighteenth-century *vers de société* mode that saw the city as a civilized and refined community that man shapes according to his rational manners, actions, and ideas; (2) the cult of artificiality and impressionism that celebrated—often in a perverse way—moods and materials of the city precisely because they were un-natural (not of nature) and unconventional; and (3) the vein that captured the city's dynamic energy, an energy and a beauty that could be both terrible and exciting. Each of these ways of seeing the city in the nineties involved certain aesthetic and political conceptions of what the role of the poet and the function of his poetry ought to be.

Poets who wrote about the city in the eighteenth-century mode felt that poets should serve as quiet and unobtrusive commentators on important social events about town. Social events could include strolling lovers in the parks, equestrian arts at Rotten Row, and processions; they would not encompass social class disorders or riots. Poetry was an activity for one's spare time and the product was to be mildly witty and always delicate and refined. An example of this practice may be seen in the writing of Frederick Locker-Lampson, who between 1857 and 1893 published twelve editions of a volume of light verse entitled *London Lyrics*.

Locker-Lampson liked to quote La Bruyère's remark that "nobody regrets having said too little." When Locker-Lampson first saw his *London Lyrics* volume prominently displayed in the window of a Piccadilly bookseller, reticence nearly overcame him: "It was a mixed feeling—the display was so painfully personal." Locker-Lampson expands on these sentiments in his autobiography, *My Confidences*, where he insists that it was "almost an accident" that he ever printed anything. He explains his humble poetic ambition: "My aim was humble. I used the ordinary metres and rhymes, the simplest language and ideas, I hope flavoured with individuality. I strove . . . not to be obscure, not to be flat, and above all, not to be tedious." [11] In an epilogue to the eighth edition of *London Lyrics* (1870), Locker-Lampson summarized his specific poetic intention and elaborated on what was eighteenth century in spirit in some of his poems.

> The kind of verse which I have attempted in some of the pieces in this volume was in repute during the era of Swift and Prior, and again during the earlier years of this century. Afterwards it fell into comparative neglect, but has now regained some of its old popularity.
>
> Light lyrical verse should be short, elegant, refined, and fanciful, not seldom distinguished by chastened sentiment, and often playful. The tone should not be pitched high, and it should be idiomatic, the rhythm crisp and sparkling, the rhyme frequent and never forced, while the entire poem should be marked by tasteful moderation, high finish, and completeness, for however trivial the subject matter may be, indeed rather in proportion to its triviality, subordination to the rules of composition and perfection of execution should be strictly enforced. Each piece cannot be expected to exhibit all these characteristics, but the qualities of brevity and buoyancy are essential. . . .
>
> It is almost needless to say that good sense will be found to underlie all the best poetry of whatever kind. [12]

Clearly, then, Locker-Lampson is a typical representative of an eighteenth-century spirit that preceded and survived throughout the 1890s. The poet of the city must be an urbane, refined observer; such a poet would always remain aloof from politics and the masses. As Locker-Lampson himself put it, "Put your poet into Parliament, or make him a peer, and he is marred—you will at once see the incongruity." [13] Other poetic revivers of eighteenth-century urbane modes include Austin Dobson and, to a certain extent, Laurence Binyon.

The second strain of poetry evident in the nineties sought to convey the artificial and impressionistic aspects of the city. The background of ideas and influences on this type of poetry is complex and multifaceted. Certainly poets like Arthur Symons, Oscar Wilde, Richard Le Gallienne, and others were attracted to the writings of the Parisian poet Charles Baudelaire, who had insisted that a perverse or shocking element be included in any true definition of beauty. Poetry could indeed effectively convey the fascination of the city, but it should focus on artificial pleasures and sensations to be found there. This was not only a choice of the city over the country, but a deliberate concentration on what was *not* nature, such as green carnations and "iron-lilies of the strand." Not only was a new choice of materials—artificial objects and situations—evident in this type of poetry, but also the new way that such materials were presented in an individualized, magical, impressionistic manner. Both the love of artifice and the presentation of such material in an impressionistic manner resulted in either a romanticized or indifferent attitude toward larger social concerns. Oscar Wilde wrote witty aphorisms advising young men to make it their first duty in life "to be as artificial as possible." He also wrote serious essays like "The Soul of Man Under Socialism" in which he argued that "art is the most intense mode of individualism that the world has known," that "a true artist takes no notice whatever of the public," and that "the form of government that is most suitable to the artist is no government at all."[14] Similar sentiments appear in prose statements made by Arthur Symons. A sentence from the preface to his second edition of *Silhouettes* affirms both Symons's love for the artificial aspects of the city and his determined individualistic stance to write in his own style: "Here it is that artificiality comes in; and if any one sees no beauty in the effects of artificial light, in all the variable, most human, and yet most factitious town landscape, I can only pity him, and go on my own way."[15]

Of the three strains of nineties poetry, this second one, the cult of artifice, was satirized and ridiculed the most. Even a popular nineties figure like Max Beerbohm could offer more irony than praise of what the aesthetes were doing. Beerbohm's satirical essay "A Defence of Cosmetics" (1894) ironically points to some of the shortcomings of the "new epoch of artifice." For one thing, the cultivation of the refined spectrum of artificial pleasures can lead to an overweening egotism: "This is a time of jolliness and glad indulgence. For the era of rouge is upon us, and as only in an elaborate era can man by the tangled accrescency of his own pleasures and emotions reach that refinement which is his highest excellence, and by making himself, so to say, independent of Nature, come nearest to God, so only in an elaborate era is woman perfect. Artifice is the strength of the world, and in that same mask of paint and powder, shadowed with vermeil tinct and most trimly pencilled, is woman's strength." Secondly, Beerbohm offhandedly points to the sneering indifference of the aesthetes toward social problems in the same essay: "Insomuch that surely the advocates of soup-kitchens and free-libraries and other devices for giving people what providence did not mean them to receive, should send out pamphlets in the praise of self-embellishment. For it will place Beauty within easy reach of many who could not otherwise hope to attain it."[16]

An even more direct attack on the aesthetes and on the *vers de société* versifiers as well was made by poets who wrote in the third predominant mode of the nineties. This third mode is perhaps the most difficult to define because it both incorporates and rejects essential elements of the other two strains. In W. E. Henley and John Davidson, there is a clear antipathy toward the light and fanciful poetry of Locker-Lampson, Dobson, and others who wrote similar verse. For Henley and Davidson both the city and poetry were serious matters of concern; new forms had to be devised to capture 'the diverse energies and problems of London. In addition, although impressionistic mood pieces such as those found most commonly in the poetry of Wilde and Symons do appear in volumes by Henley and Davidson, the perverse pleasure of such languid self-preoccupations is generally sacrificed for larger social concerns.

For Henley and Davidson there were both terrible and exciting energies in the contemporary metropolis; furthermore, poetry was a sufficiently potent literary form to capture these energies. Henley's *London Voluntaries* (1892) at once describes the awesome autumnal glow of a London that takes on the appearance of a golden city of El Dorado in October as well as the wasteland desolation wrought by the grip of the "Wind-Fiend" on the wintry city. The seasonal and symphonic structure, with its alternating seasons as well as themes and variations, gives *London Voluntaries* and its creator a prophetic dimension. The enormous city is sinister and splendid, "obscene" and "the glimmer and glamour of a dream." Rather than continuing in this comprehensive vein, however, during the course of the decade Henley turned more and more toward the eighteenth-century and impressionistic strains of poetry. In editing *A London Garland* (1895), a gift book which combined engravings of contemporary artists with selected lyrics about London life, Henley shows a preference for the impressionistic strain. Several years later, Henley's *London Types* (1898) celebrated in eighteenth-century fashion the quaint and picturesque figures to be found about town.

John Davidson's poetic career took the opposite direction from Henley's. Davidson's early poems about London—"London," "A Frosty Morning," and "November"—were short impressionistic lyrics about city life. In *Fleet Street Eclogues* and in poems such as the visionary "In the Isle of Dogs" and the dramatic monologue "Thirty-Bob a Week," Davidson touched upon some of the city's pressing social problems. By this time, Davidson recognized that London was a "subtle city of a thousand moods," a lace of "mystery [and] things that count." Poetry needed to transcend the dimension of amateur versifiers. It had to be as vibrant and grand a literary medium as the city itself. In his essay "On Poetry" (1905), Davidson's conceptions of the power of poetry are idealistically high: "I know nothing so entertaining, so absorbing, so full of contentment, as the making of blank verse; it is a supreme relief of nervous tension, the fullest discharge of emotion, the greatest deliverance of energy; it satisfies the blood and the brain, the bones and the marrow."[17]

Toward the end of their careers, Henley and Davidson wrote two very different poems about the twentieth-century invader (some would say conqueror) of the urban scene—the automobile. Henley's poem, *A Song of Speed*, celebrates the new energy that man has harnessed and welcomes the expanded and quickened pace that the vehicle is likely to bring to many other dimensions of modern life. Conversely, Davidson's poem, "The Testament of Sir Simon Simplex Concerning Automobilism," condemns the invention and records the poet's fears concerning the democratic spread of goods. Although the two late poems serve as reminders of the divergent course of the two poets' careers, in comparison to the other two strains of poetry current in the nineties, Henley and Davidson are unique in the forms and materials that their poetry encompasses. The varied, numerous, and sometimes irregular verse forms employed by Henley and Davidson surpass all those used by poets such as Locker-Lampson and Symons, just as their scale and scope go beyond Sunday walks in the park or Saturday nights at the music hall.

Locker-Lampson, Dobson, and Binyon: Diminished Visions

The poetry of Locker-Lampson, Dobson, and Binyon stands for a commitment to the inevitability of the city as a way of life. These poets did not view this acceptance of the city as a "prison" sentence, but as an appealing entry into a variety of fanciful entertainments, an introduction to a world of social companionship. The city's attractions called for poetic praise. Yet none of the three poets ever felt overwhelmed by their urban subject matter. Their self-admitted task was not to record the metropolis's stories from a wide range of perspectives, but simply to record "humble," personal impressions of what features of the town appealed to them. Rarely do Locker-Lampson or Dobson touch on the more disturbing social problems of the city; when they do, they dismiss them summarily with conventional eighteenth-century sentiments that all is well and in its proper place. In many respects, however, Binyon seems closer to an Arnoldian than an eighteenth-century outlook because at times his quiet reflections on the city lead him to react unfavorably to its ugly and depressing aspects.

By his own definition, Locker-Lampson set it as his task in *London Lyrics* to write light lyrical verse that would be "short, elegant, refined, and fanciful, not seldom distinguished by chastened sentiment, and often playful." The aspect of the eighteenth-century spirit that appeals to Locker-Lampson is not that of the heroic couplet, moral epistles, satiric castigation of vice and folly, or imitation of the ancients but that which allows the poet to be self-consciously frivolous and insouciant in short lines and trimeter. Characteristically, it is almost exclusively the urbane spirit reflected through the personal delights of the poet-about-town that makes up the volume *London Lyrics*. Some of the town's delights verge on superficial and trivial pleasures indeed: feeding a bun to a bear in "The Bear Pit in the Zoological Gardens" (1865), signing a hotel registry in "A Word That Makes Us Linger" (1888), or viewing a gallery painting in "On 'A Portrait of a Lady'" (1868). Locker-Lampson's poems are not light in content, but they can be light in attitude—thereby capturing the excitement of a downtown stir. Thus, the poet's meter and verse form capture the attractive motion of a central city hub in "Piccadilly" (1856).

> Piccadilly! Shops, palaces, bustle, and breeze,
> The whirring of wheels, and the murmur of trees;
> By night or by day, whether noisy or stilly,
> Whatever my mood is, I love Piccadilly.
>
> .   .   .   .
>
> Bright days, when a stroll is my afternoon wont
> And I meet all the people I do know, or don't:
> Here is jolly old Brown, and his fair daughter Lillie—
> No wonder, young Pilgrim, you like Piccadilly![18]

Only the last stanza of "Piccadilly" seems out of place in its presumed attempt to tack on a moral in eighteenth-century fashion.

> Life is chequer'd; a patchwork of smiles and of frowns;
> We value its ups, let us muse on its downs;
> There's a side that is bright, it will then turn us t'other,
> One turn, if a good one, deserves yet another.
> These downs are delightful, these ups are not hilly,—
> Let us try one more turn ere we quit Piccadilly.   [ll. 29–34]

Such a quasi-moralistic, bittersweet coda (other poems end similarly) points to a more poignant aspect of Locker-Lampson's presentation of city life. In fact, in his own poetic declaration, "Advice to a Poet" (1883), he alludes to this intention of projecting a bittersweet attitude.

> Oh, for the Poet-Voice that swells
> To lofty truths, or noble curses—

I only wear the cap and bells,
And yet some Tears are in my verses. [ll. 57–60]

In a few of the more substantial poems in the volume, Locker-Lampson
touches on the more significant features of the city. "Rotten Row" (1867)
loosely parallels the poet's own aging with the maturation of civilized
man. Realizing that mankind can never return to the nostalgic state of an
idyllic countryside—"I'd like the country if I could"—the poet appreci-
ates the solace that a city park in springtime offers. The fashionable people
create an atmosphere of urbanity that is as reassuring as sheep grazing
peacefully on a misty meadow. Yet even though he suppresses the ten-
dency to make a nostalgic return to an idyll, he rounds off the poem with a
note of subdued personal melancholy.

A lively scene on turf and road;
The crowd is bravely drest:
The *Ladies' Mile* has overflow'd,
The chairs are in request:
The nimble air, so soft, so clear,
Can hardly stir a ringlet here.

.   .   .   .   .   .

Ah, no—I'll linger here awhile,
And dream of days of yore;
For me bright eyes have lost the smile,
The sunny smile they wore:—
Perhaps they say, what I'll allow,
That I'm not quite so handsome now. [ll. 7–12, 43–48]

A reverent nostalgia for the city's past geniuses is combined with an ap-
preciation of the fashionable present in the poet's perception of St. James's
Street in a poem of the same name. The street has a "classic fame" and all
educated men recall the past days when men and women of genius and
flare walked its flagstones.

At dusk, when I am strolling there,
Dim forms will rise around me;
Lepel flits past me in her chair,
And Congreve's airs astound me!
And once Nell Gwynne, a frail young Sprite,
Look'd kindly when I met her;
I shook my head, perhaps,—but quite
Forgot to quite forget her. [ll. 25–32]

In the present, the street is "rich, and gay, and clever" in its fashions, but some of the old glory has faded.

> Now gilded youth loves cutty pipes,
> And slang that's rather *scaring*;
> It can't approach its prototypes
> In taste, or tone, or bearing.   [ll. 37–40]

In the penultimate stanza—which later required a footnote apology to the American people—Locker-Lampson seems to invest little hope in the future.

> Worse times may come. *Bon ton*, indeed,
> Will then be quite forgotten,
> And all we much revere will speed
> From ripe to worse than rotten:
> Let grass then sprout between yon stones,
> And owls then roost at Boodle's,
> For Echo will hurl back the tones
> Of screaming *Yankee Doodles*.   [ll. 49–56]

Locker-Lampson's essential outlook in "St. James's Street" (1867) is a reverence for the past and the elegance of the eighteenth century. He is not interested in looking at the present—and much less the future—developments in the city. In fact, in only two poems in the volume does Locker-Lampson even remotely demonstrate an awareness of poverty or other social problems that plagued nineteenth-century London. In "The Old Stonemason" (1874) a sad picture of an old man and a child is presented as the two outcasts share a meagre lunch on "the stately palace steps." The juxtaposition of the ragged, huddled figures upon the grand staircase moves Locker-Lampson enough for him to comment that "all made / A most pathetic sight." Yet the concluding stanza seems to affirm the essentially eighteenth-century notion that Providence will somehow provide.

> We had sought shelter from the storm,
> And saw this lowly Pair,—
> But none could see a Shining Form
> That watch'd beside them there.   [ll. 17–20]

The poem in which Locker-Lampson appears most ill at ease in London surroundings is "Beggars" (1865). Much to his distress, beggars haunt him in his comings and goings to the London theater. Raymond Williams's comments on the urban masses apply to this poem as they have to other poetic responses; Locker-Lampson sees the beggars as an indistinguishable group, not as individuals. He almost exclusively stresses their troublesome, physical movements. Thus, a full person is not seen, but instead a grasping, greedily extended hand. Notice how in these descriptions, the two beggars, one male and the other female, intrude on the poet's insular, private world.

> I am pacing the Mall in a rapt reverie,
> I am thinking if Sophy is thinking of me,
> When I'm roused by a ragged and shivering wretch,
> Who seems to be well on his way to Jack Ketch.
> He has got a bad face, and a shocking bad hat;
> A comb in his fist, and he sees I'm a flat
>
> . . . .
>
> He eyes my gold chain, as if greedy to crib it;
> He looks just as if he'd been blown from a gibbet.
>
> . . . .
>
> As I stroll from the club, and am deep in a strophè
> That rolls upon all that's delightful in Sophy,
> I'm humbly addressed by an "object" unnerving,
> So tatter'd a wretch must be "highly deserving."
> She begs,—I am touch'd, but I've great circumspection;
> I stifle remorse with the soothing reflection
> That cases of vice are by no means a rarity—
> The worst vice of all's indiscriminate charity.
>
> [ll. 1–6, 9–10, 13–20]

The poem ends on a confused note as Locker-Lampson feels some compassion for the beggars even though their physical appearance on the London scene deeply offends his genteel sensibilities.

> "Hopgarten protests they've no feeling, and so
> It was only their *muscular movement*, you know!"
> Thinks I (when I've said *au revoir*, and depart—
> A Comb in my pocket, a Weight—at my heart),
> And when wretched Mendicants writhe, there's a notion
> That begging is only their "muscular motion."   [ll. 39–44]

Like Locker-Lampson, Austin Dobson both celebrated the attractive pleasures of town life and condemned some of its deficiencies in his poetry. In "On London Stones" (1876) he consciously rejects the notion that residence in a rural setting is a prerequisite for the writing of good poetry.

> On London stones I sometimes sigh
> For wider green and bluer sky;—
> Too oft the trembling note is drowned
> In this huge city's varied sound;—
> 'Pure song is country born'—I cry.
>
> .   .   .   .
>
> In vain!—the woods, the fields deny
> That clearer strain I fain would try;
> Mine is an urban Muse, and bound
> By some strange law to paven ground;
> Abroad she pouts,—she is not shy
>   On London stones! [19]

In "To a Pastoral Poet," Dobson admits that he can take pleasure in pastoral poetry but he is careful to keep it in perspective; as an urbane realist, he recognizes that such idyllic retreats are no longer attainable for him.

> Among my best I put your Book,
> O Poet of the breeze and brook!
> (That breeze and brook which blows and falls
> More soft to those in city walls)
>
> .   .   .   .
>
> Then I shall take your Book, and dream
> I lie beside some haunted stream;
> And watch the crisping waves that pass,
> And watch the flicker in the grass;
> And wait—and wait—and wait to see
> The Nymph . . . that never comes to me!   {ll. 1–4, 13–18}

Several poems in Dobson's *Vers de Société* celebrate urban ingenuity or mildly protest the city's heat and clamor. In "A City Flower" (1864), the poet's spirit seems dejected by the day's turmoil—"To and fro in the City I go, / Tired of the ceaseless ebb and flow, / Sick of the crowded mart"—{ll. 1–3} but he is soon revived by the plants that he personally nurtures on his "window-sill" amidst the city's bricks and mortar. In "In Town" (1876) Dobson makes a light, playful protest against London's summer heat and noise that blunt his creativity. He wishes for a holiday escape to the green countryside.

> There is that woman again:
> 'Strawberries! fourpence a pottle!'
> Thought gets dry in the brain;
> Ink gets dry in the bottle.

. . . . . .

Oh for the green of a lane,
Where one might lie and be lazy!
'Buzz' goes a fly in the pane;
Bluebottles drive me crazy!   [ll. 5–8, 13–16]

Dobson's most significant poems about the city were written in the first decade of the twentieth century. In these more serious poems, Dobson goes beyond Locker-Lampson's earlier light, urbane sensibility and attains a new awareness of the inescapable and unsolvable social problems in the city. In "After a Holiday" (1901) he records for the first time the side of the metropolis that inflicts hardships.

And I read—here in London town,
Of a murder done at my gate,
And a goodly ship gone down,
And of homes made desolate;

And I know, with the old sick heart,
That but for a moment's space
We may shut our sense, and part
From the pain of this tarrying-place.   [ll. 17–24]

This attention to menacing urban problems is evident in several poems of this period. "The Friend of Humanity and the Rhymer" (1907) is a dialogue in which the Friend of Humanity wants to end the conversation because he feels that the poet's only response to human suffering is easy and fanciful ditties. In a remarkable retort, however, the poet expresses his desire to show deeper concern.

FRIEND OF HUMANITY.   Nay, nay, I've done.
    I did but make petition. You make fun.
RHYMER. Stay. I am grave. Forgive me if I ramble:
    But then a negative needs some preamble
    To break the blow. I feel with you, in truth,
    These complex miseries of Age and Youth;
    I feel with you—and none can feel it more
    Than I—this burning Problem of the Poor;
    The Want that grinds, the Mystery of Pain,
    The Hearts that sink, and never rise again;—
    How shall I set this to some careless screed,
    Or jigging stave, when Help is what you need,
    Help, Help,—more Help?   [ll. 17–29]

Dobson, however, really does not know *how* poetry can ameliorate the distressing urban conditions. Two short poems, "A Waif" and "Elim," offer poignant portraits of suffering, but they end quickly as conventional or biblical solutions gloss over the problems. The "grace of God" will surely transform the boy in "A Waif" (1907).

> Ragged and starved, with shifting look, and eyes
> Too old for childhood, and too full for joy,
> How shall you guess, thro' this forlorn disguise,
> The Man you hope for, in this hopeless Boy?
> *There is no heart so cold but may be warmed;*
> *And—by the grace of God—can be transformed.*   [ll. 1–6]

In like manner, the God who freed the oppressed people of Egypt will soon save the oppressed urban poor depicted in "Elim" (1909).

> Shall we ignore
> The long Procession of the Poor,
> Still faring through the night-wind keen,
> With faltering steps, to the Unseen?—
> Nay: let us seek for these once more
> Palm-trees and wells!   [ll. 10–15]

In what was to be his final speculation on the function of the poet in modern society, Dobson contemplates possible topics for poetry in "On the Future of Poetry" (1914), and he asks the Bards of the Future

> What magic will you find to stir
> The limp and languid listener?
> Will it be daring and dramatic?
> Will it be frankly democratic?
>
> Will Pegasus return again
> In guise of modern aeroplane,
> Descending from a cloudless blue
> To drop on us a bomb or two?   [ll. 5–12]

Dobson's answer indicates the typical attitude of humility that he and Locker-Lampson always maintained—"I know not." He is willing to maintain, however, that poetry should always have as its first theme "Human Life / Its hopes and fears, its love and strife" and that it should be topical, but not degradingly so.

> I hold that they who deal in rhyme
> Must take the standpoint of the time—

But not to catch the public ear,
As mountebank or pulpiteer.   [ll. 25–28]

Another poet of the early 1890s, Laurence Binyon, had little more to say than Dobson about the future prospects of poetry. Binyon, like Dobson and Locker-Lampson, had definite poetic tastes. "Poetry," he once wrote, "is made to be known, loved, enjoyed, and the poetry which wins us with a tranquil and sure power is victorious in the end over that which thrills at first reading, and chills on the third or fourth."[20] This Arnoldian ability to reflect quietly and sensitively upon a scene or a person distinguishes Binyon's two slight volumes of poems about the city, *London Visions* (1896 and 1899). In tone and in his abhorrence of bitter ranting, Binyon follows the placid lead of Locker-Lampson and Dobson. In his perplexed awareness of the social problems and the burgeoning vastness of London, Binyon is closely akin in outlook to Dobson's attitudes later in his career. Rarely does Binyon lose sight of the specifics of the city before him, and when he does, it makes for less effective poetry because he merely asserts his own inadequacy in the face of the metropolis that man has created. An example of this uncertainty occurs in "The Golden Gallery at Saint Paul's" (1896).

The Golden Gallery lifts its aery crown
O'er dome and pinnacle: there I leaned and gazed.
Is this indeed my own familiar town,
This busy dream? Beneath me spreading hazed
In distance large it lay, nor nothing broke
Its mapped immensity.[21]

Binyon was far less confused, however, than Locker-Lampson and Dobson by London's large and disturbing aspects. In choice of subject matter and use of metrical forms, Binyon makes significant departures from those poets who remained loyal to eighteenth-century modes. In fact, Binyon is a transitional figure who anticipates the grander and more ardent poetic statements of Henley and Davidson. Although Henley was the first poet in the nineties to present the splendor and squalor of the vast city in his *London Voluntaries* (1892), Binyon is the first of the minor figures to present the contradictions of the city. Basically, the poetry of *London Visions* falls into three categories as Binyon presents specific people and scenes that show the city's ability to encompass "desolations and majesties," "distress and desire." One group of poems examines progress in the city, progress that involves both construction and destruction; a second group obliquely criticizes the city by praising storms and fogs that momentarily hide the uglier aspects of urban sprawl; and a third group concentrates on pathetic individual figures who are outcasts of urban society.

G. Robert Stange has written that no poet celebrated "the building of Victorian London [which] was one of the most splendid achievements of the English spirit."[22] Yet Binyon is at his best in poems such as "The Builders" (1908) and "The Road Menders" (1899) when he captures the human energy that builds a city from inert materials. The builders shape lifeless material and thereby create a new order under stressful conditions.

> Staggering slowly, and swaying
> Heavily at each slow foot's lift and drag,
> With tense eyes careless of the roar and throng
> That under jut and jag
> Of half-built wall and scaffold stream along,
> Six bowed men straining strong
> Bear, hardly lifted, a huge lintel stone.
> This ignorant thing and prone,
> Mere dumbness, blindly weighing,
> A brute piece of blank death, a bone
> Of the stark mountain, helpless and inert,
> Yet draws each sinew till the hot veins swell
> And sweat-drops upon hand and forehead start,
> Till with short pants the suffering heart
> Throbs to the throat, where fiercely hurt
> Crushed shoulders cannot heave; till thought and sense
> Are nerved and narrowed to one aim intense.
>
> ["The Builders," ll. 1–17]

In "The Road Menders" the rhythmical beat of the workmen's hammers makes a kind of music.

> Now, with the morning shining round them, come
> Young men, and strip their coats
> And loose the shirts about their throats,
> And lightly up their ponderous hammers lift,
> Each in his turn descending swift
> With triple strokes that answer and begin
> Duly, and quiver in repeated change,
> Marrying the eager echoes that weave in
> A music clear and strange.
>
> [ll. 35–43]

From the activity in the street the poet can make his own song by noting the universal significance of man's effort to harness the earth's materials for his use. The young workers take on the significance of Promethean figures

Charmed in the sunshine and the rhythm enthralling,
As of unwearied Fates, for ever young,
That on the anvil of necessity
From measureless desire and quivering fear,
With musical sure lifting and downfalling
Of arm and hammer driven perpetually,
Beat out in obscure span
The fiery destiny of man.   [ll. 56–63]

Binyon, however, is aware of the dual consequences of the various urban activities. Although he celebrates progress and man's shaping of the urban landscape, in "The Destroyer" (1908), Binyon reminds the reader that man's appetite to conquer his environment is insatiable and that in the process many older buildings and lifestyles are destroyed in the name of progress. Again, Binyon's poetry moves from specific description to generalized significance.

He stands on high in the torch glare,
With planted feet, with lifted axe.
Behind, a gulf of crimsoned air;
Beneath, the old wall that gapes and cracks

Tossed fragments crash to dust and smoke.
Exulting life, aloft he stands
And drives his unrepentant stroke,
Nor heeds the havoc of his hands.

.   .   .   .

Man's Demon, never satiate,
That finds nought made to its desire;
How shall it to this world be mate,—
To a world of stone, a heart of fire!   [ll. 1–8, 17–20]

A second group of poems in Binyon's *London Visions* makes thematic use of natural disturbances such as storms and fogs. Robert Bridges delighted in the snow that covered London's ugliness but berated the thoughtless "trains of sombre men, past tale of number" who spoiled the white purity of the charmed urban scene in his poem "London Snow" (1880). Binyon also delights in such momentary natural transformations of cityscape, and he obliquely adds his own quiet protest against the uglier aspects of the urban environment. In "The Storm" (1908), a brief rainstorm followed by a burst of sunlight gives a momentary uplift to the weary inhabitants of squalid rooms.

Men stop in the street to wonder. The brilliance runs,
Washing with silent waves the town opprest;

> Startles squalid rooms with a sudden smile;
> Enters gloomy courts, and glories there.
> Strange as a vision the wide expanded heavens
> Open; the living wind with nearness breathes
> On weary faces of women of many cares;
> They stand at their doors and watch with a soothed spirit
> The marvellous West asleep in endless light.   [ll. 20—28]

In "Fog" (1908) a heavy mist confounds morning traffic until it finally lifts just before noon and reveals "the dwindled stream / Of traffic in slow confusion crawling by: / The baffled hive of helpless man laid bare" (ll 17—19). In "Deptford" (1896), an encompassing mist is put to a more serious and disturbing purpose as it hides the ugly specifics of both crumbling buildings and dejected spirits.

> Alas! I welcome this dull mist, that drapes
> The path of the heavy sky above the street,
> Casting a phantom dimness on these shapes
> That pass, by toil disfeatured, with slow feet
> And sad mistrustful eyes; while in the mire
> Children a mockery of play repeat,
> Drearly to satisfy their starved desire.   [ll. 8—14]

In a similar vein the poet reminds his readers in "The Bathers" (1896) that although a group of workers may momentarily experience the joys of a holiday on the seacoast, their urban-industrialized lives are dreary indeed.

> Strange now the factory's humming wheel, the cry
> Of tireless engines, the swift-hoisted bales
> Unnumbered; strange the smell of ordered wares
> In the shop's dimness: noonday traffic fails
> Out of the wave-washed ear; stiff office stool,
> And busy hush: and like a turbid dream,
> The tavern's glittering fume insensibly
> Ebbs with the hot race and the glutted stream
> Of labour, thieving the dear sands of youth.   [ll. 22—30]

Although Binyon wrote several poems that offer oblique social criticism by juxtaposing natural transformations with social abuses, in London Visions there are many specific portraits of outcast figures: "The Rag-Picker" (1908), "The Paralytic" (1908), "The Convict" (1896), "A Woman" (1896), "To a Derelict" (1899), and "The Toy-Seller" (1899). The outcast figures are as passive as they are pathetic. To Cornelius Weygandt, these poems epitomize Binyon's strengths and limitations: "The London Visions are renderings of the picturesqueness of London, some done with the art-ist's eyes wide open, others when he is in half-dream. . . . [Binyon is] a painter of pictures in words." [23] So many of Binyon's poetic pictures of urban subjects have a still-life quality to them. Unlike Buchanan, Binyon rarely tells the life stories of the city's outcast victims; furthermore, he does not capture the stir of urban movement surrounding his street figures as fully as Henley does. Yet Binyon realizes what he is up to. He avoids a poetry of "thrills" in favor of a poetry of "tranquil and sure power" that could be "loved [and] enjoyed." The effect conveyed by Binyon's picture-book presentations of social outcasts is that there is no remedy for the pas-sive, beaten-down figures. Thus, the paralytic can only shake his head at the world in dismay.

> He stands where the young faces pass and throng;
> His blank eyes tremble in the noonday sun:
> He sees all life, the lovely and the strong,
> Before him run.
>
> Eager and swift, or grouped and loitering, they
> Follow their dreams, on busy errands sped,
> Planning delight and triumph; but all day
> He shakes his head.   [ll. 1–8]

Similarly, the reader has a difficult time focusing his pity for the rag-picker because the figure is presented in the manner of nebulous passivity.

> Husk of manhood, mere
> Shrivel of his kind!—
> In a bloodless mask
> How the old eyes peer,
> With no light behind!—
> Mate of his mean task.   [ll. 19–24]

In "To a Derelict" (1899) Binyon surely expresses an ironic wish that the spectral tramp would vanish from the city; the irony backfires, however, because the poet advances no other solution for the social problem in the poem.

> O hide thyself beneath the ground!
> Trouble not our sunshine longer, lest we see
> Too clearly inscribed on thee
> All that we fear to be.
>
> What dost thou with the sun?
> Long since thy race was run.

What spectral task employs
Thy hands? . . .   [ll. 11–18]

In only two poems does Binyon attempt to relate the plight of the social
outcasts to larger social and universal statements. In "In the British Mu-
seum" (1908), Binyon goes beyond externalities to convey a poor woman's
feelings of indifference in the vast cultural storehouse.

Hither a poor woman, with sad eyes, came,
And vacantly looked around. The faces vast,
Their strange motionless features, touched with flame,
Awed her: in humble wonder she hurried past;

And shyly beneath a sombre monument sought
Obscurity; into the darkest shade she crept
And rested: soon, diverted awhile, her thought
Returned to its own trouble. At last she slept.   [ll. 9–16]

The sleeping woman dreams that the immense statues "heard her sorrow,
with ears prepared" (l. 24). Dream soon turns to nightmare as the old
woman realizes the indifference of the "civilized" city and she prepares to
return to the dreary squalor of her tenement lodging. This mode of vi-
sion—what one contemporary reviewer of *London Visions* referred to as
Binyon's "easy habit of dignifying the commonest particulars, and carry-
ing them back to a lofty universal"—is also evident in "Trafalgar Square"
(1899).[24] Here, at another London landmark, a poor woman on the point
of despair attains a sustaining and uplifting vision amidst the "dark stat-
ues and dumb fountains" of one of London's busiest intersections. The
square attracts indigents who are admittedly uneasy and dissatisfied with
society. Characteristically, Binyon focuses on one figure in the scene.

They that all night, dozing disquieted,
Huddled together on the benches cold,
Now shrank apart, distrustful and unfed,
And by the growing radiance unconsoled.

Then one, a woman, silently arose,
And came to the broad fountain, brimming cool,
And over the stone margin leaning close,
Dipped hands and bathed her forehead in the pool.   [ll. 5–12]

The fountain takes on the mystical significance of a religious shrine as its
transforming power works a miracle.

She, the rejected, had no more disgrace:
Her opening heart drew in a different truth.

. . . .

And in her spirit a still fountain springs
Deeper than hunger, faith crying for life,
That to her eyes an inward clearness brings,
And to her heart courage for any strife.   [ll. 31–32, 53–56]

Thus, the poem ends on a note of active but ineffectual resolve. That Binyon believes in the transforming vision amidst one of the most public settings in London is unquestionable. Yet he is silent concerning what specific social solutions will transform the miserable plight of the woman and the other unfortunates who share a park bench for the night's lodging. So although Binyon takes in more of London's diverse social scene than Locker-Lampson and Dobson did, he too allays his feelings of uneasiness and perplexity by dissolving them into hazy or easy resolutions. The mode of light verse practiced by these poets will not handle the larger and troubling implications of the city.

Wilde and Symons: The Cult of Artifice and Impressionism

If Binyon and Dobson at times evoked pity for isolated, miserable people, Wilde and Symons in Baudelairean fashion evoked beauty from the sordid lives of similar figures in the city. Whereas Binyon condemned the poetry of "thrills . . . too dangerously personal" that "dazzle and astonish" the reader's sensibilities and praised instead "the poetry which wins us with tranquil and sure power," Wilde and Symons were both influenced by Baudelaire's revolutionary conceptions of an urban poetry of beauty. It is well known that Baudelaire maintained that the qualities of beauty to be stressed were strangeness and shock. Or as he wrote in an unfinished poem intended for the second edition of *Les Fleurs du mal*:

Car j'ai de chaque chose extrait la quintessence,
Tu m'as donne ta boue et j'en ai fait de l'or.

(From each thing I gathered its quintessence,
You gave me your mire, and I turned it into gold.)[25]

Enid Starkie explains the implications of Baudelaire's revolutionary urban aesthetic: "Baudelaire was the first to see the beauty of the teeming modern city, to see beauty also in the dim little lives of those who inhabited these vast conglomerations. . . . Beauty for him did not lie in the subject itself but in what the artist brought to it. Beauty was the flame of the fire, the radiance of the energy, generated by the spiritual shock he received when he was moved and this spiritual shock could come from aspects hitherto considered ugly. He did not . . . see beauty in ugliness; he only said that from ugliness he could distil beauty."[26] Excerpts from two of Baudelaire's poems demonstrate how the poet could distil beauty from the raw materials of urban settings and sufferers. Whereas Binyon's presentations of the city's beggars rarely go beyond the picturesque, Baudelaire takes a vibrant and shocking interest in such figures.

> Little white girl with red hair,
> The holes in your frock
> Show poverty
> And beauty,
>
> For me, a poor poet,
> Your young and ailing body,
> Spotted with freckles,
> Has its sweetness.
>
> .   .   .   .   .
>
> In place of stockings in holes,
> May a dagger of gold
> Glitter for the eyes of rakes
> On your leg;
>
> May barely fastened knots
> Reveal for our sinning
> Your lovely breasts, radiant
> As two eyes.   ["To a Red-Haired Beggar Girl," ll. 1–8, 17–24]

> Now is the graceful evening, friend of the criminal;
> Now it comes like an accomplice, stealthily; the sky
> Closes slowly like a gigantic bedroom,
> And Man, impatient, changes to wild beast.
>
> .   .   .   .
>
> Across those lights the wind tortures
> Prostitution is ignited in the streets;
>
> .   .   .   .
>
> Here and there one hears kitchens hissing,
> The screaming of theatres and orchestras roaring;
> The plain tables, where gambling throws its pleasures,
> Fill up with bawds and cheats, accomplices,
> And thieves, who know no truce nor grace,
>
> .   .   .   .

Reflect, O my soul, in this most solemn time,
And close your ears to this roar.
It is the hour when the sorrows of the ill are sharpened.
Dark Night grips them by the throat; they fulfil
Their fate and move into the common whirlpool;
The hospitals are full of their sighing.—More than one
Will no more come back to seek the perfumed soup,
Beside the fire, at night, by a beloved soul.[27]
["Evening Twilight," ll. 1–4, 14–15, 21–25, 29–36]

The turn in "Evening Twilight" is remarkable: from a seemingly enjoyable immersion in the sinful sensations and criminal thrills of the city by night, Baudelaire withdraws to a spiritual retreat—"O my soul"—in which he contemplates the unjust sufferings of the ill and downcast victims of urban society. This perspective is what distinguishes the poetry of Baudelaire from that of Wilde and Symons. Rarely do Wilde and Symons even mention social or moral abuses in their impressionistic poems about the city because they choose to confine their observations to the shocking and exquisite thrills the city offers, especially at night. Wilde and Symons transmuted urban materials into beauty by emphasizing their artificial qualities; Baudelaire's transmutations had these qualities but had spiritual and social dimensions as well.

Poems like Wilde's "Symphony in Yellow" (1889) and "Impression du Matin" (1881) are strictly impressionistic pieces which show the poet's transforming powers of imagination at work on the city's materials and settings. "Symphony in Yellow" falls far short of attaining any intricate movements not only because of its brevity, but also because of its predominant and distracting use of similes. Although a unified tone of subdued color is sustained throughout the poem, the techniques are too direct and obvious. The poet's imaginative process is too blatant and heavy-handed. Observing an urban sight the poet immediately compares it to a rich poetic image and carefully manipulates the reader's impressions of the city.

An omnibus across the bridge
Crawls like a yellow butterfly,
And, here and there, a passer-by
Shows like a little restless midge.

Big barges full of yellow hay
Are moored against the shadowy wharf,
And, like a yellow silken scarf,
The thick fog hangs along the quay.[28]

The ultimate and most unconvincing transmutation occurs in the last two lines of the poem as "the pale green Thames" becomes "a rod of rippled jade." By linking London with exotic Oriental gems, the poet makes the more disquieting aspects of the city magically disappear. In this poem, the city is not the people or social problems (people appear as ant-size specks in lines 3–4), but a mood evoked in the poet's mind and expressed in a musical painting.

In "Impression du Matin," Wilde captures the city in another mood of delicate and shadowy unreality. In the hours just before dawn, the city appears to be a Whistlerian scene of harmonious and shrouded stillness.

> The Thames nocturne of blue and gold
> Changed to a Harmony in gray:
> A barge with ochre-colored hay
> Dropt from the wharf: and chill and cold
>
> The yellow fog came creeping down
> The bridges, till the houses' walls
> Seemed changed to shadows, and St. Paul's
> Loomed like a bubble o'er the town.   [ll. 1–8]

A turn occurs in the poem, however, in the final two stanzas. The poet's attention turns away from the "waking life" of the streets, complete with "country wagons" and "a bird," to focus on the lurid and languorous attraction of a prostitute beneath a gas street lamp. By devoting the last stanza to the prostitute, Wilde records both his fascination and ambivalence toward a common urban problem.

> But one pale woman all alone,
> The daylight kissing her wan hair,
> Loitered beneath the gas lamps' flare,
> With lips of flame and heart of stone.   [ll. 13–16]

Wilde uses the theme of prostitution again in "The Harlot's House" (1885). Here Wilde unabashedly celebrates the cult of artifice and employs the motif of the arabesque in its structure and content. The longest section of the poem consists of a description of the intricate but artificial dance movements that occur inside the harlot's house. Wilde is toeing a delicate line in this poem because he must balance mechanical grotesqueness with alluring strangeness. In the best tradition of Edgar Allan Poe, Wilde succeeds because the artificial rituals of the dance always take on the elusive and shadowy dimensions of mysterious strangeness.

> Like strange mechanical grotesques,
> Making fantastic arabesques,

The shadows raced across the blind.
We watched the ghostly dancers spin
To sound of horn and violin,
Like black leaves wheeling in the wind.

Like wire-pulled automatons,
Slim silhouetted skeletons
Went sidling through the slow quadrille,
They took each other by the hand,
And danced a stately saraband;
Their laughter echoed thin and shrill.   [ll. 7–18]

A pair of lovers who "loiter down the moonlit street" watch this revelry
and indulgence in the artificial pleasures of the city. In a dilemma remi-
niscent of the one that beset the hero in Clough's *Dipsychus*, the couple's
attitudes toward the infamous palace of sweet sin are diametrically op-
posed. The gentleman escort sees the harlot's house as a place of death and
damnation: "The dead are dancing with the dead, / The dust is whirling
with the dust" (ll. 26–27). The woman finds the music and dancing irre-
sistibly attractive, and she joins the revelers inside. The poem ends on a
note of amoral ambiguity. For the gentleman outside, the lively vision
deteriorates.

Then suddenly the tune went false,
The dancers wearied of the waltz,
The shadows ceased to wheel and whirl.   [ll. 31–33]

That deterioration, however, may be due to his own dullness in refusing
to enter the Palace of Artifice. Characteristically Wilde concludes the
poem with no moral resolution or social condemnation. Through artifice,
squalor is approached but not judged.

Deliberate intention and awareness of artistic purpose also mark Arthur
Symons's three volumes about the diurnal and nocturnal moods of the
city—*Days and Nights* (1889), *Silhouettes* (1892), and *London Nights*
(1895). To insure that his audiences understood his artistic purposes,
Symons prefaced all three volumes with either a prologue poem or a short
prose introduction (if not always in the first, then in the second edition).
Yet, as with so many artists, there are often contradictions between Sy-
mons's critical pronouncements and his poetic statements.

In the "Prologue" (1887) poem to his first volume, *Days and Nights*,
Symons concedes that Tennyson's "Palace of Art" has properly been brought
down from "some far peak" to the center of the modern metropolis. Art
seekers should

> go where cities pour
> Their turbid human stream through street and mart,
> A dark stream flowing onward evermore
> Down to an unknown ocean;—there is Art.
>
> She stands amidst the tumult, and is calm;
> She reads the hearts self-closed against the light;
> She probes an ancient wound, yet brings no balm;
> She is ruthless, yet she doeth all things right.[29]

There are two striking implications of this pronouncement: that Art "doeth all things right" and that she "brings no balm." Here is the combined arrogance and humility of the nineties aesthetes; they will write poetry that exquisitely captures transient moments, that refines material to the most intense refinement even while realizing that their task is very limited in scope and will bring no solutions to humanity's sufferings. This is not to say that Symons was indifferent to the disturbing social problems of London. Like most lyric poets, Symons rarely provides the full details of a prostitute's or a derelict's life; however, his volumes reflect his sympathetic willingness to make them subjects of poetry—on his own terms.

Although Symons's fullest social commentary on urban squalor appears in his sequence of prose essays, *London: A Book of Aspects* (1908), a wider social focus is evident in at least two poems in the *Days and Nights* volume—"A Café-Singer" (1884) and "The Street-Singer" (1888). Melodramatically grim pictures of the hard lot of the urban poor are apparent in these poems which do not exactly fit the odd collection of diverse impressions of *Days and Nights*. In an essay Symons wrote that the "ideal of Decadence [was] to fix the last fine shade, the quintessence of things; to fix it fleetingly; to be a disembodied voice, and yet the voice of a human soul."[30] In many of Symons's impressionistic poems, the emphasis falls heavily on the "disembodied voice" of a singer or the exciting dance steps of a performer in a café or music hall while the "human soul" or certainly the social plight of the performer is overlooked. "A Café-Singer" is exceptional not only because it blends dialogue with description but because it goes beyond the café and music hall to focus on the suffering of a singer's dying child at home.

> —Mother, I cannot breathe: the room swims, stifles me;
> Give me a little air!
> O that the night were over! Good God, let me see
> Another sunrise there!
>
> Mother, you will not go—to-night—to dance and sing?
> Oh, I must have you by.

They will not mind, mother: it is a little thing.
Do, wait until I die.

—Child, do you think they care, *they* care, if the heart breaks,
Unless the voice breaks too?
Do you think they'd lose one laugh one minute for our sakes,
Because of me and you?

My girl, it breaks my heart. Good-bye. I go. They wait.
These spangles—are they right?
Stay, one more dab of rouge. And if I·come too late,
Good-bye, my dear, good-night.   [ll. 1–16]

In the second poem, "The Street-Singer," Symons presents the plight of a waif who wanders through the maze of London's streets. In this poem Symons moves beyond the sentimental and overstrained pathos of "A Café-Singer" to an attitude of urbane, nearly cynical sophistication. He juxtaposes the suffering of the street singer with the ironical sneering of a rich onlooker comfortably secure in his home. The insult of urban indifference is added to the injury of social oppression.

From side to side she looks with eyes that grope,
Feverishly hungering in a hopeless hope,
For pence that will not come; and pence mean rest,
The rest that pain may steal at night from sleep,
The rest that hunger gives when satisfied;
Her fingers twitch to handle them; she sings
Shriller; her eyes, too hot with tears to weep,
Fasten upon a window, where, inside,
A sweet voice mocks her with its carollings.   [ll. 6–14]

Although the two poems about impoverished singers are interesting, they are untypical. In *Days and Nights* Symons practices imagistic exercises. Sometimes in his effort to record fleeting impressions he wanders astray—as in the two-poem sequence "Wood Notes. A Pastoral Interlude" (1884–85). Yet in the best poems in the volume he holds true to his intent to fashion art out of urban materials. A short passage from "A Winter Night" (1886) serves as a good illustration.

The dim wet pavement lit irregularly
With shimmering streaks of gaslight, faint and frayed,
Shone luminous green where sheets of glass displayed
Long breadths of faded blinds mechanically.   [ll. 5–8]

In the preface to the second edition of *Silhouettes*, Symons wrote, in defense of what he had done, that he claimed "only an equal liberty for the rendering of every mood of that variable and inexplicable and contradictory creature which we call ourselves, of every aspect under which we are gifted or condemned to apprehend the beauty and strangeness and curiosity of the visible world."[31] In the phrase "gifted or condemned to apprehend," Symons echoes Pater's conclusion to *The Renaissance*; in the association of "beauty" with "strangeness and curiosity," Symons clearly echoes Baudelaire. The two strains—Paterian and Baudelairean—combine and interact to enrich the significance and sophistication of *Silhouettes*. G. Robert Stange sees an important development between Symons's first and second volumes of poetry: "His achievement as a poet of the city involved a larger and more coherent use of his material. He becomes increasingly able to give the scattered facts of the city a metaphoric significance. . . . The poet progresses from an assembling of the diverse images of city life to poetic situations which are modified or even created by the ambient city."[32] Thus, in a poem like "Nocturne" (1889) a new dimension of pleasurable enjoyment and comforting escape are found in London after dark. Contrary to James Thomson's depiction of nighttime in the city as a burdensome oppression of cares and woes, Symons sees in the night's fleeting impressions a time of carefree enjoyment and release into a magical world that is the opposite of the mundane activities of the city by day.

> One little cab to hold us two,
> Night, an invisible dome of cloud,
> The rattling wheels that made our whispers loud,
> As heart-beats into whispers grew;
> And, long, the Embankment with its lights,
> The pavement glittering with fallen rain,
> The magic and mystery that is night's,
> And human love without the pain.
>
> The river shook with wavering gleams,
> Deep buried as the glooms that lay,
> Impenetrable as the grave of day,
> Near and as distant as our dreams.
> A bright train flashed with all its squares
> Of warm light where the bridge lay mistily.
> The night was all about us: we were free,
> Free of the day and all its cares![33]

These stanzas—with their emphasis on mystery and adventure amidst the glittering artificiality of night—constitute the Baudelairean strain. The

Paterian strain usually asserts itself as the transient nature of the experience is painfully recognized. The city's pleasures are fleeting.

> That was an hour of bliss too long,
> Too long to last where joy is brief.
> Yet one escape of souls may yield relief
> To many weary seasons' wrong.
> 'O last for ever!' my heart cried;
> It ended: heaven was done.
> I had been dreaming by her side
> That heaven was but begun.   [ll. 17–24]

The poem, then, underscores the transient security of the city. All the qualities that Blake hoped would flourish in the city—love, magic, mystery, warmth, freedom—are present in Symons's poem, but only fleetingly. Here an insulated society of two is presented and the bond is temporary at best. Throughout the volume Symons presents such fragile moods—emotional states of experience that are strangely magical and beautiful but always impermanent.

Other poems in *Silhouettes* lightly record the delight of the experience of living in London. Despite the heavy preference for the artificial expressed in the preface to the second edition, both natural and artificial settings serve as sources of pleasure in the collection of poems. All the doubts and reflections about nineteenth-century urban existence that populated Arnold's park are absent from Symons's "In Kensington Gardens" (1892), not because the problems have disappeared but because they would be disruptive to the mood.

> Under the pink and white,
> Love in her eyes alight:
> Love and the Spring and Kensington Gardens—
> Hey for the heart's delight!   [ll. 5–8]

Nature can also provide magical moods at night, as in "April Midnight" (1892).

> Good it is to be here together,
> Good to be roaming,
> Even in London, even at midnight,
> Lover-like in a lover's gloaming.
>
> You the dancer and I the dreamer,
> Children together,

> Wandering lost in the night of London,
> In the miraculous April weather. [ll. 13–20]

Nature and artifice *are* balanced in the volume. For every poem that celebrates the scent of a spring blossom, there is a corresponding one that celebrates the scent of exotic perfume. For example, on the page facing "In Kensington Gardens" appears the poem "Perfume" (1891).

In *London Nights* Symons narrowed the focus of his poetry even more by eliminating all pastoral or natural interludes in order to focus exclusively on random encounters with street soubrettes and stage girls. Poem after poem nonchalantly celebrates the momentary bliss of the one-night stand and each brief affair has its special pleasures, though the total effect of the volume is that Symons "projects a bizarre sense of the color, the harshness, the almost brutal artificiality of London and Paris at the end of the century."[34] "To One in Alienation" (1892), for example, captures the contrasting rage and shame felt by two lovers of the same woman. The poem is divided into two sections. In the first and longer section, the constant lover of the prostitute tells of his anger at the woman's decision to take on a new customer for the night. The new customer in turn speaks in the second section of the poem and records the incurable shame he feels. All three figures are totally alienated from any sort of normal human relationships. Insane and ineffectual rage overcomes the first lover as he helplessly lies awake in bed, "Cursing a sleepless brain that would but scrawl / Your image on the aching wall."[35] The prostitute herself is unable to give or receive love, and the first lover cruelly but accurately states that she is merely looked upon as "a half-forgotten point of view." The prostitute's client also suffers mental anguish that amounts to "a solitude of shame."

Symons's treatment of prostitution differs from that found in mid-century poetry. Whereas Clough, Smith, Buchanan, and others attacked prostitution as a social evil and a distressing urban problem, Symons explored the devastating effects on individual psyches. The internalization is not only psychological but literal as well. Prostitutes in mid-century poetry are usually seen walking the streets. Symons removed them from public view and made the setting in his poem a "little bedroom painted red" in a squalid garret. It is this specificity of urban imagery (often inside a sordid room or in a cheap hotel) which paves the way for T. S. Eliot's presentation of the degradation of urban living. The arrangement of the "dingy urban imagery" in a poem such as "White Heliotrope" (1893) even sounds like Eliot.[36]

> The feverish room and that white bed,
> The tumbled skirts upon a chair,

The novel flung half-open, where
Hat, hair-pins, puffs, and paints, are spread;

The mirror that has sucked your face
Into its secret deep of deeps,
And there mysteriously keeps
Forgotten memories of grace.   [ll. 1–8]

Yet Symons never puts his poetic images together as deliberately as Eliot. The majority of poems in *London Nights* simply present the shocking details of pleasurable nights of indulgence, "the savour of forbidden things," as one line would have it. The vignettes are shocking enough indeed: "Magnificat" (1895) praises God "who wrought for you and me / Your subtle body made for love" (ll. 1–2), while "Bianca" (1894) presents "drowsing heats of sense" and "aches in the hotness of her mouth" (ll. 6, 15). Another set of poems is called "Variations Upon Love" (1893). The use of a musical structure recurs here and in other poems of the nineties; this particular mode is yet another development that is relevant to the way Eliot would present the city. Many of Symons's lines are intentionally provocative: "One night's enough for love to have met and parted" and "I know your lips are bought like any fruit" (ll. 8, 29).

Critics responded censoriously to *London Nights* not because of Symons's presentation of urban material but because of his nonchalant attitude toward the seamier sides of the urban experience. The volume was attacked for its immorality. *The National Observer*, for example, cited the collection's "dreary indecencies" and stated its firm intention of not "wasting many words over a most disagreeable volume."[37] Symons countered the attacks of some of his critics— he noted that the volume had been received with "a singular unanimity of abuse"—in a preface to the second edition. In that preface Symons insists on his individual right as an artist to render the complex range of man's moods, which inevitably includes the passion and desire of the senses. After reiterating the Wildean dictum that it is a serious mistake to confuse moral and artistic judgments, Symons concludes his essay with a Paterian appeal: "I do not profess that any poem in this book is the record of actual fact; I declare that every poem is the sincere attempt to render a particular mood which has once been mine, and to render it as if, for the moment, there were no other mood for me in the world. I have rendered, well or ill, many moods, and without disguise or preference."[38]

Although Symons's artistic declaration of the individual independence of the artist is adamant in the *London Nights* preface, it is only in reading Symons's prose that one detects any hints that his social experience of Lon-

don is actually comprehensive and disturbing. Symons's six impression-
istic essays in prose are reflections on the various dimensions of the London
experience and form the slim volume *London: A Book of Aspects* (1908).[39]
This collection of integrated prose commentaries not only shows a Symons
who was able to move beyond the private moods of a man to the public
moods of a city, but it also is structurally similar to the way that Henley,
Davidson, and Eliot present the city—the device of organizing a serious
poetic statement around the movements of a symphony or the changes of
the seasons.

Henley and Davidson: London's Energies

Henley himself was overly modest in estimating that in his *London Volun-
taries* (1893) he discerned "some possibilities of London as material for
verse that may have some chance of living." Symons more accurately
sensed the importance of the poet's new achievement when he proclaimed
that "Here, at last, is a poet who can so enlarge the limits of his verse as to
take in London." Symons's proclamation suggests two questions: how ex-
actly did Henley enlarge the limits of verse? And, what aspects of London
did he treat in his poetry?

Some modern critics have seconded and elaborated Symons's assessment
of Henley's achievement. Jerome Hamilton Buckley, for example, main-
tains that "no poet before Henley had viewed the city as other than an
inanimate background for the multitudinous life it harbored; none had
concerned himself, like the Dickens of *Bleak House* and *Great Expectations*,
with the actual personality of London, with the place-spirit that brooded
over its wharves and warehouses, its cathedrals and courts of chancery.
Comparable in effect to Baudelaire's impressionistic *Tableaux parisiens*, the
Voluntaries first adapted English verse to the depiction of the metropolis
as a great organism throbbing with its own vitality. Whereas previous
London verse had served to tell the story of Londoners, Henley's poems
forsook all narrative or satiric purpose in order to create an atmosphere."[40]
This statement is important for understanding *London Voluntaries*. Henley's
sequence of five poetic sections is not dramatic, narrative, or satiric, but
essentially descriptive. In his attempt to capture London's many moods,
Henley intermingles nature and art. The overarching structure of *London
Voluntaries* is at once that of a symphony and a mural. Musical directions
such as *grave* and *andante con moto* are provided at the head of each section,
and the poet's eye moves about the city from the Thames Embankment to

Trafalgar Square. The blend of painting and music evident in the entire poem's structure also appears within sections as specific sights and sounds of London are depicted with the greatest detail. At yet another level, the poem depends on an intermingling of nature and art. The four seasons of the year are rendered as the various sections of the poem unfold (summer-spring cycle) and the poet's experience encompasses the specific attributes of trees as well as buildings. Finally, with neither bitterness nor excessive optimism, Henley demonstrates his acceptance of the squalid and splendid aspects of the London metropolis.

Although section 1 is the briefest of the five sections of *London Voluntaries*, it immediately establishes the diverse but balanced response to the city evident throughout the poem. The city is both tradition and immediate impression; it is composed of buildings as well as people. The city's buildings and its people are, in different senses, participants in nature's cycle.

> St. Margaret's bells,
> Quiring their innocent, old-world canticles,
> Sing in the storied air,
> All rosy-and-golden, as with memories
> Of woods at evensong, and sands and seas
> Disconsolate for that night is nigh.[41]

From generation to generation, a city's cultural traditions and artifacts are renewed, as is human love. Social relationships in the city will continue to be bonded by ties of love even though individuals will die and be replaced within the social community.

> The sober Sabbath stir—
> Leisurely voices, desultory feet!—
> Comes from the dry, dust-coloured street,
> Where in their summer frocks the girls go by,
> And sweethearts lean and loiter and confer,
> Just as they did an hundred years ago,
> Just as an hundred years to come they will:—
> When you and I, Dear Love, lie lost and low.　　[sec. 1. ll. 17–24]

Section 2 of *London Voluntaries* shows Henley's commitment to strenuous action. The poet will not record his impressions of the city from the vantage point of a chair in a café or music hall but from the saddle of a fast horse as he rides swiftly through London at night with his love.

> Forth from the dust and din,
> The crush, the heat, the many-spotted glare,
> The odour and sense of life and lust aflare,
> The wrangle and jangle of unrests,
> Let us take horse, Dear Heart, take horse and win
>
> .   .   .   .
>
> Through street and square, through square and street,
> Each with his home-grown quality of dark
> And violated silence, loud and fleet,
> Waylaid by a merry ghost at every lamp,
> The hansom whirls and plunges, Hark, O, hark!
>
> > [sec. 2. ll. 1–5, 21 25]

Section 2 is replete with such exclamatory expressions as "Hark, O, hark!" "And lo!" "And look, O, look!" and "Did you hear?" as the poet and his love savor the sensations of the city in the early morning hours. Whereas Symons would recommend strenuous lovemaking in a secluded room or the various artificial entertainments about town for this time of night, Henley enthusiastically stands by his recommendation of a brisk tour in a hansom pulled by a swift horse.[42] Symons's figures find delight in love and artifice; Henley's couple share the wonders that they encounter in their wanderings about the real city. In Henley's verse, transforming powers of imagination work upon the world of nature (trees and sky) as well as that built by man (streets and ships).

> At night this City of Trees
> Turns to a tryst of vague and strange
> And monstrous Majesties,
> Let loose from some dim underworld to range
> These terrene vistas till their twilight sets:
> When, dispossessed of wonderfulness, they stand
> Beggared and common, plain to all the land
> For stooks of leaves! And lo! the Wizard Hour,
> His silent, shining sorcery winged with power!
> Still, still the streets, between their carcanets
> Of linking gold, are avenues of sleep.
> But see how gable ends and parapets
> In gradual beauty and significance
> Emerge!
>
> .   .   .   .
>
> The smell of ships (that earnest of romance),
> A sense of space and water, and thereby

A lamplit bridge touching the troubled sky,
And look, O, look! a tangle of silver gleams
And dusky lights, our River and all his dreams,
His dreams that never save in our deaths can die.

[sec. 2. ll. 34–47, 57–62]

In section 3 of *London Voluntaries*, Wordsworth's childhood vision of "golden cities ten months' journey deep / Among Tartarian wilds" is presented as a dream come true. The "enchanted lustrousness" and "mellow magic" of a golden October afternoon transform "London Town" into a comforting place for all to live.

Lo! the round sun, half-down the western slope—
Seen as along an unglazed telescope—
Lingers and lolls, loth to be done with day:
Gifting the long, lean, lanky street
And its abounding confluences of being
With aspects generous and bland;

.   .   .   .

And the high majesty of Paul's
Uplifts a voice of living light, and calls—
Calls to his millions to behold and see
How goodly this his London Town can be!
For earth and sky and air
Are golden everywhere,
And golden with a gold so suave and fine
The looking on it lifts the heart like wine.
Trafalgar Square
(The fountains volleying golden glaze)
Shines like an angel-market.   [sec. 3. ll. 7–12, 39–49]

London seems to have reached Blake's ideal of the New Jerusalem not only because angels are in Trafalgar Square but because stores and churches—the material and spiritual sides of man—seem to be reconciled in joyous harmony.

The windows, with their fleeting, flickering fires,
The height and spread of frontage shining sheer,
The quiring signs, the rejoicing roofs and spires—
'Tis El Dorado—El Dorado plain,
The Golden City!   [sec. 3. ll. 65–69]

The only realistic reminder of urban squalor in this highly romantic section is the brief mention of a blind beggar.

> The very blind man pottering on the kerb,
> Among the posies and the ostrich feathers
> And the rude voices touched with all the weathers
> Of the long, varying year,
> Shares in the universal alms of light.   [sec. 3. ll. 60–64]

In both description and content, tone and image, it is the beauty and possibility of London that shine through in the first three sections of *London Voluntaries*. In stark contrast, however, Henley depicts in section 4 of the poem a nightmarish London under the grip of disease and death. A poisonous winter fog, "The Wind-Fiend," oppresses the city, robbing it of both life and beauty.

> Out of the poisonous East,
> Over the continent of blight,
> Like a maleficent Influence released
> From the most squalid cellarage of hell,
> The Wind-Fiend, the abominable—
> The Hangman Wind that tortures temper and light—
>
> .   .   .   .
>
> A craftsman at his bench, he settles down
> To the grim job of throttling London Town.
>   [sec. 4. ll. 1–6, 14–15]

Although the air is stagnating and suffocating, it does force the poet into an intenser consideration of the social problems evident in the streets of London. At the general level, Henley makes it clear that the offensive pollution comes "out of the poisonous East," from the industrial factories in the East End of London. The poet's eye also focuses on individual victims of social abuses as he describes the plight of a prostitute on a wintry night.

> And the poor, loitering harlot rather choose
> Go pinched and pined to bed
> Than lurk and shiver and curse her wretched way
> From arch to arch, scouting some threepenny prey.
>   [sec. 4. ll. 36–39]

Henley does not, however, treat any more specific outcast figures; he is not inclined to Whitmanesque cataloguing. Rather, Henley presents large and general forces at work at a given time in the city. Like the Black Plague, "The Wind-Fiend" resonates as a compact symbol of the suffering that so many endure in the city. To present a litany of these sufferings would be to detract from the impact of gripping power that such malignant forces have on the city's inhabitants. By making a general statement, Henley cogently suggests the subtle but devastating way that oppression works within the city.

> The Wind-Fiend, the insufferable,
> Thus vicious and thus patient, sits him down
> To the black job of burking London Town.   [sec. 4. ll. 76–78]

By section 5, the final section of the poem, the seasons have come around full circle. Through five voluntaries the city has experienced nature's effects, beginning in early summer, advancing through midsummer, autumn, and winter, and ending with spring. Whereas Eliot a generation later would stress the deadening, unredemptive powers of springtime in the opening section of *The Waste Land*, Henley jubilantly expands upon the redemptive and inspiring powers of nature at work on all aspects of the city—men and women as well as trees and flowers. The musical tempo of the last voluntary is to be *allegro maëstoso*, and it is with this "vigorous yet majestic" rhythm that Pan transforms both country and city.

> For Pan, the bountiful, imperious Pan—
> .   .   .   .
> Still reigns and triumphs, as he hath triumphed and reigned
> Since in the dim blue dawn of time
> The universal ebb-and-flow began,
> To sound his ancient music, and prevails,
> By the persuasion of his mighty rhyme,
> Here in this radiant and immortal street
> Lavishly and omnipotently as ever
> In the open hills, the undissembling dales,
> The laughing-places of the juvenile earth.
> For lo! the wills of man and woman meet,
> Meet and are moved, each unto each endeared.
>   [sec. 5. ll. 52, 56–66]

In this passage, as well as in several other places in section 5 of the poem, Henley unabashedly celebrates human fertility as an indispensable part of the spring rites. Certainly Henley's buxom and active matrons display no ' signs of the sexual sterility or neuroses that would afflict Eliot's urban dwellers a generation later.

> Bevies of spring clouds trooping slow,
> Like matrons heavy bosomed and aglow
> With the mild and placid pride of increase! Nay,
> What makes this insolent and comely stream
> Of appetence, this freshet of desire
> (Milk from the wild breasts of the wilful Day!),
> Down Piccadilly dance and murmur and gleam
> In genial wave on wave and gyre on gyre? [sec. 5. ll. 3–10]

All forms of sexual perversion or prostitution—favorite topics for poets like Wilde and Symons—disappear from the streets of London as the sexual impulse is openly and healthily expressed between the most ordinary couples walking through the sunlit streets of London.

> There is no man, this deifying day,
> But feels the primal blessing in his blood.
> There is no woman but disdains—
> The sacred impulse of the May
> Brightening like sex made sunshine through her veins—
> To vail the ensigns of her womanhood. [sec. 5. ll. 26–31]

Ninety years earlier, Wordsworth closed his sonnet "Composed upon Westminster Bridge" on the contented note which depicted a city in a calm, if suspended, tranquility.

> Ne'er saw I, never felt, a calm so deep!
> The river glideth at his own sweet will:
> Dear God! the very houses seem asleep;
> And all that mighty heart is lying still! [ll. 11–14]

Henley closes his poem on a similar note of contentment but the heartbeat of the city that he celebrates so optimistically is one actively alive with life and the promise of fertility and renewal.

> Incomparably nerved and cheered,
> The enormous heart of London joys to beat
> To the measures of his rough, majestic song;
> The lewd, perennial, overmastering spell
> That keeps the rolling universe ensphered,
> And life, and all for which life lives to long,
> Wanton and wondrous and for ever well. [sec. 5. ll. 70–76]

Although Henley lived up to Symons's claim that in *London Voluntaries* the poet had "enlarge[d] the limits of his verse as to take in London," the voluntaries were to be Henley's last major poetic effort to capture the mystery and wonder of the London metropolis. Toward the end of the nineties, Henley once again wrote about the people and places of London, but on a far diminished scale. In *London Types* (1898) and as editor and contributor to *A London Garland* (1895), Henley did what Laurence Binyon did in verse: he rendered the picturesqueness of London; he became a painter of pictures in words. A contemporary reviewer of *London Types* stressed the inadequacies of the small collection of poems: "These are capital photographs, which may be interesting a hundred years hence; but they are not pretty, and we are loth to call them art. When slang intrudes into serious poetry, the result is lamentable."[43] The critic's condemnation is two-fold: Henley has superficially captured the sights of the city (as a photographer would) and he has offensively recorded street sounds that are inappropriate to the dignity of poetry. Now only the first of the critic's complaints seems justified. The excitement of Henley's street figures in *London Types* derives in part from the vigor of their own words, but they have little to say. Essentially, Henley follows the pattern of *London Voluntaries* in that he writes descriptive verse rather than dramatic monologues. In *London Types* a familiar set of urban figures are introduced. There is, for example, the "'Bus-Driver" who

> challenged, or chafed, or chaffed,
> *Back-answers* of the newest he'll explode;
> He reins his horses with an air; he treats
> With scoffing calm whatever powers there be;
> He *gets it straight*, puts *a bit on*, and meets
> His losses with both *lip* and £ *s. d.*   [ll. 3–8]

Whereas the bus-driver moves through a maze of streets, the news-boy exhibits intense activity on London's street corners.

> That imp of power, is powerless! Ever he dares,
> And, daring, lands his public neck and crop.
> Even the many-tortured London ear,
> The much enduring, loathes his *Speeshul* yell,
> His shriek of *Winnur*! But his dart and leer
> And poise are irresistible.   [ll. 7–12]

Objective description and careful restraint from all inclinations toward sentimental pathos characterize Henley's portrait of London's flower-girls who bring spring beauty to all ranks of society.

> And forth from Drury Lane,
> Trapesing in any of her [London's] whirl of weathers,
> Her flower-girls foot it, honest and hoarse and vain,

> All boot and little shawl and wilted feathers:
> Of populous corners right advantage taking,
> And, where they squat, endlessly posy-making.   [ll. 9–14]

Henley's editorship of *A London Garland* also demonstrates his interest in the pictorial aspects of London and in the mode of short descriptive lyrics. This special gift book marries the arts of painting and poetry as drawings by Beardsley, Whistler, Pennell, and members of the Society of Illustrators are set across the pages from poems by Bridges, Dobson, Locker-Lampson, and others. Henley himself contributed three poems to the volume and all three are impressionistic descriptions of sights about London. An illustration by Whistler accompanies Henley's "Nocturn" and in the poem the Thames River, "jaded and forlorn," as well as "the old skeleton bridge" and "the piles" are presented.[44]

The last poem that Henley wrote just before his death in 1903 predicts an entirely new life for twentieth-century urban man. In *A Song of Speed* (1903) Henley not only describes his exhilarating ride in his friend's new Mercédes but also makes the automobile a central symbol of the poem. The automobile is a "message from God," an emblem of progress and an indication of the quickened pace of all aspects of modern life. With characteristic enthusiasm, Henley welcomes the changes that it will bring.

> Speed as a chattel:
> Speed in your daily
> Account and economy;
> One with your wines,
> And your books, and your bath—
> Speed!
> Speed as a rapture:
> An integral element
> In the new scheme of Life
> Which the good Lord, the Master,
> Wills well you should frame
> In the light of His laugh
> And His great, His ungrudging,
> His reasoned benevolence—
> Speed!   [ll. 8–22]

In linking the exciting energy of speed to the power of God, Henley sounds yet another variation on the theme of the transforming powers that possess the potential to change the city and its inhabitants.

This marvellous Mercédes,
This triumphing contrivance,
Comes to make other
Man's life than she found it.   [ll. 340–43]

At the time that Symons praised Henley for "so enlarg[ing] the limits
of his verse as to take in London" and for passing the "test of poetry which
professes to be modern," John Davidson was quietly emerging as the poet
of the decade who would most comprehensively live up to the new poetic
directions that Symons talked about. In 1890 Davidson gave up his teach-
ing job in a private school in Greenock, Scotland, and moved with his
family to London. He was determined to create for himself a full-time
literary career in London. During the course of the decade Davidson had
tried his hand at every strain of nineties verse discussed so far. In addition
to his dramatic and fictional compositions, he wrote in a wide range of
poetic forms including lyrics, dramatic monologues, ballads, eclogues,
and verse essays. Davidson's newly adopted urban environment nurtured
his creative powers and caused his poetry to flourish in its fresh percep-
tions and varied forms. As Maurice Lindsay points out in his introduction
to a selection of Davidson's verse, "Davidson was probably the last of the
nineteenth-century poets who tried to make poetry their principal sup-
port."[45] In the first half of the nineties, Davidson's efforts met with suc-
cess; his most popular volume, *Ballads and Poems*, appeared in 1894. In
the second half of the nineties, however, the sale of Davidson's volumes
declined, and as life became harder for him and his family, the poet be-
came increasingly bitter. Toward the close of his life he wrote with great
bitterness of the London days: "Nine tenths of my time in London was
wasted in the endeavor to earn a livelihood." The tone and content of Da-
vidson's poetry corresponds closely to the ups and downs of his economic
condition. In his early poems, Davidson celebrates London and transforms
its people and landmarks into something "rich and strange." Poems of the
middle period tend toward mild social protest as Davidson takes a melio
ristic or wait-for-change attitude. Davidson's last poems, which extend
into the first decade of the twentieth century, are remarkable for their bit-
ter, pessimistic tone as the poet becomes a prophetic commentator and
social critic. In these last poems Davidson's peculiar brand of melancholy
is most evident; it is the side of melancholy that is marked by irascibility
and rage.

Davidson's early lyrical and descriptive pieces about London are impres-
sionistic and highly romanticized. In the sonnet "London" (1894), for ex-
ample, there are clear echoes of Wordsworth's 1803 sonnet "Composed

upon Westminster Bridge." The transforming power of the poet's imagination paints a community of ethereal peace and harmony. After focusing on "the clouds [that] on viewless columns bloomed" in the opening lines of the poem, the poet is moved to make a direct lyrical outcry.

> 'Oh sweetheart, see! how shadowy,
> Of some occult magician's rearing,
> Or swung in space of heaven's grace
> Dissolving, dimly reappearing,
> Afloat upon ethereal tides
> St. Paul's above the city rides!'[46]

The poet here relies on a combination of magically distorting "thin smoke" and optimistic faith to make his assertion that all is well in London.

> A rumour broke through the thin smoke
> Enwreathing abbey, tower, and palace,
> The parks, the squares, the thoroughfares,
> The million-peopled lanes and alleys,
> And even-muttering prisoned storm,
> The heart of London beating warm.   [vol. 1. ll. 13–18]

Almost ten years later Davidson wrote a similar poem of observation called "London, W." (1905). It shows a firmer and more realistic grasp of urban details and rhythms as the sometimes contradictory complexities and forces which make up the life of a great city are presented.

> Deep delight in volume, sound, and mass,
> Shadow, colour, movement, multitudes,
> Murmurs, cries, the traffic's rolling bass—
> Subtle city of a thousand moods!   [vol. 1. ll. 1–4]

Even here, however, the possibility of delight in the concrete variety of the city is maintained.

Several other descriptive and impressionistic poems demonstrate that in various ways, another dimension of vision—magical transcendence and poetic transformation of the city—is also still attainable at the end of the nineteenth century. In "In the Isle of Dogs" (1898), the transformation is especially impressive because of the setting (the East London neighborhood of the West India Docks), but it is equally strange because the precise motivation of the moment of heightened vision seems to be lacking. As the poet walks through the dusty street lined with "shameful houses" on a sultry afternoon the "turbulent pulse of sound" produced by "hammers, wheels and hoofs" subsides as his attention is drawn to a hymn played by an old organ-grinder. Davidson experiences one of those Wordsworthian moments of unexpected elevation as the "alchemy" and "magic" of poetic imagination transmute the urban scene before him and figuratively carry him off to "a green isle."

Because the poet sees the area in the deserted stillness of a Sunday afternoon, and rejoices in it not as it is but as he can magically transform it, he sees none of the East End's social problems that would provide material for some of his other poems. "A Frosty Morning" (1895) relies on a more common method of transforming the city in the nineties—the chance workings of nature. The pure white frost hides the uglier aspects of the industrialized city.

> On window-sill and door-post,
> On rail and tramway rust,
> Embroidery of hoar-frost
> Was sewn like diamond dust.   [vol. 1. ll. 9–12]

Several other poems of Davidson's early period strike a fairly optimistic note as figures reach contentment in the city. The poem "A Loafer" (1894), for example, is a dramatic monologue in which a colorful tramp affirms his contentment with his lot in the vast metropolis. The tramp recognizes that his "clothes are worn to threads and loops" and that his "tangled beard" matches his "tangled hair," but he looks beyond external appearances—even beyond the sparkling eyes and rouged cheeks of the passersby in Piccadilly—to an awareness and acceptance of "pain and death" as the core of life. Lacking in material comforts, the tramp is content because he is secure in his philosophy of *amor fati*.

> I know no handicraft, no art,
> But I have conquered fate;
> For I have chosen the better part,
> And neither hope, nor fear, nor hate.
> With placid breath on pain and death,
> My certain alms, alone I wait.   [vol. 1 ll. 31–36]

Around 1895 optimism gave way to meliorism as Davidson's poetic statements portrayed some of the more disturbing aspects of London life. Bitterness or despair had not yet set in, however, since Davidson hopes that conditions might improve. Again in this period, Davidson used a wide range of poetic forms to express his ideas. The two series of *Fleet Street Eclogues* (1893 and 1895) are the longest of his poems from this period. In their movement through the various seasons of the year and in their scope, they are similar to Henley's *London Voluntaries*. The notable difference of Davidson's series, however, is that the London scene is presented dramatically rather than descriptively. The old poetic form of pastoral dialogue is modernized as shepherds become contemporary journalists commenting on the urban condition. Although Menzies is the speaker whose views are closest to Davidson's own, it is the presentation of diverse points of view, and of the lively discussion of how to adjust to the city, that expands and captures the dimensions of the complexities of urban existence. As Hayim Fineman suggests, the revamped eclogue was well suited to a new urban poetry because it both expressed the diversity of urban opinion and captured the disjointed, fragmented pace of conversation in the city: "In the eclogue, as adapted by Davidson, he is enabled to indulge in digressions and produce a crescent growth of mood by means of passionate choral outbursts on the part of loosely conceived imaginary characters. The thought moreover can be dropped, resumed, and varied at pleasure; alternations of lyric and hortatory passages can be introduced and the length of the verse be varied to suit the mood. All this can be done without the author speaking in his own name and, therefore, according to Davidson's theory, frankly and unrestrainedly."[47] This intermingling of different voices and this dramatization of fragmented impressions of the city would attain full fruition in Joyce's *Ulysses* and Eliot's early volumes of poetry.

Throughout the changing seasons and passing holidays in the city, several speakers emerge in *Fleet Street Eclogues* as representatives of different ways to cope with urban existence. The speakers do not deliver long monologues, but interact and exchange ideas. Herbert, for example, nostalgically longs for an escape to a pastoral Arcadia that now, thirty years after Buchanan's country and city ambivalence, has only a quaint appeal and even less relation to the facts. Interspersed with Herbert's vision is the conversion testament of Basil. Since Basil is impatient with the city's "odour stale" and "the bruit loud / Of hoof and wheel on road and rail, / The rush and trample of the crowd," Herbert's pastoral daydreaming has a potent effect on Basil's mood. Momentarily, Basil forgets the turmoil of the city as he concentrates on the peace of the country.

> Go on: of rustic visions tell
> Till I forget the wilderness
> Of sooty brick, the dusty smell,
> The jangle of the printing-press.
>
> .   .   .   .
>
> You have pronounced the magic sign!
> The city with its thousand years,
> Like some embodied mood of mine,
> Uncouth, prodigious, disappears.   [vol. 1. ll. 25–28, 37–40]

Another vital interplay within the *Fleet Street Eclogues* occurs between Basil, the activist patriot, and Menzies, the sensitive and emerging social critic. Since Basil's patriotic flag-waving is predictable, it is more fruitful to concentrate on Menzies's observations of London's social problems. What makes Menzies's social commentaries the most memorable in the poem is their calculated placement. His first stunning remark is delivered with the force of a blow. After many good-natured exchanges in "St. Valentine's Eve," Menzies puts an end to all conversation as he startlingly proclaims: "I mock not, I shall see earth and be glad: / London's a darksome cell where men go mad" (vol. 1. ll. 165–66). In another eclogue, "St. George's Day," Menzies assumes the cosmic "I" stance of Walt Whitman as he catalogues and takes in the sufferings of the city.

> I hear the idle workman sigh;
> I hear his hungry children cry.
>
> .   .   .   .
>
> I see the loafer-burnished wall;
> I hear the rotting match-girl whine;
> I see the unslept switchman fall;
> I hear the explosion in the mine;
> I see along the heedless street
> The sandwichmen trudge through the mire;
> I hear the tired quick tripping feet
> Of sad, gay girls who ply for hire.   [vol. 1. ll. 3–4, 43–50]

But at this point in the development of his social criticism, Menzies is not ready to offer any concrete solutions to the social problems that have come to his attention. Although mankind has temporarily gone astray—"But though we wander far astray, / And oft in gloomy darkness grope"—Menzies's attitude is that there are still faint grounds for hope: "Fearless we face the blackest day, / For we are the world's forlorn hope" (vol. 1. ll. 255–58). Menzies is incapable of evolving any social solutions through the course of the eclogues. He does, however, at the end of the poem make the melioristic gesture of joining in the Christmas Eve celebration where a small "fire of faith" is lit from "a smouldering brand."

Davidson's best-known poem, the dramatic monologue "Thirty Bob a Week" (1894), is an example of the melioristic stance of his middle period. J. Benjamin Townsend remarks that it "offers the comfort of stoic resolution in place of social revolution."[48] The humble clerk in the poem is barely able to suppress his frustrations as he tells himself that it is right for him to stay on the honorable side of the economic struggle for survival because society is in God's hands (an echo of Hopkins's "Tom's Garland").

> But I don't allow it's luck and all a toss;
> There's no such thing as being starred and crossed;
> It's just the power of some to be a boss,
> And the bally power of others to be bossed:
> I face the music, sir; you bet I ain't a cur;
> Strike me lucky if I don't believe I'm lost!   [vol. 1. ll. 7–12]

The poem "Waiting" (1897) echoes on a larger scale the moderate social protest evident in the underpaid clerk's acceptance of his poor lot. "Waiting" divides into two equal parts: an exposition of the socioeconomic problems, and a litany of pleas and suggestions for solutions. The problems are set forth forcefully and bluntly in the best tradition of William Morris's chants.

> Is there any help or hail
> For the tenants of the alleys,
> Of the workhouse and the jail?
>
> .   .   .   .   .   .
>
> We cringe for orts and doles—
> Prosperity's accustomed foil,
> Millions of useless souls.
> In the gutters and the ditches
> Human vermin festering lurk—
> We, the rust upon your riches;
> We, the flaw in all your work.   [vol. 1. ll. 8–10, 14–20]

However, in proposing solutions, Davidson's tone and approach are diametrically opposed to Morris's. Whereas Morris calls for the workers to overthrow their oppressors and to take charge of shaping the new social order, Davidson, in the resolution stanzas of his poem, is fawningly polite as if he would have the idle say "thank you" to the rich for meager changes.

> Come down from where you sit;
> We look to you for aid.
> Take us from the miry pit,
> And lead us undismayed:
> Say, 'Even you, outcast, unfit,
> Forward with sword and spade!'
> And myriads of us idle
> Would thank you through our tears,
> Though you drove us with a bridle,
> And a whip about our ears!   [vol. 1. ll. 21–30]

The oppressed themselves call for a Carlylean captain of industry to take charge of the deplorable situation.

> Will no one help us to escape?
> We scarce have room to breathe.
> You might try to understand us:
> We are waiting night and day
> For a captain to command us,
> And the word we must obey.   [vol. 1. ll. 35–40]

"Most of Davidson's writing after 1895," writes J. Benjamin Townsend, "is the product of a mind egocentric, hypersensitive, and easily unbalanced, intent upon the primary task of justifying a life of disappointment."[49] As biographers indicate, the reasons behind the increasing bitterness in both his life and work during his last years—he committed suicide in 1909—are multifaceted. It is clear, however, that he had concluded that there was no hope for mankind: neither democratic nor socialistic schemes could relieve the wrong and waste he saw in the city. With Davidson's increasing bitterness in outlook came the growing conviction that he had a mission as a poet to take up the irascible role of prophet and social critic. Henceforth, he would employ blank verse because it echoed the dignity of Milton and Wordsworth. Davidson's verse became more and more vehement and at times turgid. Yet to the end, he did not sacrifice his focus upon urban details. Poems of his late period, in blank and rhymed verses, denounce everything from the ugliness of the Crystal Palace to the frenzied and callous pace of people in the London Bridge Railway Station.

Poems like "A Northern Suburb" (1896), "The World's Failure" (1904), and "In the City" (1905) express Davidson's detestation of the uglier aspects of urban existence combined with his despairing belief that no salvation or redemption of the city was possible. In these poems, Davidson most clearly points a finger toward the twentieth-century response of T. S. Eliot. "A Northern Suburb" describes the cancerous growth of the expanding urban ugliness.

> But here the whetted fangs of change
> Daily devour the old demesne—
> The busy farm, the quiet grange,
> The wayside inn, the village green.
>
> In gaudy yellow brick and red,
> With rooting pipes, like creepers rank,

> The shoddy terraces o'erspread
> Meadow, and garth, and daisied bank.
>
> With shelves for rooms the houses crowd,
> Like draughty cupboards in a row—
> Ice-chests when wintry winds are loud,
> Ovens when summer breezes blow.   [vol. 1. ll. 5–16]

Davidson perceptively recognizes that ugly urban structures and monotonous neighborhoods foster not seething discontent but stifling dullness and apathy.

> For here dwell those who must fulfil
> Dull tasks in uncongenial spheres,
> Who toil through dread of coming ill,
> And not with hope of happier years—
>
> The lowly folk who scarcely dare
> Conceive themselves perhaps misplaced,
> Whose prize for unremitting care
> Is only not to be disgraced.   [vol. 1. ll. 21–28]

"The World's Failure" includes a bitter denunciation of the urban business ethic. What is distinctly new in this poem, however, is Davidson's elevation of the "elaborate torture" of the capitalistic system to the wider statement of the cosmic condition, much as Thomson transformed the view of the city to make it an emblem of conditions throughout the cosmos. Davidson takes on the voice of the enraged prophet as he moves to the grand pronouncement that the earth itself is "the torture-chamber of the universe." "In the City" portrays further shadows of doom engulfing the city as Davidson proclaims that no storm of nature could possibly wash away the ugly smoke of London. Trapped in the "city's labyrinth," "the storms themselves are wrapped / In draggled shrouds of soot" (vol. 1. ll. 10–12).

In another trio of late poems—"The Crystal Palace," "Railway Stations: London Bridge," and "The Testament of Sir Simon Simplex Concerning Automobilism" (all 1908)—Davidson attacked specific landmarks and aspects of the already fading Victorian London scene. In these poems, Davidson noticeably restrains the scope of his prophetic utterances, even though he intensifies the vehemence of his more narrowly concentrated attacks. Davidson bitterly attacks not only Victorian landmarks and achievements but also the attitudes of that society. The Crystal Palace, for example, stands as an ugly reminder of Victorian industrialism and commercialism which ravished nature and had no sense of beauty.

Contraption,—that's the bizarre, proper slang,
Eclectic word, for this portentous toy,
The flying-machine, that gyrates stiffly, arms
A-kimbo, so to say, and baskets slung
From every elbow, skating in the air

.   .   .   .

Victorian temple of commercialism,
Our very own eighth wonder of the world,
The Crystal Palace.

.   .   .   .

No idea of its purpose, and no mood
Can make your glass and iron beautiful.

[vol. 2. ll. 1–5, 14–16, 28–29]

Davidson couples his objections to the ugliness of the architectural structure with a denouncement of the ignorant and foolish crowds that such a monstrosity attracts. The repeated tendency of nineteenth-century poets to view collections of people as "the masses" or "a blur of faces featureless, / Of forms inane" was certainly not put to rest with the turn of the new century. Davidson never distinguishes between the individual and the social order of which the individual was a distinct part.

In the main floor the fretful multitude
Circulates from the north nave to the south
Accross [sic] the central transept [sic]—swish and tread
And murmer [sic], like a seaboard's mingled sound.

.   .   .   .

For this is Mob, unhappy locust-swarm,
Instinctive, apathetic, ravenous.
Beyond a doubt a most unhappy crowd!

.   .   .   .

Crowd; Mob; a blur of faces featureless,
Of forms inane, a stranded shoal of folk.

[vol. 2. ll. 52–55, 132–34, 144–45]

Similarly, in "Railway Stations: London Bridge" Davidson condemns both the ugly structure itself and the callous, greedy people who pass through it day after day.

And yet this human tide,
As callous as the glaciers that glide
A foot a day, but as a torrent swift,

> Sweeps unobservant save of time—for thrift
> Or dread disposes clockwards every glance—
> Right through a station which a seismic dance
> Chimerical alone can harmonize
> Even in imagination's friendly eyes.
> Clearly a brimming tide of mind as well
> As blood, whose ebb and flow is buy and sell,
> Engulfed by London's storm and stress of trade
> Before it reached the civic sea, and made
> Oblivious, knowing nought terrestrial
> Except that time is money, and money all.   {vol. 2. ll. 55–68}

Finally, Davidson's "The Testament of Sir Simon Simplex Concerning Automobilism" stands in contrast to Henley's *A Song of Speed*. Whereas Henley celebrated the automobile as an exciting new means of urban and rural transportation, Davidson (mistakenly, given later developments in the twentieth century that democratically extended the automobile to almost everyone) welcomes the automobile because he feels that it will allow a few wealthy individualists to escape the use of trains (which he condemned as decadent dens of democracy). The "testament" is spoken by an aristocratic individualist and is meant to be a poetic protest against democracy. At points in the poem, the language is so heightened and vehement that it is difficult for the reader to glean Davidson's real message, wrapped as it is amongst rhetoric and bombast.

> The motor stops the decadence: not all
> Are in the same train with the prodigal,
> The Christian scientist, the *souteneur*,
> The Gothamite, the man from anywhere,
> Domestic Gill and idiomatic Jack,
> The wheedling knave, the sneak, the hectoring quack;
> The man of broader mind and farther goal
> Is not entrained with Lubin Littlesoul;
> Your gentleman by birth with quickened sense,
> Refined requirements and abundant pence,
> And men of faculty and swelling aim
> Who conquer riches, power, position, fame,
> Are not entrained with loafers, quibblers, cranks,
> Nor with the Mob who never leave the ranks,
> With plodding dullness, unambitious ease,
> And discontented incapacities.
>
> .   .   .   .

I call Democracy archaic, just
As manhood suffrage is atavic lust
For folkmotes of the prime, whose analogue
In travel was the train, a passing vogue:
The automobile put an end to that,
And left Democracy as fallen and flat
As railway-stock.   [vol. 2. ll. 167–82, 203–9]

Again, in the case of John Davidson, coming down from Scotland to London to make a career as writer and prophet is important. The way to make a literary reputation is to write about the city. Davidson makes his complex and developing view of the city the *matter* of the poetry in which he is to make his mark. Like Buchanan and Thomson before him, for at least a decade Davidson finds energies to celebrate, occasions for imaginative transcendence, and finally tests in the city for the hard and bleak messages of a poet.

This chapter began with Helmut E. Gerber's question as to whether the 1890s marked "a beginning, an end, or a transition" in literary forms and outlooks. Of course, all three terms are part of the answer. Besides the diversity of poetic forms and experimentation in the nineties, from the eighteenth-century modes of Locker-Lampson and Dobson to the avant-garde impressionism of Symons and Wilde, the most striking development in the decade is the tendency of most poets to abandon any hope of applying poetry to the pressing social problems of the urban environment and to seek instead individual pleasure and salvation in the city. Granted there are a few exceptions: an awareness of poverty and other social problems emerges in the later poetry of Henley and Davidson. But although these two poets do touch a radical hope for change, they do not stay there long. The predominant emphasis that emerges in the poetry written during the 1890s, then, is on working out individual salvation and pleasure rather than using poetry as an aid to communal reconstruction and social regeneration in the city as poets such as Blake and Morris advocated.

In the early twentieth century two of the most interesting poets who both build upon and modify nineteenth-century traditions are D. H. Lawrence and T. S. Eliot. Lawrence traveled extensively seeking to merge his individuality with a just and humane Blakean community, the golden city ideal. Eliot on the other hand looks back to the pessimism of James Thomson and seems to suggest strongly that there are no social or communal solutions in the wasteland city; poetry can only help an individual strive for a private salvation out of historical time.

Epilogue

Continuities: The Urban Responses of D. H. Lawrence and T. S. Eliot

In nineteenth-century English poetry, the predominant responses to the city involved the concepts of: the real versus the ideal city, that is the actual (sometimes labeled "false"), temporal, and industrial city versus the imaginatively envisioned "true" golden or celestial city; the contrasting awareness of a more desirable past, a nostalgia which often stressed the more attractive moral, social, and physical health of the countryside; and the possibilities for redemption in and of the city. These themes and modes of nineteenth-century poets' responses to the city continued into the twentieth century—sometimes altered slightly, but at other times modified and transformed extensively.

Two early twentieth-century poets who had more than sporadic contact with London and in whose works all of these themes are present were D. H. Lawrence and T. S. Eliot. The comparisons and contrasts between Lawrence's and Eliot's backgrounds, responses, and works nevertheless reveal two different and typical understandings of human possibility, both of which have precedents in nineteenth-century poetry about the city. Yet they point toward new solutions to old problems. So far as their direct responses to the modern city, both describe the physical city in ways which were current since Blake and Wordsworth: that is, they depict confusion and ugliness as well as represent societal abuses and oppressive "mind-forg'd manacles." Both of the modern poets draw attitudes and images from late nineteenth-century poets such as James Thomson—deadness, vacuity, despair—and aesthetes such as Oscar Wilde and Arthur Symons—impressionistic perspectives involving yellow fog, mist, and a concentrated focus.

In another sense, both Lawrence and Eliot saw beyond the present metropolis to the past and future conditions of human community. Each poet compares the present city to a more attractive past. In the case of Lawrence, the comparison is made to the more healthful (moral, social, and physical) countryside; in the case of Eliot, the comparison harks back to a classical age of Roman civic grandeur or to a time of beauty and swans recorded in the Spenserian tradition. But poetic vision looks forward as well and Lawrence and Eliot sought, in their own ways, redemption of the city and the ills of civilization. In their analyses of these ills, Lawrence and Eliot are, literally, radical. For Lawrence (as for Blake and Morris) the city is as it is because of *laissez-faire* capitalism; for Eliot (as for Hopkins and Noel) the city's abuses can be traced to the general decline of faith.

The similarities between Lawrence and Eliot seem almost at this point to outweigh the differences. Both Lawrence and Eliot hated the ugliness, the boredom, and the violence of the modern industrial or temporal city, which they labeled as "false" and "unreal"; both looked back to a past that was assuredly better than the sordid present in numerous respects; and both came to long for a redemption of urban waste and a realization of human potential. On the final point of redemptive schemes for the city, however, the differences between the two poets are most apparent. Lawrence always maintained that the present city built by industrial and commercial capitalism was "false," but he also maintained that the only way it would ever be transformed was by creative and vital men regenerating the actualities of that city.[1] By contrast, Eliot stepped out of the historic dimension that made the city into the peace of a garden of eternal intimations—the personal and lonely vision of "the moment in the rose-garden" and "the moment in and out of time."[2]

Lawrence and Eliot, then, in their responses to the question of whether redemption will come from inside or outside of the city align themselves on opposite sides of a controversy that reaches back through the nineteenth century to the romantic poetry of Blake and Wordsworth. The persistence of these two responses to the city spans the nineteenth century and beyond into the twentieth century. From Blake to Lawrence, there were poets who not only optimistically believed but recorded such thoughts and feelings in their poetry that the "false" or real city could be imaginatively transformed by the poet and perhaps be redeemed by its human inhabitants. Several statements by Lawrence—drawn from various writings—apply here. To Bertrand Russell he wrote: "We live in towns from choice, when we subscribe to our great civilized form. The nostalgia for the country is not *so* important. What is important is that our towns are *false* towns—every street a blow, every corner a stab."[3] To Lady Cynthia Asquith he wrote: "We must rid ourselves of this ponderous incubus of falsehood, this massive London, with its streets and streets of nullity: we must, with one accord and in purity of spirit, pull it down and build up a beautiful thing."[4] In *Sons and Lovers*, Lawrence refers to "the splendour of

London," a city full of infinite products and possibilities. At the end of the novel, Paul Morel walks "towards the city's gold phosphorescence."[5] A final example of Lawrence's desire to transform the "false" city into a harmonious community for human fulfillment is his impressive vision of "a golden city" that "had come true" in his "Autobiographical Fragment."[6]

An opposing line of development to the one just described runs from Wordsworth to' T. S. Eliot wherein poets saw impending doom in the condition of the city and recorded their belief that redemption would have to be carried on outside the city, outside social history, outside human time. Concerning this specific outlook, his friend and fellow poet Stephen Spender reports: "There is much evidence that Eliot thought that Western civilization was confronted by impending ruin. Many of his writings at the time and for some years afterward, including his *Criterion* Commentaries, show how convinced he was that the civilization would collapse. In 1929, when I myself as a very young man had lunch with him for the first time, I asked him what form he had thought the collapse would take. 'Internecine warfare,' he answered. Puzzled by this, I pressed him for a more precise answer. He said, 'People killing one another in the streets.'"[7]

Curiously, in the case of these two major twentieth-century poets, biographical background seems to reverse itself; whereas Blake and Eliot spent nearly all of their lives in an urban setting, the ties of Wordsworth and Lawrence were to the land and the traditions of rural community. Nevertheless, the pronouncements of the two twentieth-century poets became disjunctive as their careers unfolded. Lawrence left his boyhood rural home and always tried to reach a golden or utopian state of human community *through* a transformation of the city's present reality. Eliot moved from Wordsworthian apprehensions and misgivings about the city through Thomsonian despair in *The Waste Land* to the mystical "rose-garden" of *Four Quartets*, a vision that was more often "out of" than "in" time. Even though Eliot himself served as a part-time fire-watcher on the rooftop of Faber and Faber and later in the Kensington district of the war-torn London of the early forties, the spiritual realm depicted in *Four Quartets* was safely removed from the actualities of the modern city. With Eliot's poetry the positive impulse to assimilate and accommodate the urban environment's possibilities that was evident in the works of so many nineteenth-century poets takes dramatically new directions in his early volumes. This willingness to deal openly and directly with the city is not as strong in his later poetry. Further, the contemporary poets of Eliot have not matched the variety of responses to London found in the poetry of their Victorian predecessors.

Notes

Notes to Introduction

1. Raymond Williams, *The Country and the City*, p. 217.
2. Numerous studies have interpreted the city as it appears in Dickens's many novels. Alexander Welsh in *The City of Dickens* notes, among other things, that as the social facts of the city became increasingly disturbing, satire and comedy were no longer adequate or even possible responses. In a fine blend of biography and literary analysis with urban and social history, F. S. Schwarz-bach's more recent study, *Dickens and the City*, illuminates the important relationship between Dickens's novels and the emergent experience of Victorian London. Recently, scholars have also studied how various artists and historians portrayed the urban experience. Two interesting articles by Donald J. Gray, "Picturesque London" and "General Histories, Guidebooks and Handbooks" comprise part of a study of the holdings on Victorian London at Indiana University's Lilly Library [*The Indiana University Bookman*, No. 12, December 1977]. *Victorian Artists and the City*, edited by I. B. Nadel and F. S. Schwarzbach, is a more comprehensive work which collects essays by eleven scholars on how artists from George Scharf to Gustave Doré portrayed London life in the nineteenth century.
3. G. Robert Stange, "The Frightened Poets," in *The Victorian City: Images and Realities*, eds. H. J. Dyos and Michael Wolff, pp. 475–94.
4. Williams, *The Country and the City*, pp. 5–6.

Notes to Chapter One

1. Hazard Adams, *William Blake: A Reading of the Shorter Poems*, p. 275.
2. Ibid., p. 280.
3. Martin K. Nurmi, "Fact and Symbol in 'The Chimney Sweeper' of Blake's *Songs of Innocence*," *Bulletin of the New York Public Library* 68 (1964): 249–56.
4. William Blake, *The Poems of William Blake*, ed. W. H. Stevenson (Harlow, England: Longman Group, 1971), ll. 8, 10, 12. Subsequent citations of Blake's poetry are from this edition.
5. Raymond Williams, *The Country and the City*, p. 148.
6. Ibid., pp. 148–49.
7. The allusions to the traditional imagery connected with biblical Babylon which underlies some of Blake's descriptions are succinctly outlined by S. Foster Damon, *A Blake Dictionary* (New York: Dutton, 1971), pp. 33–34. Briefly, the relevant passages can be found in Revelation 17:5; Psalm 87:4; and Isaiah 51:9.

Notes

8. Kenneth R. Johnston, "Blake's Cities: Romantic Forms of Urban Renewal," in *Blake's Visionary Forms Dramatic*, eds. David V. Erdman and John E. Grant, p. 426. Johnston stresses that "the struggle between these two opposite but equal orders is a central organizing principle in both *Milton* and *Jerusalem*."

9. Raymond Williams, *Culture and Society, 1780–1950*, pp. 297–300.

10. Johnston, "Blake's Cities," pp. 413, 422.

11. Ibid., p. 441.

12. Raymond Williams, "Prelude to Alienation," *Dissent* 11 (1964): 303–15.

13. William Wordsworth, *Wordsworth: Poetical Works*, rev. ed., ed. Ernest de Selincourt (New York: Oxford University Press, 1969). Subsequent citations of Wordsworth's poetry, except *The Prelude*, are from this edition.

14. For example, in the 1850 text, both unrealistic and stronger terms of dissatisfaction with the large city appear. London is called a "Fairy-land" (l. 98), "Thou monstrous ant-hill on the plain / Of a too busy world!" (ll. 149–50), and a "vast domain" (l. 765). Some passages which describe the specifics of street din are excluded entirely from the 1850 text (around l. 155) while at other times what was initial excitement now becomes "the shock / Of the huge town's first presence" (ll. 67–68). Other revisions and exclusions are also interesting and deserve to be worked out in a separate study.

15. William Wordsworth, *William Wordsworth: The Prelude, A Parallel Text*, ed. J. C. Maxwell (Baltimore: Penguin Books, 1971). bk. 1. ll. 5–10. Subsequent citations of Wordsworth's *Prelude* are from the 1805 text in this edition.

16. Williams, *The Country and the City*, p. 5.

17. Georg Simmel, "The Metropolis and Mental Life," in *Classic Essays on the Culture of Cities*, ed. Richard Sennett, p. 48.

18. Williams, *The Country and the City*, p. 150.

19. Williams, "Prelude to Alienation," p. 311.

20. Ibid., p. 312.

21. G. Robert Stange, "The Frightened Poets," in *The Victorian City: Images and Realities*, eds. H. J. Dyos and Michael Wolff, pp. 477–78.

22. Alfred Tennyson, *The Poems of Tennyson*, ed. Christopher Ricks (Harlow, England: Longman Group, 1969). ll. 7–12. Subsequent citations of Tennyson's poetry are from this edition.

23. Jerome Hamilton Buckley, *Tennyson: The Growth of a Poet*, p. 32.

24. Christopher Ricks, *Tennyson*, pp. 34–35.

25. Ricks argues in *Tennyson* (p. 33) that the poet must have made up the epigraph to "Timbuctoo" on his own since the lines have never been found in George Chapman or anywhere else.

26. There is ample evidence that Tennyson was aware of and interested in the social conditions of nineteenth-century London. For example, Sir Charles Tennyson maintains that the social criticism in *Maud* "sprang from his long talks with Charles Kingsley and F. D. Maurice about the terrible conditions in the rapidly growing industrial cities" (*Alfred Tennyson* [New York: Macmillan, 1949], p. 281). Furthermore, Jerome C. Hixson and Patrick Scott document

that Tennyson "had a long-standing interest in the 'condition-of-England' question, from Edwin Chadwick's epoch-making report on the *Sanitary Condition of the Labouring Population* (1842, item 1049), to General Booth's late-Victorian appeal *In Darkest England, and the Way Out* (1890, item 586)" ("Tennyson's Books," *Tennyson Research Bulletin*, 2 [1976]: 197).

27. Stange, "The Frightened Poets," p. 478.

28. John D. Rosenberg, *The Fall of Camelot: A Study of Tennyson's Idylls of the King*, p. 11.

29. Donald J. Gray, "Arthur, Roland, Empedocles, Sigurd, and the Despair of Heroes in Victorian Poetry," *Boston University Studies in English* 5 (1961): 1–17.

30. Patrick Brantlinger, *The Spirit of Reform: British Literature and Politics, 1832–1867*, pp. 186–87.

31. Hallam Tennyson, *Alfred Lord Tennyson: A Memoir by His Son*, 2:303.

32. Buckley, *The Growth of a Poet*, p. 228.

33. Hallam Tennyson, *Alfred Lord Tennyson*, 2:337.

34. Buckley, *The Growth of a Poet*, p. 234.

35. Stange, "The Frightened Poets," p. 478.

36. Buckley, *The Growth of a Poet*, p. 252.

Notes to Chapter Two

1. Walter E. Houghton, *The Victorian Frame of Mind, 1830–1870*, p. 1.

2. Ibid., p. 3.

3. H. J. Dyos, *Victorian Suburb: A Study of the Growth of Camberwell*, p. 111.

4. Ibid., p. 51.

5. Ibid.

6. Ibid., pp. 111, 31

7. W. R. Greg, "Prostitution," *Westminster Review* 53 (1850): 448–506.

8. Hippolyte Taine, *Notes on England*, p. 36.

9. Charles Kingsley, *Alton Locke, Tailor and Poet*, 1:251, 258.

10. Kingsley, *Alton Locke*, pp. 259–60.

11. F. G. Stephens, "Modern Giants," *The Germ* no. 4 (1850): 169.

12. Ibid., p. 172.

13. Ibid., pp. 170, 171

14. Arthur Hugh Clough, "Recent English Poetry," *North American Review* 77 (1853): 1–30.

15. Ibid., pp. 2–3.

16. Ibid., p. 5.

17. Ibid.

18. Ibid., pp. 11, 12.

19. Ibid., p. 17.

20. Ibid., p. 20.

21. Ibid., p. 27.

22. Wendell V. Harris, *Arthur Hugh Clough*, p. 118.

23. Walter E. Houghton, *The Poetry of Clough: An Essay in Revaluation*, p. 156.

24. Arthur Hugh Clough, *The Poems of Arthur Hugh Clough*, 2d ed., ed. F. L. Mulhauser (London: Oxford University Press, 1974), ll. 1–4. Subsequent citations of Clough's poetry are from this edition.

25. Stange, "The Frightened Poets," p. 485.

26. Arthur Hugh Clough, "Recent Social Theories," *North American Review* 77 (1853): 106–17.

27. Clough, "Recent English Poetry," p. 3.

28. For example, Donald J. Gray argues that "it is exactly the tension of living and acting as poet in the world that is the energy of Clough's poetry, and it was in expressing that tension that he did best and most tellingly what it was in him to do" (*Victorian Literature: Poetry*, eds. Donald J. Gray and G. B. Tennyson, p. 392), while Barbara Hardy in an essay on "Clough's Self-Consciousness" (*The Major Victorian Poets: Reconsiderations*, ed. Isobel Armstrong, pp. 257, 259, 265) talks about the "duality, tension and contradiction" in *Dipsychus*, pointing to the poem's "pivoting 'yets'" and "the vagueness and ambiguity of action," among other things.

29. Clyde de L. Ryals, "An Interpretation of Clough's *Dipsychus*," *Victorian Poetry* 1 (1963): 188.

30. Raymond Williams, *Culture and Society, 1780–1950*, pp. 297–300.

31. In a long passage set in a London café, the Spirit also points out how money can be used to serve as a distancing, discriminating device from the masses. Money builds artificial barriers in the city; it separates and distinguishes one from other people (sc. 5. ll. 130–203).

32. Alexander Smith does not fit exactly the pattern of emigration that applies to Buchanan, Thomson, and Davidson. However, his early poems about city life were of some importance and his volumes were read and reviewed seriously in London. In an illuminating article, Mary Jane W. Scott argues that "Smith made only one trip to England (in 1853), and it remained for him remote." Scott has an interesting discussion of the *City Poems* volume and of Smith's Glasgow experience. See "Alexander Smith: Poet of Victorian Scotland," *Studies in Scottish Literature* 14 (1979): 98–111.

33. Stange, "The Frightened Poets," p. 485.

34. Alexander Smith, *Poems*, 4th ed. (London: David Bogue, 1856). Subsequent citations of Smith's *A Life Drama* are from this edition.

35. Clough, "Recent English Poetry," p. 4. Smith may have read this advice since he did include such imagery in his *City Poems* (1857).

36. Scott, "Alexander Smith," pp. 106–7. Scott notes that the minor pedlar-poet from Glasgow, James Macfarlan, published his *City Songs* in 1855. Also, Raymond Williams in *Keywords: A Vocabulary of Culture and Society*, p. 47, points out that the word "*city* as a really distinctive order of settlement, implying a whole different way of life, is not fully established, with its modern implications, until the early nineteenth century" and that "the increasing abstraction of *city* as an adjective" did not occur until mid-nineteenth century.

37. Alexander Smith, *City Poems* (Cambridge: Macmillan, 1857), ll. 415–20. Subsequent citations of Smith's poetry are from this edition.

38. Stange, "The Frightened Poets," p. 485.

39. Clough, "Recent English Poetry," p. 4.

40. Ibid., pp. 17, 20.

41. Ibid., p. 12.

42. Alan Roper, *Arnold's Poetic Landscapes*, p. 247.

43. Stange, "The Frightened Poets," pp. 485–86.

44. Matthew Arnold, *The Poems of Matthew Arnold*, ed. Kenneth Allott (Harlow, England: Longman Group, 1965), ll. 1–10. Subsequent citations of Arnold's poetry are from this edition.

45. Matthew Arnold, *The Letters of Matthew Arnold to Arthur Hugh Clough*, ed. H. F. Lowry (London: Oxford University Press, 1932), p. 65. Cited hereafter as *Letters to Clough*.

46. Lionel Trilling, *Matthew Arnold*, pp. 114–15.

47. Roper, *Arnold's Poetic Landscapes*, pp. 158, 165.

48. Francis Sheppard, *London 1808–1870: The Infernal Wen*, p. 356.

49. Françoise Choay, *The Modern City: Planning in the Nineteenth Century*, pp. 23, 24.

50. Roper, *Arnold's Poetic Landscapes*, p. 52.

51. Patrick Brantlinger, *The Spirit of Reform*, p. 185.

52. Stange, "The Frightened Poets," p. 486. Of course, one could also argue that such later poems as "The Scholar Gypsy" (1853), "Rugby Chapel" (1857), and "Thyrsis" (1864) treat the dilemmas of the modern condition with its "sick hurry" and "divided aims" and are thus meaningful statements about city life, albeit in the form of fable or antiurban pastoral.

53. In the "General Report for the Year 1855," for instance, Arnold contrasted the situations of country and city schools that he had inspected: "It appears, at first sight, as if the schools of a metropolis had advantages over schools in the country, which ought to ensure to the former the superiority. They exist in a great centre of wealth and intelligence, where their promoters have remarkable facilities for combination of effort." But while there may have been greater educational opportunities available in the city, Arnold was not entirely pleased with what he saw in some London schools and he pointed out that the greater challenges of the London environment could often prove to be sources of distraction for both students and teachers: "Is it that the excitement and intensity of London life are *too* powerful; that they operate on those connected with elementary schools not as stimulants, but as distractions. . . . Is it, in short, that the activity of all kinds, which in other large towns exerts a favourable effect on the development of elementary schools, exists in London in an overpowering degree, and becomes prejudicial to them?" (*Reports on Elementary Schools, 1852–1882* [London: Wyman, 1908], pp. 35–37).

54. Matthew Arnold, *Passages from the Prose Writings of Matthew Arnold* (New York: Macmillan and Co., 1880), p. 129.

55. Arnold, *Prose Writings*, p. 130.

56. J. Moultrie, Introduction to *The Poetical Remains of William Sidney Walker, with a Memoir of the Author*, p. cxvii.

57. Ibid., p. cxxxiv.

58. Ibid., p. cxviii.

59. Ibid., p. cxxxiv.

60. William Sidney Walker, *The Poetical Remains of William Sidney Walker, with a Memoir of the Author*, ed. J. Moultrie (London: John W. Parker, 1852). Subsequent citations of Walker's poetry are from this edition.

61. R. A. Forsyth, "Nature and the Victorian City: The Ambivalent Attitude of Robert Buchanan," *Journal of English Literary History* 36 (1969): 387.

62. Ibid., p. 386.

63. Ibid., p. 396.

64. Robert Buchanan, "David Gray, a Memoir," in *A Poet's Sketch–Book*, p. 51.

65. John A. Cassidy, *Robert W. Buchanan*, pp. 25–26.

66. Robert Buchanan, "On My Own Tentatives," in *David Gray and Other Essays*, pp. 290–91.

67. Robert Buchanan, *The Complete Poetical Works of Robert Buchanan*, vol. 1 (London: Chatto and Windus, 1901), ll. 7–12. Subsequent citations of Buchanan's poetry, except "Summer Song in the City," are from this edition.

68. Raymond Williams, *The Country and the City*, pp. 149, 71, 129.

69. "Summer Song in the City" was not reprinted in *The Complete Poetical Works of Robert Buchanan*. At least five of the poems treated in this section appeared first under the heading "London Lyrics" in such popular journals as *Fortnightly* and *London Society*. "Summer Song in the City" appeared in *London Society* 13 (1868): 89–90. ll. 5–6, 45–48.

70. Cassidy, *Robert W. Buchanan*, p. 89.

71. Ibid., pp. 34–35.

Notes to Chapter Three

1. Alistair Horne, *The Terrible Year: The Paris Commune, 1871*, p. 95.

2. Melvin Kranzberg, *The Siege of Paris, 1870–1871: A Political and Social History*, p. 182.

3. Gustave Doré and Blanchard Jerrold, *London: A Pilgrimage*, pp. 122, 124.

4. George M. Young, *Victorian England: Portrait of an Age*, 2d ed., p. 24.

5. B. I. Coleman, ed., *The Idea of the City in Nineteenth-Century Britain*, p. 16.

6. Raymond Williams, *Keywords: A Vocabulary of Culture and Society*, p. 274.

7. Raymond Williams, *Culture and Society, 1780–1950*, pp. 293–94.

8. Gareth Stedman Jones, *Outcast London: A Study in the Relationship between Classes in Victorian Society*, p. 301.

9. Ibid., p. 284.

10. Matthew Arnold, *Culture and Anarchy*, ed. J. Dover Wilson, pp. 193, 192, 105, 205.

11. Wilfrid Ward, *The Life of John Henry, Cardinal Newman*, 2:344.

12. G. R. Sims, *How the Poor Live in Horrible London*, p. 44.

13. Gerard Manley Hopkins, *Letters*, 1:27–28. Three volumes of Hopkins's letters will be referred to: volume 1, *The Letters of Gerard Manley Hopkins to Robert Bridges*; volume 2, *The Correspondence of Gerard Manley Hopkins and Richard Watson Dixon*; volume 3, *Further Letters of Gerard Manley Hopkins*. Volumes 1 and 2 were published in 1955; volume 3 in 1956. All three volumes were edited by Claude Colleer Abbott and published by Oxford University Press, New York. Subsequent citations of Hopkins's letters are from these editions.

14. The concluding sentences to one of Hopkins's meditations are very Ruskinian in their sanctification of work—see *The Note-books and Papers of Gerard Manley Hopkins*, ed. Humphry House, p. 305. Referred to hereafter as *Note-books*. Two studies, Wendell Stacy Johnson's *Gerard Manley Hopkins: The Poet as Victorian* and Alison G. Sulloway's *Gerard Manley Hopkins and the Victorian Temper*, have extensive treatments of the relationship between Hopkins and Ruskin but brief discussions of "Tom's Garland."

15. In his article "The Dating of 'Tom's Garland,'" *Notes and Queries* 18 (1971): 258, John Sutherland provides a concise summary of the cultural history surrounding the poem: "The poem was thus in Hopkins' hands until late December, and it was in the period from early October until mid-November that 'the Unemployed' became spectacularly notorious. . . . On 7 October a number of angry demonstrators unfurled a red flag in Trafalgar Square and proclaimed the cause of the unemployed. On 12 October a larger procession of unemployed men marched through London. Between this date and 8 November there were unruly meetings in Trafalgar Square and Hyde Park and these culminated in 'Bloody Sunday' on 13 November."

16. Hopkins never mentions Ford Madox Brown's "Work" sonnet in his letters. W. H. Gardner, *Gerard Manley Hopkins: A Study of Poetic Idiosyncrasy in Relation to Poetic Tradition*, 2:12, seems to be most accurate, however, in maintaining that "it is probably the seed from which 'Tom's Garland' grew." Gardner quotes the sonnet in full.

17. Gerard Manley Hopkins, *The Poems of Gerard Manley Hopkins*, ed. W. H. Gardner and N. H. MacKenzie, 4th ed. (London: Oxford University Press, 1970). Subsequent citations of Hopkins's poetry are from this edition.

18. A narrator in William Morris's poem, *The Pilgrims of Hope* (1886), is struck by a London crowd's "dull and hang-dog gait" and their "joyless, hopeless, shameless, angerless" stare. This "thing" with "their rags of filth o'erlaid" has been invented by the age, but "the teeth of the dragon shall grow": (*The Collected Works of William Morris*, ed. May Morris, vol. 24, sec. 3. ll. 28, 32, 36, 37–38).

19. Mr. Podsnap's confused equations—"Providence has declared that you shall have the poor always with you. . . . It is not for me to impugn the workings of Providence"—seem very close to Hopkins's views.

20. Coventry Patmore, *The Poems of Coventry Patmore*, ed. Frederick Page (London: Oxford University Press, 1949), p. 56. Subsequent citations of Patmore's poetry are from this edition.

21. *Georg Lukács: Writer and Critic and Other Essays*, ed. and trans. Arthur D. Kahn, pp. 115, 121, 126.

22. Ibid., pp. 111, 127, 130, 144.

23. J. A. Symonds, "The Red Flag, and Other Poems," *The Academy* 4 (1873): 4–5.

24. Ibid., p. 4.

25. Roden Noel, *The Collected Poems of Roden Noel*, ed. Victoria Buxton (London: Kegan Paul, Trench, Trübner 1902), ll. 1–15. Subsequent citations of Noel's poetry are from this edition.

26. Stange, "The Frightened Poets," p. 479.

27. Noel, *The Collected Poems of Roden Noel*, p. 504.

28. Cosmo Monkhouse, "Songs of the Heights and Deeps," *The Academy* 27 (1885): 179–80.

29. Also interesting are the juxtaposed descriptive sets of the fairy loom-weaver from mythology with the factory worker-weaver from reality (ll. 557–94). Note also the contrast between the nineteenth-century Thames and the river of Spenser's day (ll. 101–4).

30. Walter Bagehot, "Charles Dickens," in *Works*, ed. Mrs. Russell Barrington, pp. 84–85.

31. William Morris, *The Letters of William Morris to His Family and Friends*, ed. Philip Henderson, p. 180.

32. William Morris, *The Collected Works of William Morris*, ed. May Morris, 24 vols. (London: Longmans, Green, 1910–1915), vol. 9. ll. 7–12. Subsequent citations of Morris's poetry as well as citations from *News from Nowhere* are from the various volumes of this edition.

33. Quoted in Edward P. Thompson, *William Morris: Romantic to Revolutionary*, p. 774.

34. William Morris, *The Letters of William Morris to His Family and Friends*, p. 234.

35. Ibid., p. 261.

36. Williams, *Culture and Society*, p. 148.

37. Ibid., p. 158.

38. Imogene B. Walker, *James Thomson, B. V.: A Critical Study*, p. 76, describes Thomson's bleak London lodging after 1866. It was "a room in a densely populated section of London, only a few blocks from main business streets, where the rows and rows of three- and four-story houses were built the one against the other, their doors separated from the sidewalk only by areaways, where the only openness was an occasional tree-filled square."

39. James Thomson, *Poems and Some Letters of James Thomson*, ed. Anne Ridler (Carbondale: Southern Illinois University Press, 1963), ll. 1–14. Subsequent citations of Thomson's poetry are from this edition.

40. R. A. Foakes in *The Romantic Assertion*, pp. 169–79, deals with Thomson as the final figure in his book because the poet's later poem "The City of Dreadful Night" marks the disintegration of the romantic assertion: it "inverts the rhetoric and the images of the Romantic vision, and applies them to an assertion of despair, the negation of that vision."

41. Bertram Dobell, "A Memoir," in *The Poetical Works of James Thomson*, 1:li.

42. Quoted from Thomson's diary, April 9, 1880, in Walker, *James Thomson*, p. 122.

43. Walker, *James Thomson*, p. 86 and Anne Ridler, Introduction to *The Poems and Some Letters of James Thomson*, p. xliii.

44. Walker, *James Thomson*, pp. 76–77.

45. Williams, *The Country and the City*, p. 236.

46. William D. Schaefer, "The Two Cities of Dreadful Night," *PMLA* 77 (1962): 609.

47. Ibid., p. 613.

48. Ibid., p. 611.

Notes to Chapter Four

1. Helmut E. Gerber, "The Nineties: Beginning, End, or Transition?" in *Edwardians and Late Victorians*, ed. Richard Ellmann, pp. 50–79.

2. John Henry Robertson [John Connell], *W. E. Henley*, p. 203.

3. Walter Pater, *Marius the Epicurean*, p. 197.

4. Arthur Symons, "Mr. Henley's Poetry," *Fortnightly Review* 58 (1892): 184.

5. Arthur Symons, "A Prelude to Life," in *The Collected Works of Arthur Symons: Spiritual Adventures*, 5:31–32.

6. Arthur Symons, "Preface to the Second Edition of *Silhouettes*: Being a Word on Behalf of Patchouli," in *The Collected Works of Arthur Symons*, 1:95–97.

7. Lionel Johnson, *The Complete Poems of Lionel Johnson*, ed. Ian Fletcher, ll. 1–8.

8. "The Poetry of London," *The Spectator* 81 (1898): 826–27.

9. G. K. Chesterton, "A Defence of Detective Stories," in *The Defendant*, pp. 158–60.

10. William Dean Howells, *London Films*, pp. 47–49.

11. Frederick Locker-Lampson, *My Confidences: An Autobiographical Sketch Addressed to My Descendants*, pp. 153, 154, 175.

12. Frederick Locker-Lampson, *London Lyrics*, pp. 193, 195.

13. Locker-Lampson, *My Confidences*, p. 185.

14. Oscar Wilde, "The Soul of Man under Socialism," in *The Soul of Man under Socialism and Other Essays*, ed. Philip Rieff, pp. 246, 260, 262.

15. Symons, "Preface to the Second Edition of *Silhouettes*," pp. 95–97.

16. Max Beerbohm, "A Defence of Cosmetics" (later changed to "The Pervasion of Rouge"), *The Works of Max Beerbohm*, pp. 107–38.

17. John Davidson, "On Poetry," in *The Poems of John Davidson*, ed. Andrew Turnbull, 2:532, 533, 536.

18. Frederick Locker-Lampson, *London Lyrics* (London: Macmillan, 1904), ll. 1–4, 9–12. Subsequent citations of Locker-Lampson's poetry are from this edition.

19. Austin Dobson, *The Complete Poetical Works of Austin Dobson* (London:

Oxford University Press, 1923), ll. 1–5, 10–15. Subsequent citations of Dobson's poetry are from this edition.

20. Laurence Binyon, "Mr. Bridges' 'Prometheus' and Poetic Drama," *The Dome* 2 (1899): 200.

21. Laurence Binyon, *London Visions* (London: Elkin Mathews, 1908), ll. 1–6. Subsequent citations of Binyon's poetry are from this edition.

22. G. Robert Stange, "The Frightened Poets," p. 493.

23. Cornelius Weygandt, *The Time of Yeats*, p. 107.

24. Unsigned review of Laurence Binyon's *Second Book of London Visions*, in *The Dome* 2 (1899): 89–90.

25. Charles Baudelaire, *Oeuvres Posthumes*, p. 20. For an excellent discussion of Baudelaire's poetic perspective on the city, see Walter Benjamin, "On Some Motifs in Baudelaire," in *Illuminations*, ed. Hannah Arendt, pp. 155–200.

26. Charles Baudelaire, *Selected Poems of Charles Baudelaire*, ed. Enid Starkie, pp. 11, 13.

27. Ibid., ll. 1–8.

28. Oscar Wilde, *The First Collected Edition of Oscar Wilde*, ed. Robert Ross, vol. 9 (London: Methuen, 1908), ll. 1 8. Subsequent citations of Wilde's poetry are from this edition.

29. Arthur Symons, *Days and Nights* (1889; reprint ed., London: Martin Secker, 1923), ll. 17–24. Subsequent citations from Symons's *Days and Nights* are from the 1923 edition.

30. Arthur Symons, "The Decadent Movement in Literature," *Harper's Magazine* 87 (1893): 862.

31. Arthur Symons, "Preface to the Second Edition of *Silhouettes*," pp. 95–97.

32. Stange, "The Frightened Poets," p. 491.

33. Arthur Symons, *Silhouettes* (London: Elkin Mathews and John Lane, 1892), ll. 1–16. Subsequent citations from Symons's *Silhouettes* are from this edition.

34. Stange, "The Frightened Poets," p. 492.

35. Arthur Symons, *London Nights* (1895; reprint ed., Boston: John W. Luce, 1923), ll. 15–16. Subsequent citations from Symons's *London Nights* are from the 1923 edition.

36. To acknowledge his indebtedness to the poetry of John Davidson, Eliot used the phrase "dingy urban imagery" in a preface to *John Davidson: A Selection of His Poems*, ed. Maurice Lindsay, p. xii.

37. *Aesthetes and Decadents of the 1890's*, ed. Karl Beckson, p. 164n.

38. Arthur Symons, "Preface to the Second Edition of *London Nights*," in *The Collected Works of Arthur Symons*, vol. 1, pp. 165–67.

39. See Arthur Symons, "London: A Book of Aspects," in *Cities and Sea-Coasts and Islands*, p. 161.

40. Jerome Hamilton Buckley, *A Study in the "Counter-Decadence" of the 'Nineties*, p. 185.

41. W. E. Henley, *The Works of W. E. Henley: Poems*, vol. 2 (London: David Nutt, 1908), sec. 1. ll. 1–6. Unless otherwise noted, subsequent citations of Henley's poetry are from this edition.

42. Symons did write "Nocturne," a poem in which two lovers tour London by night in a hansom cab. Yet, even in that poem, the interaction is more between the lovers themselves than with the sights and sounds of the actual city.

43. "Recent Verse," *The Athenaeum* no. 3869 (Dec. 21, 1901): 838.

44. The text of Henley's "Nocturn" appears in *A London Garland*, ed. W. E. Henley, p. 195.

45. *John Davidson: A Selection of His Poems*, ed. Maurice Lindsay, p. 41.

46. John Davidson, *The Poems of John Davidson*, ed. Andrew Turnbull, 2 vols. (Edinburgh: Scottish Academic Press, 1973), 1: ll. 7–12. Subsequent citations of Davidson's poetry are from the two volumes of this edition.

47. Hayim Fineman, *John Davidson: A Study of the Relation of His Ideas to His Poetry*, p. 16.

48. J. Benjamin Townsend, *John Davidson: Poet of Armageddon*, p. 272.

49. Ibid., p. 281.

Notes to Epilogue

1. For a more extensive discussion of Lawrence's response to the city, see William B. Thesing, "D. H. Lawrence's Poetic Response to the City: Some Continuities with Nineteenth-Century Poets," *Modernist Studies: Literature and Culture 1920–1940*, 4 (1981–82).

2. For a more extensive discussion of Eliot's response to the city, see the two chapters—"The Temporal City of Total Conditioning" and "Toward the City Outside Time"—in Stephen Spender's excellent study, *T. S. Eliot* (New York: Penguin Books, 1976). Spender draws "a very decisive line between the temporal city of European civilization become the waste land . . . and the spiritual world of the City of God, not dependent on the condition of civilization" (p. 127).

3. D. H. Lawrence, *Letters to Bertrand Russell*, ed. Harry T. Moore (New York: Gotham Book Mart, 1948), p. 80.

4. D. H. Lawrence, *The Letters of D. H. Lawrence*, ed. Aldous Huxley (New York: Viking Press, 1932), p. 252.

5. D. H. Lawrence, *Sons and Lovers* (New York: Penguin Books, 1976), pp. 82, 420.

6. D. H. Lawrence, "Autobiographical Fragment," in *Phoenix: The Posthumous Papers*, ed. Edward McDonald (New York: Viking Press, 1936), p. 829.

7. Spender, *T. S. Eliot*, pp. 119–120.

Selected Bibliography

The following bibliography is divided into three parts: the first part lists general studies of the city and of the Victorian period; the second part comprises studies that focus on literary responses to the city; the third part lists general anthologies as well as works and criticisms of individual poets.

I

Altick, Richard D. *Victorian People and Ideas*. New York: W. W. Norton, 1973.

Ashworth, William. *The Genesis of Modern British Town Planning: A Study in the Economic and Social History of the Nineteenth and Twentieth Centuries*. London: Routledge and Kegan Paul, 1954.

Barker, Felix, and Peter Jackson. *London, Two Thousand Years of a City and Its People*. New York: Macmillan, 1974.

Batho, Edith, and Bonamy Dobrée. *The Victorians and After, 1830–1914*. 3d rev. ed. New York: Dover, 1962.

Bell, Aldon D. *London in the Age of Dickens*. Norman: University of Oklahoma Press, 1967.

Besant, Sir Walter. *London in the Nineteenth Century*. London: Adam and Charles Black, 1909.

Booth, Charles. *Life and Labour of the People in London*. 10 vols. London: Macmillan, 1892–97.

Brantlinger, Patrick. *The Spirit of Reform: British Literature and Politics, 1832–1867*. Cambridge, Mass.: Harvard University Press, 1977.

Briggs, Asa. *The Age of Improvement*. New York: Oxford University Press, 1962.

———. *Victorian Cities*. New York: Harper and Row, 1963.

Bryant, Arthur. *The Pageant of England, 1840–1940*. New York: Harper, 1941.

Buckley, Jerome Hamilton. *A Study in the "Counter-Decadence" of the Nineties*. Princeton. Princeton University Press, 1945.

———. *The Victorian Temper: A Study in Literary Culture*. Cambridge, Mass.: Harvard University Press, 1951.

Burn, William L. *The Age of Equipoise: A Study of the Mid-Victorian Generation*. London: G. Allen and Unwin, 1968.

Chadwick, George F. *The Park and the Town: Public Landscape in the Nineteenth and Twentieth Centuries*. New York: F. A. Praeger, 1966.

Chapple, J. A. V. *Documentary and Imaginative Literature, 1880–1920*. New York: Barnes and Noble, 1970.

Selected Bibliography

Charlesworth, Barbara. *Dark Passages: The Decadent Consciousness in Victorian Literature*. Madison: University of Wisconsin Press, 1965.

Choay, Françoise. *The Modern City: Planning in the Nineteenth Century*. New York: George Braziller, 1969.

Cockshut, A. O. J. *The Unbelievers: English Agnostic Thought, 1840–1890*. London: Collins, 1964.

Coleman, B. I., ed. *The Idea of the City in Nineteenth-Century Britain*. London: Routledge and Kegan Paul, 1973.

Daiches, David. *Some Late Victorian Attitudes*. New York: W. W. Norton, 1969.

Doré, Gustave, and Blanchard Jerrold. *London: A Pilgrimage*. 1872. Reprint. New York: Dover, 1970.

Dunning, John H., and E. Victor Morgan. *An Economic Study of the City of London*. London: George Allen and Unwin, 1971.

Dyos, H. J. *Victorian Suburb: A Study of the Growth of Camberwell*. Leicester, England: Leicester University Press, 1961.

————, and Michael Wolff, eds. *The Victorian City: Images and Realities*. 2 vols. London: Routledge and Kegan Paul, 1973.

Ensor, Robert C. K. *England, 1870–1914*. London: Oxford University Press, 1936.

Fletcher. Ian. "The 1890's, A Lost Decade." *Victorian Studies* 4 (1961): 345–54.

Gerber, Helmut E. "The Nineties: Beginning, End, or Transition?" In *Edwardians and Late Victorians*. Edited by Richard Ellmann. New York: Columbia University Press, 1960, pp. 50–79.

Glass, Ruth D., ed. *London, Aspects of Change*. London: MacGibbon and Kee, 1964.

Gray, Donald J. "General Histories, Guidebooks and Handbooks." *Indiana University Bookman*. 12 (1977): 26–40.

————. "Picturesque London." *Indiana University Bookman* 12 (1977): 41–62.

Greg, W. R. "Prostitution." *Westminster Review* 53 (1850): 448–506.

Gregg, Pauline. *Modern Britain: A Social and Economic History Since 1760*. 5th rev. ed. New York: Pegasus, 1965.

Gretton, Richard H. *A Modern History of the English People, 1880–1922*. London: G. Richards, 1923.

Handlin, Oscar, and John Burchard, eds. *The Historian and the City*. Cambridge, Mass.: MIT Press and Harvard University Press, 1963.

Horne, Alistair. *The Terrible Year: The Paris Commune, 1871*. New York: Viking Press, 1971.

Houghton, Walter E. *The Victorian Frame of Mind, 1830–1870*. New Haven, Conn.: Yale University Press, 1957.

Jackson, Holbrook. *The Eighteen-Nineties*. Harmondsworth: Penguin, 1950.

Jones, Gareth Stedman. *Outcast London: A Study in the Relationship between Classes in Victorian Society*. London: Oxford University Press, 1971.

Kitson Clark, George S. R. *An Expanding Society: Britain 1830–1900*. London: Cambridge University Press, 1967.

————. *The Making of Victorian England.* Cambridge, Mass.: Harvard University Press, 1962.

Kranzberg, Melvin. *The Siege of Paris, 1870–1871: A Political and Social History.* Ithaca, N.Y.: Cornell University Press, 1950.

Lucas, John. *Literature and Politics in the Nineteenth Century.* London: Methuen, 1971.

Madden, William A. "The Victorian Sensibility." *Victorian Studies* 7 (1963): 67–97.

Marcus, Steven. *Engels, Manchester, and the Working Class.* New York: Random House, 1974.

Mayhew, Henry. *London Labour and the London Poor: A Cyclopaedia of the Condition and Earnings of Those That Will Work, Those That Cannot Work, and Those That Will Not Work.* 4 vols. London: Griffin, Bohn, 1862–64.

Mearns, Andrew. *The Bitter Cry of Outcast London. An Enquiry into the Condition of the Abject Poor.* London: London Congregational Union, 1883.

Metcalf, Priscilla. *Victorian London.* New York: Praeger, 1972.

Mumford, Lewis. *The Culture of Cities.* New York: Harcourt, Brace, 1938.

Nadel, Ira Bruce, and F. S. Schwarzbach, eds. *Victorian Artists and the City: A Collection of Critical Essays.* New York: Pergamon, 1980.

Olsen, Donald J. *The Growth of Victorian London.* New York: Holmes and Meier, 1977.

Pierson, Stanley. "The Way Out." In *The Victorian City: Images and Realities.* Edited by H. J. Dyos and Michael Wolff. 2 vols. London: Routledge and Kegan Paul, 1973.

Roebuck, Janet. *The Making of Modern English Society from 1850.* New York: Charles Scribner, 1973.

————. *The Shaping of Urban Society.* New York: Charles Scribner, 1974.

Rose, Millicent. *The East End of London.* London: Cresset Press, 1951.

Seaman, L. C. B. *Life in Victorian London.* London: B. T. Batsford, 1973.

————. *Victorian England: Aspects of English and Imperial History, 1837–1901.* London: Methuen, 1973.

Sennett, Richard, ed. *Classic Essays on the Culture of Cities.* New York: Meredith, 1969.

Sheppard, Francis H. W. *London, 1808–1870: The Infernal Wen.* Berkeley: University of California Press, 1971.

Simmel, Georg. "The Metropolis and Mental Life." In *Classic Essays on the Culture of Cities.* Edited by Richard Sennett. Englewood Cliffs, N.J.: Prentice-Hall, 1969.

Sims, George Robert. *How the Poor Live* and *Horrible London.* London: Chatto and Windus, 1889.

Taine, Hippolyte. *Notes on England.* New York: Henry Holt, 1876.

Thomson, David. *England in the Nineteenth Century.* Harmondsworth: Penguin, 1950.

Traill, Henry D., ed. *Social England: A Record of the Progress of the People in Religion, Laws, Learning, Arts, Industry, Commerce, Science, Literature, and Man-*

Selected Bibliography

ners. Vol. 6. London: Cassell, 1897–1902.

Trevelyan, G. M. *British History in the Nineteenth Century, and After, 1782–1919*. London: Longmans, 1938.

Vicinus, Martha. "Dark London." *Indiana University Bookman* 12 (1977): 63–92.

———. "Introduction." In *Indiana University Bookman* 12 (1977): 1–4.

Walford, L. B. *Memories of Victorian London*. London: Edward Arnold, 1912.

Webb, R. K. *Modern England, From the Eighteenth Century to the Present*. New York: Dodd, Mead, 1968.

Weber, Adna F. *The Growth of Cities in the Nineteenth Century: A Study in Statistics, 1899*. Reprint. Ithaca, N.Y.: Cornell University Press, 1963.

Young, George M., *Victorian England: Portrait of an Age*. 2d ed. New York: Oxford University Press, 1953.

———, ed. *Early Victorian England: 1830–1865*. 2 vols. London: Oxford University Press, 1934.

II

Altick, Richard D. "The Sociology of Authorship: The Social Origins, Education, and Occupations of 1,100 British Writers, 1800–1935." *Bulletin of the New York Public Library* 66 (1962): 389–404.

Auden, W. H. *The Enchafèd Flood*. New York: Random House, 1950.

Bagehot, Walter. "Charles Dickens." In *Works*. Edited by Mrs. Russell Barrington. 10 vols. London: Longmans, Green, 1915.

Beerbohm, Max. "A Defence of Cosmetics." *The Works of Max Beerbohm*. New York: Dodd, Mead, 1896.

Byrd, Max. *London Transformed: Images of the City in the Eighteenth Century*. New Haven, Conn.: Yale University Press, 1978.

Chesterton, G. K. "A Defence of Detective Stories." *The Defendant*. London: J. M. Dent, 1914.

Clark, Jeanne Gabriel. "London in English Literature, 1880–1955." Ph.D. dissertation, Columbia University, 1957.

Clough, Arthur Hugh. "Recent English Poetry." *North American Review* 77 (1853): 1–30.

———. "Recent Social Theories." *North American Review* 77 (1853): 106–17.

Dahl, Curtis. "The Victorian Wasteland." In *Victorian Literature: Modern Essays in Criticism*. Edited by Austin Wright. New York: Oxford University Press, 1961.

Dougherty, James. *The Fivesquare City: The City in the Religious Imagination*. Notre Dame, Ind.: University of Notre Dame Press, 1980.

Forsyth, R. A. *The Lost Pattern: Essays on the Emergent City Sensibility in Victorian England*. Nedlands: University of Western Australia Press, 1976.

———. "The Victorian Self-Image and the Emergent City Sensibility." *University of Toronto Quarterly* 33 (1963): 61–77.

Howe, Irving. "The City in Literature." In *The Critical Point, On Literature and Culture*. New York: Horizon Press, 1973.

Howells, William Dean. *London Films*. New York: Harper, 1905.

Jaye, Michael C. and Ann Chalmers Watts, eds. *Literature and the Urban Experience: Essays on the City and Literature*. New Brunswick, N.J.: Rutgers University Press, 1981.

Johnson, E. D. H. "Victorian Artists and the Urban Milieu." In *The Victorian City: Images and Realities*. 2 vols. London: Routledge and Kegan Paul, 1973.

Johnson, Lionel. *The Complete Poems of Lionel Johnson*. Edited by Iain Fletcher. London: Unicorn Press, 1953.

Johnston, Kenneth R. "Blake's Cities: Romantic Forms of Urban Renewal." In *Blake's Visionary Forms Dramatic*. Edited by David V. Erdman and John E. Grant. Princeton, N.J.: Princeton University Press, 1970.

Kahn, Arthur D., ed. and trans. *Georg Lukács: Writer and Critic and Other Essays*. New York: Grosset and Dunlap, 1970.

Kingsley, Charles. *Alton Locke, Tailor and Poet*. Vol. 1. New York: J. F. Taylor, 1898.

Knoepflmacher, U. C. "The Novel between City and Country." In *The Victorian City: Images and Realities*. 2 vols. London: Routledge and Kegan Paul, 1973.

Korg, Jacob, ed. *London in Dickens' Day*. Englewood Cliffs, N.J.: Prentice-Hall, 1960.

Miller, Stephen. "Studies in the Idea of the City in Western Literature." Ph.D. dissertation. Rutgers University, 1970.

Pater, Walter. *Marius the Epicurean*. New York: Macmillan, 1900.

Peters, Robert L. "Whistler and the English Poets of the 1890's." *Modern Language Quarterly* 18 (1957): 251–61.

Pike, Burton. *The Image of the City in Modern Literature*. Princeton, N.J.: Princeton University Press, 1981.

Pinto, Vivian de Sola. *Crisis in English Poetry, 1880–1940*. London: Longmans, 1951.

Raleigh, John H. "The Novel and the City: England and America in the Nineteenth Century." *Victorian Studies* 11 (1968): 291–328.

Schwarzbach, F. S. *Dickens and the City*. London: Athlone, 1979.

Stange, G. Robert. "The Frightened Poets," In *The Victorian City: Images and Realities*. 2 vols. Edited by H. J. Dyos and Michael Wolff. London: Routledge and Kegan Paul, 1973.

Starkie, Enid. *From Gautier to Eliot: The Influence of France on English Literature, 1851–1939*. London: Hutchinson, 1960.

Stephens, F. G. "Modern Giants." *The Germ* no. 4 (1850): 169–73.

Vicinus, Martha. *The Industrial Muse: A Study of Nineteenth Century British Working-Class Literature*. New York: Harper and Row, 1974.

Warburg, Jeremy. "Poetry and Industrialism: Some Refractory Material in Nineteenth Century and Later English Verse." *Modern Language Review* 53 (1958): 161–70.

Ward, Wilfrid. *The Life of John Henry, Cardinal Newman*. 2 vols. New York: Longmans, Green, 1912.

Selected Bibliography

Weimer, David R. *The City as Metaphor*. New York: Random House, 1966.
Welsh, Alexander. *The City of Dickens*. New York: Oxford University Press, 1971.
Williams, Raymond. *The Country and the City*. New York: Oxford University Press, 1973.
————. *Culture and Society, 1780–1950*. New York: Harper and Row, 1958.
————. *The English Novel from Dickens to Lawrence*. New York: Oxford University Press, 1970.
————. *Keywords: A Vocabulary of Culture and Society*. New York: Oxford University Press, 1976.
————. "Literature and Sociology: In Memory of Lucien Goldmann." *New Left Review* no. 67 (1971): 3–18.
————. *The Long Revolution*. New York: Columbia University Press, 1961.
————. "Prelude to Alienation." *Dissent* 11 (1964): 303–15.

III

Anthologies and General Survey Studies of Poetry of the Period

Armstrong, Isobel, ed. *Victorian Scrutinies: Reviews of Poetry, 1830–1870*. London: Athlone Press, 1972.
Beckson, Karl, ed. *Aesthetes and Decadents of the 1890's*. New York: Random House, 1966.
Dixon, C. J., ed. *Fin de Siècle: Poetry of the Late Victorian Period, 1860–1900*. London: Norton Bailey, 1968.
Evans, Sir Ifor. *English Poetry in the Later Nineteenth Century*. 2d rev. ed. New York: Barnes and Noble, 1966.
Gray, Donald J., and G. B. Tennyson, eds. *Victorian Literature: Poetry*. New York: Macmillan, 1976.
Greever, Garland, and Joseph M. Bachelor, eds. *The Soul of the City: An Urban Anthology*. Boston: Houghton Mifflin, 1923.
Hamilton, G. Rostrevor, and John Arlott, eds. *Landmarks: A Book of Topographical Verse for England and Wales*. Cambridge: Cambridge University Press, 1943.
Henley, William E., ed. *A London Garland*. London: Macmillan, 1895.
Hyatt, Alfred H. *The Charm of London: An Anthology*. London: Chatto and Windus, 1925.
A London Omnibus. London: Chatto and Windus, 1927.
Low, D. M., ed. *London Is London: A Selection of Prose and Verse*. London: Chatto and Windus, 1949.
Lucas, E. V., ed. *The Friendly Town: A Little Book for the Urbane*. London: Methuen, 1905.
Messenger, N. P., and J. R. Watson, eds. *Victorian Poetry: "The City of Dreadful Night" and Other Poems*. Totowa, N.J.: Rowman and Littlefield, 1974.

Miles, Alfred H., ed. *The Poets and the Poetry of the Nineteenth Century.* 12 vols. London: George Routledge, 1905.

Munro, John M., ed. *English Poetry in Transition, 1880–1920.* New York: Pegasus, 1968.

Perkins, David. *A History of Modern Poetry: From the 1890s to the High Modernist Mode.* Cambridge, Mass.: Harvard University Press, 1976.

"The Poetry of London." *The Spectator* 81 (Dec. 3, 1898): 826–27. [Unsigned review of *London in Song.*]

Scott, Walter S., Joan Stevenson, and Sidney Scott, eds. *Pride of London: A Day Book.* London: John Green, 1947.

Shmiefsky, Marvel. *Sense at War with Soul: English Poetics, 1865–1900.* The Hague: Mouton, 1972.

Thornton, R. K. R., ed. *Poetry of the 'Nineties.* Baltimore: Penguin, 1970.

Whitten, Wilfred, ed. *London in Song.* London: Grant Richards, 1898.

Wiley, Paul L., and Harold Orel, eds. *British Poetry, 1880–1920: Edwardian Voices.* New York: Appleton-Century-Crofts, 1969.

Individual Poets

MATTHEW ARNOLD (1822–1888)

Arnold, Matthew. *Culture and Anarchy.* Edited by Dover J. Wilson. Cambridge: Cambridge University Press, 1960.

———. *The Letters of Matthew Arnold to Arthur Hugh Clough.* Edited by H. F. Lowry. London: Oxford University Press, 1932.

———. *The Poems of Matthew Arnold.* Edited by Kenneth Allott. Harlow, England: Longman Group, 1965.

Roper, Alan. *Arnold's Poetic Landscapes.* Baltimore: Johns Hopkins University Press, 1969.

Trilling, Lionel. *Matthew Arnold.* New York: Columbia University Press, 1949.

CHARLES BAUDELAIRE (1821–1867)

Baudelaire, Charles. *Oeuvres Posthumes.* Paris: Mercure de France, 1908.

———. *Selected Poems of Charles Baudelaire.* Edited by Enid Starkie. New York: Grove Press, 1974.

Benjamin, Walter. "On Some Motifs in Baudelaire." In *Illuminations.* Edited by Hannah Arendt. New York: Schocken, 1969.

LAURENCE BINYON (1869–1943)

Binyon, Laurence. *London Visions.* London: Elkin Mathews, 1908.

———. "Mr. Bridges' 'Prometheus' and Poetic Drama." *The Dome* 2 (1899): 199–206.

Unsigned review of *Second Book of London Visions.* In *The Dome* 2 (1899): 89–90.

Weygandt, Cornelius. *The Time of Yeats.* New York: Appleton-Century, 1937.

Selected Bibliography

WILLIAM BLAKE (1757–1827)

Adams, Hazard. *William Blake: A Reading of the Shorter Poems*. Seattle: University of Washington Press, 1963.

Blake, William. *The Poems of William Blake*. Edited by W. H. Stevenson. Harlow, England: Longman Group, 1971.

Erdman, David V. *Blake: Prophet Against Empire*. 2d rev. ed., Princeton, N.J.: Princeton University Press, 1969.

Frye, Northrop. *Fearful Symmetry: A Study of William Blake*. Princeton, N.J.: Princeton University Press, 1947.

Nurmi, Martin K. "Fact and Symbol in 'The Chimney Sweeper' of Blake's *Songs of Innocence*." *Bulletin of the New York Public Library* 68 (1964): 249–56.

ROBERT BUCHANAN (1841–1901)

Buchanan, Robert. *The Complete Poetical Works of Robert Buchanan*. 2 vols. London: Chatto and Windus, 1901.

———. "David Gray, a Memoir." In *A Poet's Sketch-Book*. London: Chatto and Windus, 1883.

———. "On My Own Tentatives." In *David Gray and Other Essays*. London: Sampson Low and Marston, 1868.

———. "Summer Song in the City" (poem). *London Society* 13 (1868): 89–90.

Cassidy, John A. *Robert W. Buchanan*. New York: Twayne, 1973.

Forsyth, R. A. "Nature and the Victorian City: The Ambivalent Attitude of Robert Buchanan." *Journal of English Literary History* 36 (1969): 382–415.

ARTHUR HUGH CLOUGH (1819–1861)

Clough, Arthur Hugh. *The Poems of Arthur Hugh Clough*. 2d ed. Edited by F. L. Mulhauser. London: Oxford University Press, 1974.

Hardy, Barbara. "Clough's Self-Consciousness." In *The Major Victorian Poets: Reconsiderations*. Edited by Isobel Armstrong. London: Routledge and Kegan Paul, 1969.

Harris, Wendell V. *Arthur Hugh Clough*. New York: Twayne, 1970.

Houghton, Walter E. *The Poetry of Clough: An Essay in Revaluation*. New Haven, Conn.: Yale University Press, 1963.

Ryals, Clyde de L. "An Interpretation of Clough's *Dipsychus*." *Victorian Poetry* 1 (1963): 182–88.

JOHN DAVIDSON (1857–1909)

Davidson, John. *The Poems of John Davidson*. Edited by Andrew Turnbull. 2 vols. Edinburgh: Scottish Academic Press, 1973.

Fineman, Hayim. *John Davidson: A Study of the Relation of His Ideas to His Poetry*. Philadelphia: University of Pennsylvania Press, 1916.

Lindsay, Maurice, ed. *John Davidson: A Selection of His Poems*. London: Hutchinson, 1961.

Townsend, J. Benjamin. *John Davidson: Poet of Armageddon.* New Haven, Conn.: Yale University Press, 1961.

AUSTIN DOBSON (1840–1921)

Dobson, Austin. *The Complete Poetical Works of Austin Dobson.* London: Oxford University Press, 1923.

WILLIAM E. HENLEY (1849–1903)

Buckley, Jerome Hamilton. *William Ernest Henley: A Study in the "Counter-Decadence" of the Nineties.* Princeton, N.J.: Princeton University Press, 1945.

Henley, William E. *The Works of W. E. Henley: Poems.* Vol. 2. London: David Nutt, 1908.

Noyes, Alfred. "The Poetry of W. E. Henley." In *Some Aspects of Modern Poetry.* London: Hodder, 1924.

"Recent Verse." *The Athenaeum* no. 3869 (1901): 838.

Robertson, John Henry [John Connell]. *W. E. Henley.* London: Constable, 1949.

Symons, Arthur. "Mr. Henley's Poetry." *Fortnightly Review* 58 (1892): 182–92.

———. "Some Makers of Modern Verse." *Forum* 66 (1921): 476–88.

GERARD MANLEY HOPKINS (1844–1889)

Gardner, W. H. *Gerard Manley Hopkins: A Study of Poetic Idiosyncrasy in Relation to Poetic Tradition.* 2 vols. New Haven, Conn.: Yale University Press, 1948–49.

Hopkins, Gerard Manley. *Further Letters of Gerard Manley Hopkins.* Edited by Claude Colleer Abbott. New York: Oxford University Press, 1956.

———. *The Letters of Gerard Manley Hopkins to Robert Bridges.* Edited by Claude Colleer Abbott. 2 vols. New York: Oxford University Press, 1955. Vol. 1, *The Letters of Gerard Manley Hopkins to Robert Bridges;* Vol. 2, *The Correspondence of Gerard Manley Hopkins and Richard Watson Dixon.*

———. *The Notebooks and Papers of Gerard Manley Hopkins.* Edited by Humphry House. New York: Oxford University Press, 1937.

———. *The Poems of Gerard Manley Hopkins.* Edited by W. H. Gardner and N. H. MacKenzie. 4th ed. London: Oxford University Press, 1970.

Johnson, Wendell Stacy. *Gerard Manley Hopkins: The Poet as Victorian.* Ithaca, N.Y.: Cornell University Press, 1968.

Sulloway, Alison G. *Gerard Manley Hopkins and the Victorian Temper.* London: Routledge and Kegan Paul, 1972.

Sutherland, John. "The Dating of 'Tom's Garland.'" *Notes and Queries* 18 (1971): 258.

FREDERICK LOCKER-LAMPSON (1821–1895)

Locker-Lampson, Frederick. *London Lyrics.* London: Macmillan, 1904.

———. *My Confidences: An Autobiographical Sketch Addressed to My Descendants.* New York: Charles Scribner, 1896.

Selected Bibliography

WILLIAM MORRIS (1834–1896)

Henderson, Philip. *William Morris: His Life, Work, and Friends*. London: Thames and Hudson, 1967.

Mackail, J. W. *Life of William Morris*. 2 vols. London: Longmans, Green, 1901.

Morris, William. *The Collected Works of William Morris*. Edited by May Morris. 24 vols. London: Longmans, Green, 1910–15.

———. *The Letters of William Morris to His Family and Friends*. Edited by Philip Henderson. London: Longmans, 1950.

Symons, Arthur. "William Morris." In *Studies in Two Literatures*. London: Secker, 1924.

Thompson, Edward P. *William Morris: Romantic to Revolutionary*. London: Lawrence and Wishart, 1955.

RODEN NOEL (1834–1894)

Monkhouse, Cosmo. "Songs of the Heights and Deeps." *The Academy* 27 (1885): 179–80.

Noel, Roden. *The Collected Poems of Roden Noel*. Edited by Victoria Buxton. London: Kegan Paul, Trench, Trübner, 1902.

Symonds, J. A. "The Red Flag and Other Poems." *The Academy* 4 (1873): 4–5.

COVENTRY PATMORE (1823–1896)

Patmore, Coventry. *The Poems of Coventry Patmore*. Edited by Frederick Page. London: Oxford University Press, 1949.

ALEXANDER SMITH (1830–1867)

Scott, Mary Jane W. "Alexander Smith: Poet of Victorian Scotland." *Studies in Scottish Literature* 14 (1979): 98–111.

Smith, Alexander. *City Poems*. Cambridge: Macmillan, 1857.

———. *Poems*. 4th ed. London: David Bogue, 1856.

ARTHUR SYMONS (1865–1945)

Symons, Arthur. *Days and Nights*. 1889. Reprint. London: Martin Secker, 1923. [1923 edition includes introduction by Walter Pater.]

———. "The Decadent Movement in Literature." *Harper's Magazine* 87 (1893): 858–67.

———. "London: A Book of Aspects." In *Cities and Seacoasts and Islands*. 1908. Reprint. New York: Brentano's, 1919.

———. *London Nights*. 1895. Reprint. Boston: John W. Luce, 1923.

———. "Preface to the Second Edition of *London Nights*." In *The Collected Works of Arthur Symons*. Vol. 1. London: Martin Secker, 1924.

———. "Preface to the Second Edition of *Silhouettes*: Being a Word on Behalf of Patchouli." In *The Collected Works of Arthur Symons*. Vol. 1. London: Martin Secker, 1924.

———. "A Prelude to Life." In *The Collected Works of Arthur Symons: Spiritual Adventures*. Vol. 5. London: Martin Secker, 1924.

————. *Silhouettes*. London: Elkin Mathews and John Lane, 1892.

————. *Wanderings*. London: J. M. Dent, 1931.

ALFRED, LORD TENNYSON (1809–1892)

Buckley, Jerome Hamilton. *Tennyson: The Growth of a Poet*. Cambridge, Mass.: Harvard University Press, 1960.

Gray, Donald J. "Arthur, Roland, Empedocles, Sigurd, and the Despair of Heroes in Victorian Poetry." *Boston University Studies in English* 5 (1961): 1–17.

Ricks, Christopher. *Tennyson*. New York: Macmillan, 1972.

Rosenberg, John D. *The Fall of Camelot: A Study of Tennyson's Idylls of the King*. Cambridge, Mass.: Harvard University Press, 1973.

Tennyson, Alfred. *The Poems of Tennyson*. Edited by Christopher Ricks. Harlow, England: Longman Group, 1969.

Tennyson, Hallam. *Alfred Lord Tennyson: A Memoir by His Son*. 2 vols. New York: Macmillan, 1897.

JAMES THOMSON (B. V.) (1834–1882)

Dobell, Bertram. "A Memoir." In *The Poetical Works of James Thomson*. Vol. 1. London: Reeves and Turner, 1895.

Foakes, R. A. *The Romantic Assertion*. New York: Barnes and Noble, 1958.

LeRoy, Gaylord C. "James Thomson." In *Perplexed Prophets*. Philadelphia: University of Pennsylvania Press, 1953.

Marks, Jeannette. "Disaster and Poetry: A Study of James Thomson." *North American Review* 212 (1920): 93–109.

Ridler, Anne. Introduction to *Poems and Some Letters of James Thomson*. Carbondale: Southern Illinois University Press, 1963.

Schaefer, William D. *James Thomson (B. V.): Beyond "The City."* Berkeley: University of California Press, 1965.

————. "The Two Cities of Dreadful Night." *PMLA* 77 (1962): 609–15.

Thomson, James. *Poems and Some Letters of James Thomson*. Edited by Anne Ridler. Carbondale: Southern Illinois University Press, 1963.

————. *The Speedy Extinction of Evil and Misery: Selected Prose of James Thomson (B. V.)*. Edited by William D. Schaefer. Berkeley: University of California Press, 1967.

Walker, Imogene D. *James Thomson, B. V.: A Critical Study*. Ithaca, N.Y.: Cornell University Press, 1950.

WILLIAM SIDNEY WALKER (1795–1846)

Walker, William Sidney. *The Poetical Remains of William Sidney Walker, with a Memoir of the Author*. Edited by J. Moultrie. London: John W. Parker, 1852.

OSCAR WILDE (1854–1900)

Wilde, Oscar. *The First Collected Edition of Oscar Wilde*. Edited by Robert Ross. Vol. 9. London: Methuen, 1908.

————. "The Soul of Man under Socialism." In *The Soul of Man under Social-*

ism and Other Essays. Edited by Philip Rieff. New York: Harper and Row, 1970.

WILLIAM WORDSWORTH (1770–1850)

Wordsworth, William. *William Wordsworth: The Prelude, A Parallel Text*. Edited by J. C. Maxwell. Baltimore: Penguin, 1971.

———. *Wordsworth: Poetical Works*. Rev. ed. Edited by Ernest de Selincourt. New York: Oxford University Press, 1969.

Index